Library of Congress Cataloging-in-Publication Data

Levey, Judith S., 1936–
    Scholastic first dictionary / Judith S. Levey.
        p.   cm.
    Includes index.
    Summary: Entries include pronunciations, simple definitions, sentences, and plurals and other forms of the words.
    ISBN 0-590-96786-X
    1. English language—Dictionaries, Juvenile.   [1.English language—Dictionaries.]
I. Scholastic Inc.   II. Title.
    PE1628.5.L45   1998
    423'.1—dc21   97-25050
                                                                  CIP

                                                                 AC

Contents

A B C D E F G H I J K L M N O P Q R S T U V W X Y Z

Using Your Dictionary

On this page and the next one, you can learn about the different parts of the dictionary, what they look like and what they are called. You will see that the words in the dictionary are listed in alphabetical order from A to Z. The dictionary shows how to spell words and how to say them, what words mean, how to use words in sentences, and how words change form. The guide words at the top of the page make it easy to find the words you are looking for in the dictionary. The pictures help make the meaning of a word clearer.

GUIDE WORDS show the first word and the last word on a page.

THE ALPHABET BAR shows which letter of the alphabet you are looking at.

A LABEL names something in a picture.

A PICTURE illustrates the main entry and helps make the meaning clearer.

A CAPTION shows which main entry is being illustrated.

snail ▶ soccer

snail (snayl)
A **snail** is a small animal that lives in a shell and has a soft, slippery body. Niki found **snails** at the beach and in the garden. **[snails]**

snake (snayk)
A **snake** is a long, thin reptile that has no legs and slides along the ground by moving first one part of its body and then another. **Snakes** have scales, and some have beautiful colors and patterns. **[snakes]**

king snake

boa constrictor

cobra

snakes

sneaker (snee-kuhr)
A **sneaker** is a kind of shoe made with rubber on the bottom and cloth or leather on top. People wear **sneakers** when they play basketball or other sports, when they jog, and for many other activities. My aunt wears **sneakers** to her job as a waitress because she stands a lot. **[sneakers]**

sneeze (sneez)
When you **sneeze**, a lot of air comes out of your nose and mouth very suddenly. "Please cover your mouth when you **sneeze**," the school nurse told us. **[sneezing, sneezed]**

playing in the **snow**

snow (snoh)
1. Snow is tiny pieces of frozen water that are white and soft. **Snow** falls from clouds in cold weather. A **snowball** is made by pressing snow together with your hands. A **snowman** is a shape of a person made from **snow**.
2. To **snow** means to fall from the sky as snow. If it **snows** tonight, let's play in the snow tomorrow. **[snowing, snowed]**

soap (sohp)
Soap is something that you mix with water and use for washing and cleaning things. Some **soap** is liquid and some is solid. When I fell down and scratched my leg, Mom washed it with **soap** and water.

soccer (sahk-uhr)
Soccer is a game played on a field by two teams made up of 11 players each. Players try to get the **soccer** ball into the goal by kicking it or hitting it with any part of the body except their hands or arms.   **soccer** player

Dictionary Entries Close-up

A MAIN ENTRY is in green and is listed in alphabetical order.

The PRONUNCIATION shows how to say the main entry.

chalkboard (chawk-bord)
A **chalkboard** is a dark, smooth surface used for writing with chalk.
A **chalkboard** is also called a **blackboard**. The word **board** is short for **chalkboard**. [**chalkboards**]

ANOTHER WORD for the main entry is shown in dark letters.

A SHORT FORM of a main entry is shown in dark letters.

diamond (die-muhnd)
1. A **diamond** is a very hard, clear stone that comes from inside the earth. **Diamonds** are shiny and are used in rings and other jewelry.
2. A **diamond** is also a shape with four sides and four corners. A **diamond** looks like this: ◆.
[**diamonds**]

A NUMBER may be used when there is more than one definition.

A DEFINITION tells what the main entry means.

When two main entries are spelled alike, they are shown separately with NUMBERS.

tear¹ (tir)
A **tear** is a drop of salt water that comes from your eye when you cry or sometimes when you laugh. **Tears** ran down Ken's cheeks when he dropped his ice cream cone. [**tears**]

A SAMPLE SENTENCE shows how the main entry word can be used in a sentence. The main entry word is shown in dark letters.

tear² (tair)
To **tear** means to pull apart. When Madeleine's shirt got caught on the gate, we could hear the material **tear**. [**tearing, torn**]

FORMS of the main entry are shown in brackets.

Pronouncing Words

Pronunciation is the way we say words. When words are written, letters of the alphabet are used for different sounds. The list below gives the letters that are used to show each sound in a pronunciation in this dictionary. Sometimes a letter or group of letters can stand for different sounds. When they are used in a pronunciation, these letters have only one sound. The pronunciation appears in parentheses after each main entry. The very dark letters in the pronunciation are said louder than the lighter letters. In a pronunciation, a group of dark letters is called a *stressed syllable*. A group of lighter letters is called an *unstressed syllable*.

a	as in **mad** (mad), **bat** (bat)		ng	as in **sing** (sing), **single** (sing-guhl)
ah	as in **father** (fahTH-uhr), **dark** (dahrk), **dot** (daht)		oh	as in **no** (noh), **grow** (groh), **toe** (toh), **alone** (uh-lohn)
air	as in **fair** (fair), **care** (kair)		oi	as in **soil** (soil), **toy** (toi)
aw	as in **paw** (paw), **tall** (tawl)		oo	as in **pool** (pool), **rude** (rood), **music** (myoo-zik), **few** (fyoo)
ay	as in **day** (day), **made** (mayd), **same** (saym)		or	as in **corn** (korn), **more** (mor)
b	as in **bad** (bad), **tub** (tuhb)		ou	as in **out** (out), **allow** (uh-lou)
ch	as in **chin** (chin), **bench** (bench)		p	as in **pan** (pan), **top** (tahp)
d	as in **deer** (dir), **red** (red)		r	as in **rip** (rip), **pour** (por)
e	as in **net** (net), **send** (send)		s	as in **side** (side), **miss** (mis), **race** (rays), **yes** (yes)
ee	as in **teeth** (teeth), **bean** (been)		sh	as in **ship** (ship), **rush** (ruhsh)
f	as in **far** (fahr), **enough** (i-nuhf)		t	as in **tub** (tuhb), **hat** (hat)
g	as in **get** (get), **flag** (flag)		th	as in **thin** (thin), **bath** (bath)
h	as in **hand** (hand), **ahead** (uh-hed)		TH	as in **this** (THis), **breathe** (breeTH)
hw	as in **white** (hwite), **whale** (hwayl)		u	as in **put** (put), **book** (buk)
i	as in **big** (big), **sit** (sit), **dear** (dir), **here** (hir)		uh	as in **above** (uh-buhv), **listen** (lis-uhn), **pencil** (pen-suhl), **lemon** (lem-uhn), **fun** (fuhn)
ie	as in **lie** (lie), **iron** (ie-uhrn), or i-e as in **ripe** (ripe), **find** (finde)		uhr	as in **later** (late-uhr), **burn** (buhrn), **work** (wuhrk)
j	as in **jar** (jahr), **edge** (ej),		v	as in **very** (ver-ee), **five** (five)
k	as in **keep** (keep), **sock** (sahk)		w	as in **well** (wel), **between** (bi-tween)
l	as in **lap** (lap), **tell** (tel), **bottle** (baht-l)		y	as in **yes** (yes), **few** (fyoo), **music** (myoo-zik)
m	as in **mad** (mad), **lamb** (lam)		z	as in **zebra** (zee-bruh), **rose** (rohz)
n	as in **now** (nou), **ten** (ten), **know** (noh), **mitten** (mit-n)		zh	as in **measure** (mezh-uhr)

above (uh-**buhv**)

Above means higher than or over. When the airplane went **above** the clouds, we couldn't see the ground. We turned on the light **above** the table. The glasses are on the shelf **above** the sink. The train rides on a bridge **above** the river. **Above** is the opposite of below.

absent (**ab**-suhnt)

If you are **absent** from a place, you are not there. Erik caught a bad cold and was **absent** from school on Thursday.

accident (**ak**-si-duhnt)

An **accident** is something that happens that you did not plan and that may upset you. Nicole hurt her arm in a bicycle **accident**. **[accidents]**

acorn (**ay**-korn)

acorns

An **acorn** is the fruit or seed of an oak tree. Oak trees grow from **acorns**. In the fall, squirrels collect **acorns** for food to eat in the winter. **[acorns]**

circus **acrobat**

acrobat (**ak**-ruh-bat)

An **acrobat** is a person who is very good at gymnastics and has good balance. An **acrobat** does surprising things with his or her body on the ground or in the air. At the circus, the **acrobat** balanced herself between two elephants. **[acrobats]**

across (uh-**kraws**)

Across means from one side to the other. Janelle can now swim **across** the pool.

act (akt)

1. To **act** means to pretend to be someone else or to be in a play or movie. In the school play, Peter was chosen to **act** as the wizard.
2. To **act** also means to do something. Mom said, "Toni, please stop **acting** so silly, and listen to me." **[acting, acted]**

activity

activity (ak-**tiv**-uh-tee)

An **activity** is something that a person does. Nicky and Tim like to draw, color, swim, and read, but their favorite **activity** is riding their bikes. **[activities]**

actor (ak-tuhr) and actress (ak-truhs)

An **actor** is a person who acts in a play or a movie. An **actor** who is a girl or woman is also called an **actress**. **[actors, actresses]**

add (ad)

To **add** means to put something together with something else. If you **add** the number 1 to the number 3, you get 4. If you **add** 2 plus 3, you get 5. **[adding, added]**

address (uh-**dress**)

An **address** tells people where a place is, so they can go there or send mail there. A home **address** is the street and town where you live. On a computer, an **address** is the place where computer mail can be sent to you. **[addresses]**

adult (uh-**duhlt**)

An **adult** is a grown-up person. Men and women are **adults**. The library has a room where **adults** can sit and read and another room where children can read. **[adults]**

adventure (ad-**ven**-chuhr)

An **adventure** is something you do that is new and exciting. An **adventure** may be scary or dangerous. Climbing up a mountain is an adventure for Crystal. **[adventures]**

adventure

afraid (uh-**frayd**)

When you are **afraid**, you feel frightened and think that something bad might happen. Rosa is **afraid** of big dogs that bark, but she likes cats a lot. Mack is **afraid** of scary movies.

after (af-tuhr)

After means at a later time. Mom promised us ice cream **after** lunch. The opposite of **after** is before.

afternoon (af-tuhr-**noon**)

Afternoon is the time of day after twelve noon and before the beginning of evening. At camp we work with clay in the **afternoon**. Tomorrow **afternoon** Tony is going shopping for a pet turtle. **[afternoons]**

again (uh-**gen**)

Again means one more time. Let's play that game **again**. The piano teacher asked Billy to play the song **again**, but this time a little slower.

against (uh-**genst**)

1. Against means touching or pressing something. The worker leaned his ladder **against** the house to climb up to the roof.
2. When two teams play **against** each other, they are in a contest to win. The soccer team in our town won when it played **against** the team in the next town.
3. When a person is **against** something, the person does not agree with it. The parents were **against** children riding bicycles in the street.

age (ayj)

Age means how old something is or how many years a person has lived. Ebony's three cousins are **ages** four, seven, and nine. **[ages]**

agree (uh-**gree**)

When you **agree** with someone else, you and the other person think the same way. Scientists **agree** that the earth is round. Rosana and Juan **agreed** that they would rather go to the beach than to the zoo. **[agreeing, agreed]**

air (air)

Air is a gas that is all around us. Most living things need to breathe **air** to stay alive. We cannot see **air** unless it has drops of water or dirt in it.

airplane

airplane (air-**playn**)

An **airplane** is a machine that flies in the air. **Airplanes** have wings and engines. The word **plane** is short for **airplane**. **[airplanes]**

airport (air-**port**)

An **airport** is a place where airplanes take off and land. The road in an **airport** where airplanes take off and land is called a **runway**. We looked out of the huge windows at the **airport** and counted three airplanes in the sky and four on the runway. **[airports]**

smoke **alarm**

alarm (uh-**lahrm**)

An **alarm** makes a loud sound to let people know that something may be wrong. The **alarm** in Uncle Ted's car makes a loud buzzing noise when he opens the door. Marsha put new batteries in the smoke **alarm** near the stairs. **[alarms]**

alien (ay-lee-uhn)

1. An **alien** is a person who comes from another country. Another word for an **alien** from another country is **foreigner**.

2. In stories, an **alien** is also someone who comes from outer space. Another word for an **alien** from outer space is **extraterrestrial**. [**aliens**]

alike (uh-like)

Things that are **alike** are the same. All the dishes in the set are **alike**. The puppies are brown with white spots and look **alike**. *Right* and *write* are words that sound **alike**.

dressed **alike**

alive (uh-live)

Alive means to be living. People need food and water to stay **alive**. When plants and animals grow, they are **alive**. When they die, they will no longer be **alive**.

all (awl)

All means every part of something or everyone. Kim and her friends ate **all** the birthday cake. Some of the tomatoes were green when we picked them, but two days later they were **all** red.

alligator (al-uh-gayt-uhr)

An **alligator** is a large, flat reptile with a long tail, short legs, and a large head with many sharp teeth. American **alligators** live in rivers and swamps in warm places in the United States. [**alligators**]

allow (uh-lou)

When someone **allows** you to do something, that person lets you do it. Mom **allows** us to watch television for one hour a day. The dog is not **allowed** to jump on the furniture. [**allowing, allowed**]

almost (awl-mohst)

Almost means close to or not far from completing something. Jared is **almost** eight years old. Abby has **almost** finished her glass of milk.

alone (uh-lohn)

When you are **alone**, there is no one else there. You are by yourself. Our dog, Albert, is **alone** when we are in school and Mom and Dad are at work.

a dog **alone** in the grass

along (uh-lawng)
1. Along means next to something. A fence runs **along** the edge of the field to keep the sheep in.
2. Along also means together. Melanie baked cookies for the party, **along** with her friend Marta and Marta's mother. Would your friend Roger like to come **along** with us to the zoo?

reading **aloud**

aloud (uh-loud)
Aloud means in a voice that other people can hear. Pedro read his story **aloud** to the class.

alphabet (al-fuh-bet)
The letters of a language that people use for writing are called the **alphabet**. There are 26 letters in our **alphabet**. The **alphabet** has large letters, called capital letters, and small letters. The small letters of the **alphabet** are a, b, c, d, e, f, g, h, i, j, k, l, m, n, o, p, q, r, s, t, u, v, w, x, y, and z. Look under the word **capital** to see the large letters. **[alphabets]**

always (awl-wayz)
Always means every time or all the time. Your birthday **always** falls on the same date every year. Summer **always** comes after spring and before autumn. It is **always** cold in winter in Alaska.

amount (uh-mount)
Amount means how much of something there is. Cattle eat a large **amount** of food every day. The painter needed a small **amount** of green paint to paint the steps outside. **[amounts]**

amphibian (am-fib-ee-uhn)
An **amphibian** is an animal that is born in water and lives in water while it is young. Later, as an adult, an **amphibian** lives on land. Toads and frogs are **amphibians**. **[amphibians]**

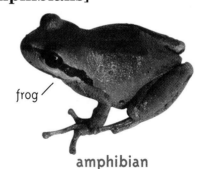

frog

amphibian

angry (ang-gree)
People feel **angry** when their feelings are hurt or when something happens that makes them very unhappy. Ellie felt **angry** when Mickey made fun of her new haircut. Grandpa was **angry** when a deer ate all his flowers. **[angrier, angriest]**

different kinds of **animals**

animal (an-uh-muhl)

An **animal** is anything that is living that is not a plant. Kittens, dogs, elephants, whales, squirrels, ants, and people are all **animals**. [animals]

anniversary (an-uh-vur-suh-ree)

An **anniversary** is a date that is remembered because something special or important happened on that date at an earlier time. July 7 is Mom and Dad's wedding **anniversary**. [anniversaries]

another (uh-nuhth-uhr)

Another means one more. It is so cold that Earl needs **another** sweater. May I please have **another** drink of water?

answer (an-suhr)

When someone says something to you, what you say back to that person is your **answer**. When Morgan asked the police officer for directions to the post office, the **answer** was, "Go to the third traffic light and turn right." [answers]

ant (ant)

An **ant** is a tiny animal that lives in tunnels in the ground. **Ants** are insects. [ants]

apart (uh-pahrt)

1. Apart means away from each other. My friend and I live far **apart**, but we send letters to each other. We pushed our chairs closer together because they were too far **apart**. An elephant's eyes are far **apart**.
2. Apart also means in pieces or in parts. Uncle Gaby took the toaster **apart** to fix it. After finishing the jigsaw puzzle, Jackson took it **apart** and put the pieces back in the box.

apartment (uh-pahrt-muhnt)

An **apartment** is one room or a group of rooms where people live. There are six **apartments** on each floor in our building. You can walk up the stairs or take an elevator to our **apartment** on the second floor. [apartments]

ape (ayp)

An **ape** is an animal that looks like a large monkey with very long arms and no tail. An **ape** can stand on two legs. **Apes** are mammals. **[apes]**

small **apes** called gibbons

apologize (uh-**pahl**-uh-jize)

To **apologize** is to say you are sorry about something you have done or said. Eric is going to **apologize** to Mr. Grady for breaking his window with a ball. Tish **apologized** to Ellen for stepping on her toe. **[apologizing, apologized]**

appear (uh-**pir**)

When something **appears**, it means you are able to see it. Sometimes a rainbow **appears** in the sky after it rains. **[appearing, appeared]**

apple (ap-uhl)

An **apple** is a round fruit with small seeds inside. **Apples** grow on trees. The skin of an **apple** is red, yellow, or green. **[apples]**

apple

aquarium (uh-**kwair**-ee-uhm)

An **aquarium** is a glass or plastic bowl or box where fish and plants live in water. Our cat sits on the floor and watches the fish swimming in the **aquarium**. **[aquariums]**

area (air-ee-uh)

An **area** is a place that is often part of a larger space. Our park has one **area** for playing on swings, another **area** for basketball and baseball, and a third **area** with benches and a sandbox. Let's clear off an **area** of the table, so we will have a place to write. **[areas]**

argue (ahr-gyoo)

When people **argue** with each other, they tell each other why they do not agree. Sometimes when people **argue**, they feel angry and speak in loud voices. **[arguing, argued]**

arm (ahrm)

1. Your **arm** is the part of your body between your shoulder and your hand.
2. An **arm** is also something that looks like an **arm** or moves like one. The **arm** of the chair is weak, so please don't sit on it. **[arms]**

armor (ahr-muhr)

Armor is a metal suit that men wore a long time ago to protect themselves when they fought in wars. Knights were soldiers who wore **armor**. **[armor]**

armor

army (ahr-mee)

An **army** is a group of people who fight together during a war. The **army** was small, but it was also strong. **[armies]**

around (uh-round)

1. Around means on all sides of something or somebody. Aunt Kim put her arms **around** Lois and gave her a big hug. The castle had a stone wall and water **around** it to protect it.
2. Around also means in a circle. Jamaal and Duane skated **around** and **around** until they were tired.

arrive (uh-rive)

When you **arrive**, you are at a place. Every morning we **arrive** at school just as the bell rings. The train **arrived** on time. **[arriving, arrived]**

arrow (ar-oh)

arrow

1. An arrow is a stick with a point on one end and sometimes feathers at the other end.
2. An arrow is also a sign that points in a direction to show you which way to go. The **arrow** sign on the street means that all the cars and bicycles must go in the same direction. **[arrows]**

art

art (ahrt)

Paintings, drawings, and sculpture are kinds of **art**. On Saturdays, Mr. Rizzo has **art** classes for children and adults. People who create **art** are called **artists**. At the museum downtown the fourth-grade class saw an **art** show with paintings by famous American **artists**. Writing, music, and dance are also known as **arts**.

ask (ask)

When you **ask** something, you use words to find out the answer to a question. Please **ask** your dad if you can come with us to the zoo. "Do you know the words to that song?" **asked** Sean. The bird in the cage kept **asking**, "Where's a cookie?" **[asking, asked]**

asleep (uh-sleep)

When you are **asleep**, you are resting and your eyes are closed. Dad sometimes falls **asleep** in the middle of a television program. **Asleep** is the opposite of awake.

astronaut (as-truh-nawt)

An **astronaut** is a person who is trained to go into outer space. In 1969 American **astronauts** walked on the moon. In 1996 the American **astronaut** Shannon Lucid spent 188 days in space. [**astronauts**]

ate (ayt)

Ate comes from **eat**. We **ate** pizza and salad for supper.

attach (uh-tach)

Attach means to put one thing onto another so it will stay there. We used magnets to **attach** our pictures to the refrigerator door. [**attaching, attached**]

attic (at-ik)

An **attic** is a room or space under the roof of a building. There are suitcases and cartons with old toys and clothes in the **attic**. [**attics**]

audience (awd-ee-uhns)

An **audience** is the group of people who watch a play, movie, puppet show, or some other kind of program. [**audiences**]

audience watching a clown

aunt (ant) or (ahnt)

Your **aunt** is the sister of your mother or father. The wife of your uncle is also called your **aunt**. [**aunts**]

author (aw-thuhr)

An **author** is a person who writes stories or articles that are in books, magazines, or newspapers. **Author** is another word for **writer**. [**authors**]

autumn (awt-uhm)

Autumn is the season after summer and before winter. **Autumn** is also called **fall**. The leaves on some trees turn bright red, orange, and yellow during the **autumn**. [**autumns**]

autumn in Maine

awake (uh-wayk)

A person who is **awake** is not asleep. Nellie stayed so still that her mom thought she was asleep, but she was really **awake**.

away (uh-way)

1. Away means not near. When something has gone **away**, it has gone from a place that is near to a place that is not near. The bird flew **away** when the baby tried to touch it.
2. Away also means in a safe place. Please put your money **away** so you don't lose it.

Bb

baby (bay-bee)

A **baby** is a very young child. Juliana gave the **baby** a bottle of apple juice. **[babies]**

baby-sit (bay-bee-sit)

To **baby-sit** is to take care of a child when the child's parents are away. My older sister **baby-sits** the neighbor's children to earn money. A person who **baby-sits** is called a **baby-sitter**. **[baby-sitting, baby-sat]**

back (bak)

1. The **back** is the upper part of the body that is behind the chest. The **back** cannot be seen from the front. Emily's rabbit loves to have its **back** rubbed.
2. Back is the opposite of front. Joey and Alex are the first children on the bus to school and always choose the two seats in the **back**. **[backs]**

backpack (bak-pak)

A **backpack** is a cloth bag worn on the back, used to carry books, clothes, and other things you want to take with you. A **backpack** sometimes has pockets and zippers. **[backpacks]**

wearing **backpacks**

wearing caps **backward**

backward (bak-wuhrd)

1. Backward means in the direction that the back is facing. As Kassim ran with the ball, he looked **backward** quickly to see if anyone was near him.
2. Backward also means in a way that is opposite to what it should be. Some words, like *mom* and *dad,* are spelled the same way forward and **backward**. Another word for **backward** is **backwards**.

bad (bad)

1. Bad means not good. Lee is **bad** at spelling but good at numbers.
2. Bad also means not acting the right way. Our dog knew it was **bad** to get on the bed with muddy paws.
3. Bad also means not good to eat. Abby knew the milk was **bad** because it tasted sour.
4. When something is **bad**, it may hurt in some way or be dangerous. A tree fell down during the **bad** storm on Monday. **[worse, worst]**

bag (bag)

A **bag** is a container open at one end and used for carrying things. **Bags** are made of paper, plastic, or cloth and sometimes have handles. **Bags** with handles are called **shopping bags**. [bags]

bake (bayk)

To **bake** something is to cook it in an oven. Grandmother promised to teach me how to **bake** pies the way she does. Someone who **bakes** bread, cookies, cakes, or similar kinds of food is called a **baker**. A **bakery** is a place where these foods are **baked** and sold.
[baking, baked]

balance (bal-uhns)

Balance means to keep yourself or something else from falling over. Have you ever seen a seal **balance** a ball on the tip of its nose? The dancer **balanced** herself on one foot.
[balancing, balanced]

balance

ball (bawl)

A **ball** has a round shape. People play games with **balls** like baseballs and tennis balls. A beach ball is a large, light **ball**. There are also **balls** of string. You can roll your socks up into a **ball**. [balls]

ballet (ba-lay)

Ballet is a special kind of dancing that takes a lot of practice and training. A person who dances **ballet** is called a **ballet dancer**. A girl or woman who dances **ballet** is also called a **ballerina**. [ballets]

at a party with lots of **balloons**

balloon (buh-loon)

A **balloon** is a very thin bag that is filled with gas and can float in the air. [balloons]

banana (buh-nan-uh)

A **banana** is a long fruit with yellow skin that is peeled away. The fruit of a **banana** is soft and light in color and tastes sweet. [bananas]

band (band)

A **band** is a group of musicians who play music together. Melanie plays the drum in the marching **band** at school. [bands]

bandage (ban-dij)

A **bandage** is a piece of clean cloth used to put over a cut to protect it from dirt. [bandages]

toy **bank**

bank (bangk)

A **bank** is a place where people save their money. Sometimes children save money in a toy **bank** at home. **[banks]**

barber (bahr-buhr)

A **barber** is a person who cuts people's hair. Joey likes to watch in the mirror as the **barber** cuts his hair. **[barbers]**

bare (bair)

When something is **bare**, nothing is covering it. The basement light is a **bare** bulb. In winter many trees are **bare**. **[barer, barest]**

barefoot (bair-fut)

If you are **barefoot**, you are not wearing anything on your feet. Emily likes to feel the sand when she walks **barefoot** on the beach.

bark¹ (bahrk)

Bark is the outside layer of a tree. **Bark** can be rough or smooth.

bark² (bahrk)

A **bark** is a loud sound that dogs and some other animals make. **[barks]**

barn (bahrn)

A **barn** is a building on a farm where animals are kept warm and dry and where they often sleep. **[barns]**

baseball (bays-bawl)

Baseball is a game played by two teams. Players take turns using a bat to hit a small white ball called a **baseball**. They catch the **baseball** with a glove. **[baseballs]**

basement (bay-smuhnt)

A **basement** is the floor below the ground in a building. When it rains very hard, water comes into the **basement** of our house. **[basements]**

basket (bas-kit)

A **basket** is used for holding things. It is a kind of container. Some **baskets** are made of straw or small branches, and some are made of plastic or wire. Becky looked for clean socks in the laundry **basket**. Brian has a **basket** on his bicycle. **[baskets]**

basketball (bas-kit-bawl)

Basketball is a game played by two teams using a large ball called a **basketball**. The players win points by throwing the **basketball** through a large ring with a net attached to it. **[basketballs]**

a **basketball**

bat (bat)

1. A **bat** is a long stick that is wide at one end. **Bats** are made of wood, plastic, or metal and are used in baseball to hit the ball.
2. A **bat** is also an animal with wings. **Bats** sleep upside down and often live in caves. At the museum we learned that **bats** are mammals, not birds. **[bats]**

holding a **bat**

bath (bath)

When you take a **bath**, you get into a bathtub full of water and wash your body. **[baths]**

bathroom (bath-room)

A **bathroom** is a room that usually has a toilet, a sink, and a bathtub or shower. Bettina's towel hangs on a hook on the back of the **bathroom** door. **[bathrooms]**

bathtub (bath-tuhb)

A **bathtub** is a large tub, usually in the bathroom, that is filled with water for taking a bath. **[bathtubs]**

battery (bat-uh-ree)

A **battery** makes electricity and is used to make things work. When the flashlight doesn't light, I know it needs new **batteries**. **[batteries]**

beach (beech)

A **beach** is the area with sand or rocks next to oceans and lakes. I flew a kite on the **beach** while my sister played under an umbrella. **[beaches]**

bead (beed)

A **bead** is a small piece of plastic, clay, or metal that has a hole in it. Margarita put 12 **beads** on a string to make a necklace. **[beads]**

beak (beek)

The **beak** is the hard part at the end of a bird's mouth. **Beaks** are pointed or round. Some birds use their **beaks** to open seeds. **[beaks]**

bean (been)

A **bean** is the seed of a plant that can be cooked and eaten. Tim likes green **beans**, black **beans**, and pinto **beans**. **[beans]**

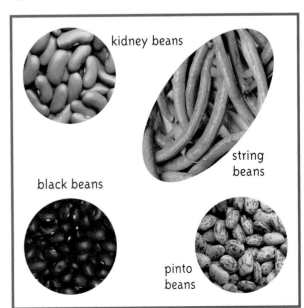

kidney beans

string beans

black beans

pinto beans

different kinds of **beans**

bear (bair)

A **bear** is a large animal with brown, black, or white fur and sharp claws and teeth. **Bears** can stand on their back legs, but usually move on all four legs. **Bears** are mammals. **[bears]**

beard (beerd)

A **beard** is the hair that grows on the lower part of the face around the chin. When Elizabeth hugs her dad, his **beard** tickles her face. **[beards]**

beat (beet)

1. When you **beat** something, you hit it. When you **beat** a drum, you can make music that is fast or slow. **2. Beat** also means to win. When Millie and her uncle play games, her uncle **beats** her at tennis, but she **beats** him at computer games. **[beating, beaten]**

beating a huge drum

beautiful (byoot-i-fuhl)

When something is **beautiful**, you enjoy looking at it or listening to it. In the spring we walk through the park to look at the **beautiful** flowers. The singer has a **beautiful** voice.

beaver (bee-vuhr)

beaver

A **beaver** is an animal with dark fur, a wide, flat tail, and sharp teeth to cut wood. A **beaver** is a mammal. **Beavers** build dams in water and make their homes there. **[beavers]**

bed (bed)

A **bed** is a piece of furniture for sleeping. Aunt Jan has a sofa that opens into a **bed**, where I sleep when I stay with her. **[beds]**

bee (bee)

A **bee** is a flying insect that lives in a hive. Some **bees** make honey. **[bees]**

bee   beetle

beetle (beet-l)

A **beetle** is an insect with hard wings that cover a pair of soft wings used to fly. **[beetles]**

before (bi-for)

1. If something happens **before** something else, it happens first or earlier. **Before** Danielle learned to write, she learned the letters of the alphabet. **2. Before** also means in front of. At the supermarket, there were three people **before** us in line.

begin (bi-gin)

Begin means start. The puppet show **begins** at two o'clock. Everyone clapped when the musicians **began** to play. **[beginning, began, begun]**

behind (bi-hinde)

Behind means in back of. In the photograph the tall students stood **behind** the shorter ones so everyone could be seen. There are places to park **behind** the store.

believe (bi-leev)

If you **believe** something, you think that it is true. Do you **believe** that witches, dragons, and ghosts are real? **[believing, believed]**

bell (bel)

A **bell** is a round, hollow piece of metal that makes a sound when it is hit. When the school **bell** rings at noon, we know it is time for lunch. Tina and Milo saw the famous Liberty **Bell** when they visited Philadelphia. **[bells]**

bell

belong (bi-lawng)

1. If something **belongs** to you, it is yours. Does this glove **belong** to you?
2. When something **belongs** somewhere, that is where it should be. These cassettes **belong** on the shelf, not all over the floor. **[belonging, belonged]**

below (bi-loh)

Below means under or lower than. The toys belong on the shelf **below** the books. The bottom of the boat is **below** the surface of the water.

belt (belt)

A **belt** is a long, narrow piece of leather, cloth, or plastic that you wear around your waist. Kate likes to wear her silver **belt** with blue pants or a black skirt. **[belts]**

sharing a **bench**

bench (bench)

A **bench** is a long, narrow piece of furniture that is big enough for at least two people to sit on. We sat on a **bench** at the railroad station to wait for the next train. **[benches]**

bend (bend)

Bend means to curve. If something **bends** or you **bend** something, it curves and is not straight. The doll's arms and legs **bend**, and its head turns. Arlen **bent** down to pick up the nickel he found on the sidewalk. **[bending, bent]**

raspberries   blueberries   strawberries

three kinds of **berries**

berry (ber-ee)

A **berry** is a seed or fruit of a plant. **Berries** are often small and round and sometimes you can eat them. Strawberries, raspberries, and blueberries are **berries** you can eat. In summer we pick **berries** and make fruit pies with them. **[berries]**

beside (bi-side)

Beside means next to. I like to sit **beside** my best friend on the bus. When you set the table, please put the spoon **beside** the knife. May I sit **beside** you?

best (best)

If something is the **best**, it is better than the rest or all others. My oldest cousin is the **best** swimmer in our family. Reid tried on three sweaters and bought the one she liked **best**.

between (bi-tween)

Between means in the middle, with something on either side. The parade marched down the middle of the street, **between** the crowds of people on the sidewalk. To make a sandwich, Nicholas put some turkey and lettuce **between** two pieces of bread.

bicycle (bie-sik-uhl)

A **bicycle** has two wheels, a seat, and two handles and is used for riding. Alicia pushed hard on the pedals to get her **bicycle** up the hill without stopping on the way. A short word for **bicycle** is **bike**. **[bicycles]**

handlebars

seat

crossbar

tire

pedal

training wheel

wheel

bicycle

big (big)

When something is **big**, it takes up a lot of space. My feet keep growing and are almost too **big** for my boots. An elephant is a very **big** animal. Another word for **big** is **large**. **[bigger, biggest]**

bill¹ (bil)

Bill is another word for **beak**. It is the hard part at the end of a bird's mouth. [**bills**]

bill² (bil)

1. Bill is a word for a piece of paper money. A picture of the first president of the United States is on the one-dollar **bill**.

2. A **bill** is also a word for how much money is owed for something bought or for work that has been done. [**bills**]

bird (buhrd)

A **bird** is an animal that has wings and feathers and that lays eggs. Most **birds** fly, but ostriches and penguins cannot fly. Many **birds** fly south when the weather gets cold and return north when it gets warm. [**birds**]

birthday (burth-day)

Your **birthday** is the day you were born. We have a family party every April for Grandma's and Andrew's **birthdays**. [**birthdays**]

bite (bite)

If you **bite** something, you use your teeth to take hold of it and cut it. Michele could not **bite** into the candy. I **bit** into the pear to see if it was sweet. [**biting, bit, bitten**]

black (blak)

Black is the darkest color there is. **Black** is the opposite of **white**. Pandas, skunks, and zebras are **black**-and-white animals. Our neighbor has a **black** cat with a bell on a ribbon around its neck.

blanket (blang-kit)

A **blanket** is a large piece of cloth that fits on a bed to keep people warm while they sleep. We slept under two **blankets** all winter long. Marco's family keeps extra **blankets** in the closet. [**blankets**]

blew (bloo)

Blew is from **blow**. When something was blowing at an earlier time, we say that it **blew**. In the storm yesterday, it rained hard and a strong wind **blew**.

different kinds of **birds**

scarlet ibis

flamingo

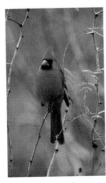
cardinal

snowy egret

seagull

peregrine falcon

blind (blinde)

Blind means not able to see. Pam's cat is going **blind** and sometimes runs into the chairs. People who are **blind** can learn to read by using their fingers to read braille. Mrs. Block, who is **blind**, has a special dog to help her cross the street.

block (blahk)

1. A **block** is an area in a city with a street on all four sides. Mrs. Martinez walks her dog around the **block** three times a day.
2. Block also means a street between two other streets. There is a school at the end of Tina's **block**.
3. A **block** is a toy that usually has flat sides and is made of wood or plastic. Sean spells words and builds towers with **blocks** that have letters on them. **[blocks]**
4. To **block** means to be in the way of or keep something from passing by. When snow **blocks** the road, no cars can pass until it is cleared. **[blocking, blocked]**

blocks

blood (bluhd)

Blood is a red liquid inside your body. **Blood** keeps your heart and other parts of your body healthy. When you cut yourself, sometimes you see **blood. [blood]**

flowers in **bloom**

bloom (bloom)

When flowers **bloom**, they open up. When trees **bloom**, flowers grow on them. The flowers on cherry trees **bloom** every spring. The roses in the garden **bloomed** all summer long. **[blooming, bloomed]**

blouse (blous)

A **blouse** is clothing that you wear on the upper part of your body. Camille is wearing a green and yellow **blouse** that matches her skirt. **[blouses]**

blow (bloh)

Blow means to use air to move or fill something. Let's **blow** up balloons for the party. The wind **blew** the paper plates off the picnic table. **[blowing, blew]**

blue (bloo)

Blue is a color. The sky on a sunny day is **blue**. If you mix **blue** paint with yellow paint, you will get green paint. Arnold's eyes are **blue**.

board (bord)

A **board** is a long, flat piece of wood that is used to build things. We watched the carpenter place one **board** next to another to make a new floor. [**boards**]

using **boards** to build a house

boat (boht)

A **boat** is used to ride in water or to carry things through water. Early in the morning the fishermen go out in a **boat** with a large net to catch fish. Tugboats, sailboats, and ferries are different kinds of **boats**. [**boats**]

body (bahd-ee)

Your **body** is all of you, from the top of your head to the bottom of your feet and everything inside, like your brain, heart, and bones. We bend our **bodies** in many different ways when we do gymnastics. Whenever I go to the doctor, she measures my **body** to see how tall I am. [**bodies**]

boil (boil)

When water or other liquids **boil**, they get very hot and have bubbles on the surface. When we cook rice on the stove, we wait for the water to **boil** in the pot before we pour in the rice. [**boiling, boiled**]

bone (bohn)

A **bone** is the hard part of your body that helps you sit up and stand up straight. When Vince broke a **bone** in his leg, he walked with crutches until the **bone** healed. A word for all the **bones** in the body is **skeleton**. [**bones**]

book (buk)

A **book** has pages with words or pictures on the inside and a cover on the outside. You are reading a **book**. Some **books** have hard covers and some have soft covers. Sarah borrows two **books** from the library every week. [**books**]

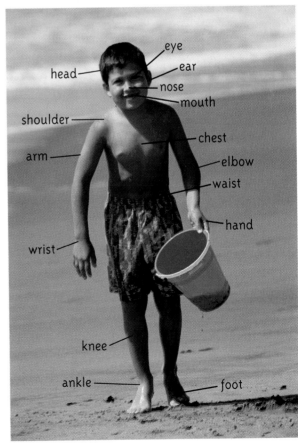

body

boot (boot)

A **boot** is a kind of shoe with a high top that covers part of the leg. **Boots** keep your feet warm and dry. **[boots]**

born (born)

When babies are **born**, they come out of their mother's body to live in the world. The day you are **born** is called your **birthday**. The monkey **born** at the zoo in March was named Bebe.

borrow (bahr-oh)

When you **borrow** something, you use something that belongs to someone else. Mariah **borrowed** videos from a friend to watch on a rainy day. **[borrowing, borrowed]**

both (bohth)

When there are two people or things, we use **both** to mean the two of them. I'm taking **both** of my bathing suits on vacation. **Both** of my parents work.

bottle (baht-l)

A **bottle** is a container that holds liquid. **Bottles** are usually made of plastic or glass. Elbert carries a plastic **bottle** of water with him when he goes hiking. **[bottles]**

bottom (baht-uhm)

The lowest part of something is called the **bottom**. Let's ski to the **bottom** of the hill. Kelley wrote her name at the **bottom** of the paper. **[bottoms]**

bought (bawt)

Bought comes from **buy**. We **bought** popcorn for our party.

bounce (bouns)

When something **bounces**, it hits a surface and goes up and down by itself. I hate it when the soccer ball misses the net and **bounces** off the post. **[bouncing, bounced]**

gift with a **bow**

bow¹ (boh)

1. To make a **bow**, you tie ribbon or string into small circles and make a knot. The best part of wrapping packages is tying the **bow**.
2. A **bow** is also a long stick with strings that is used to play musical instruments like the violin. **[bows]**

bow² (bou)

When you **bow**, you bend your body forward at the waist. At the end of the play, the audience claps and the actors stand together in a line and **bow**. **[bowing, bowed]**

a **bow**

bowl (bohl)

A **bowl** is a round container with deep sides for holding food like soup or cereal. **Bowls** come in many sizes and are made of glass, plastic, clay, metal, and wood. **[bowls]**

a tool **box**

box (bahks)
A **box** holds things and is often in the shape of a rectangle or a square. **Boxes** are made of heavy paper, plastic, or wood. The worker at the post office weighed the **box** I was mailing to my friend and then put stamps on it. Will collects baseball cards and keeps them in an orange **box** on a shelf. [**boxes**]

boy (boi)
A **boy** is a young male person who is still a child. When **boys** grow up, they become men. The **boys** sat together in the back of the bus. [**boys**]

braille (brayl)
Braille is a kind of writing that uses raised dots to make letters. People who are blind read **braille** by touching it with their fingers.

brain (brayn)
The **brain** is a part of the body inside the head. People and animals have **brains**. It is because of your **brain** that you can move, think, and feel. [**brains**]

brake (brayk)
A **brake** is something you use to make a wheel stop moving. The train stopped so quickly that the **brakes** made a very loud noise. [**brakes**]

branch (branch)
A **branch** is a part of a tree or bush that grows out from the trunk. A bird has built its nest between two of the **branches** in the apple tree. Mr. Caro took a picture of children on the **branches** of a tree in the park. [**branches**]

children on **branches** of a tree

brave (brayv)
When people are **brave**, they act strong and without fear even if they feel afraid. Firefighters are **brave** when they go into burning buildings to save people. Tommy wanted to be **brave** when the dentist pulled out his tooth. [**braver, bravest**]

bread (bred)
Bread is food that is made of flour and is baked. My favorite sandwich is smooth peanut butter and jelly on whole wheat **bread**. [**breads**]

break (brayk)

When something **breaks**, it comes apart or stops working. Dad said that if we **break** a window playing ball, we have to save our money for a new window. When Jared's headphones **broke**, he could hear music in only one ear.
[breaking, broke, broken]

breakfast (brek-fuhst)

Breakfast is the first meal of the day. I have juice and cereal for **breakfast** before I go to school. What do you eat for **breakfast**?
[breakfasts]

breathe (breeTH)

When you **breathe**, air goes in and out of your body through your nose or your mouth.
[breathing, breathed]

brick (brik)

A **brick** is a small block of clay that is used to build things. The apartment house on the corner is made of red **bricks**. A small bird built a nest in the chimney where the **bricks** are missing. **[bricks]**

bricks

bridge

bridge (brij)

A **bridge** is a road that is built over water or over a valley so that cars and people can go from one side to the other. People can travel from New Jersey to New York over a **bridge**, through a tunnel, or on a ferry. **[bridges]**

bright (brite)

When something is **bright**, it gives off light and shines. The campers packed a **bright** light for their trip so they could read and play games in their tent at night. The moon was so **bright** at the beach that we could see all the boats in the water even in the dark.
[brighter, brightest]

bring (bring)

When you **bring** something, you have it with you. I'll **bring** the balls and you **bring** the bats to baseball practice tomorrow. Anna **brought** sandwiches, drinks, and some cookies to share with us at lunch.
[bringing, brought]

broken (broh-kuhn)

Broken is from **break**. When something is **broken**, it has stopped working. The leg of the chair is **broken** and needs to be glued together.

sweeping with a **broom**

broom (broom)

A **broom** has a long handle and a brush at one end. A **broom** is used to sweep up dirt. The **broom** is in the kitchen closet. Ted is sweeping the sidewalk with a **broom**. **[brooms]**

brother (bruhth-uhr)

If you have a **brother**, he is a boy who has the same parents you have. Hillary has an older **brother** and a younger **brother. [brothers]**

brown (broun)

Brown is a color. Chocolate, mud, pinecones, birds' nests, hamsters, and some people's eyes are **brown**.

brush (bruhsh)

A **brush** is used to make hair and fur smooth, to clean the surface of things, or to paint. Michael got out his dog's shampoo, **brush**, and towel before giving Baxter a bath. At the end of the art class, the children wash out their **brushes** and put them in cans to dry. **[brushes]**

bubble (buhb-uhl)

A **bubble** is very light and round and has air in it. **Bubbles** float in the air like tiny, clear balloons. **Bubbles** are usually made from soap or some other liquid. **[bubbles]**

blowing a **bubble**

bucket (buhk-it)

A **bucket** is a round container that is open at the top. A **bucket** has high sides and a round, flat bottom. **Bucket** is another word for **pail**. The farmer filled a **bucket** with grain to feed his chickens. **[buckets]**

bud (buhd)

A **bud** is a flower before it has opened. The roses we bought yesterday are starting to open today as **buds**. **[buds]**

bug (buhg)

A **bug** is an insect or other tiny animal. Some **bugs** fly and others crawl. We have screens on our windows to keep the **bugs** out when the windows are open. [**bugs**]

build (bild)

Build means to make something out of different parts. At the playground, workers are **building** three ladders to climb on, two ramps, and a curved slide. [**building, built**]

building (bil-ding)

A **building** is a place that has been built, where people live, work, play, or go to school. **Buildings** can have many rooms and many floors. **Buildings** can be small like an igloo, huge like a castle, or tall like a skyscraper. [**buildings**]

garlic bulb

light bulb

bulbs

bulb (buhlb)

1. A **bulb** is the part of a plant that grows in the soil and makes roots below it and flowers above it. A **bulb** has a round shape and a short stem. Tulips are flowers that grow from **bulbs**.
2. A light **bulb** is a different kind of bulb. A light **bulb** uses electricity to make light. [**bulbs**]

bulldozer

bulldozer (bul-doh-zuhr)

A **bulldozer** is a machine with a large piece of metal in front that pushes dirt and rocks away. People usually use **bulldozers** to clear land to build buildings. [**bulldozers**]

bulletin board (bul-uht-n bord)

A **bulletin board** is a board that notes and pictures can be attached to. We put postcards, photographs, and pictures from magazines on the **bulletin board** in our room. [**bulletin boards**]

bulletin board

bump (buhmp)
1. A **bump** is a round place that is above the area around it. William got a **bump** on his head when he hit it on a low branch of a tree. When something has many **bumps** on it, we say it is **bumpy**. The country road was **bumpy**. **[bumps]**
2. When you **bump** into something, your body hits something you didn't mean to hit. **[bumping, bumped]**

bunch (buhnch)
A **bunch** is a group of things. We bought tomatoes, lettuce, and a **bunch** of carrots. **[bunches]**

burn (buhrn)
When something **burns**, it is on fire. Let's take the bread out of the toaster before it **burns**. **[burning, burned]**

bury (ber-ee)
When you **bury** something, you put it in the ground or in the sea. We watched the squirrel **bury** acorns in the dirt. **[burying, buried]**

bus (buhs)
A **bus** is like a long van with many windows and rows of seats. A yellow **bus** takes the children in our town to school. **[buses]**

bush (bush)
A **bush** is a plant with many branches, but it is smaller than a tree. The birds like to eat the berries on the **bushes**. **[bushes]**

busy (biz-ee)
Busy means doing something or doing a lot of things. The whole family was **busy** preparing the holiday meal. **[busier, busiest]**

butter (buht-uhr)
Butter is a yellow food that is made from cream or milk. **Butter** is hard when it is cold and soft when it is warm. I like to put **butter** on corn.

butterfly (buht-uhr-flie)
A **butterfly** is an insect with two pairs of wings that are often brightly colored. **Butterflies** develop from caterpillars. **[butterflies]**

butterflies

button (buht-n)
A **button** is something small and often round that goes through a hole to hold clothes together. Heidi's sweater has red **buttons** in the shape of hearts. **[buttons]**

buy (bie)
If you **buy** something, you spend money to get it. William and Megan are saving their money to **buy** a skateboard. **[buying, bought]**

cabin (kab-uhn)

A **cabin** is a small house or building made of logs or plain boards. When Dad and his friends go fishing, they stay in a **cabin** by a stream. **[cabins]**

caboose (kuh-boos)

A **caboose** is the last car of a train. The workers on the train sleep in the **caboose**. **[cabooses]**

cactus plants

saguaro cactus   organ pipe cactus

cactus (kak-tuhs)

A **cactus** is a plant with a thick stem, sharp points, and no leaves. **Cactuses** grow in deserts and come in many shapes and sizes. Some **cactuses** grow berries and flowers. **[cactuses or cacti]**

cafeteria (kaf-uh-tir-ee-uh)

A **cafeteria** is a place to eat. In a **cafeteria**, people look at different kinds of food, choose the ones they want, and then carry their food to a table to eat. **[cafeterias]**

cage (kayj)

A **cage** is a box with open sides made of wire or bars. Pets or animals in zoos are sometimes kept in **cages** to keep them from running away. The kindergarten class has a bird in a **cage** with a swing and a hamster in a **cage** with a running wheel. **[cages]**

cake (kayk)

A **cake** is a sweet food that is baked. **Cakes** have different flavors. Most **cakes** are made of flour, butter, eggs, milk, and sugar. Josh's favorite **cake** is chocolate, but Polly likes carrot **cake** with raisins. **[cakes]**

calculator (kal-kyuh-layt-ur)

A **calculator** is a machine that adds, subtracts, multiplies, divides, and does many other things with numbers. **Calculators** have keys to press and a screen that shows the answer. **[calculators]**

calculator

calendar (kal-uhn-duhr)

A **calendar** shows all the days, weeks, and months in a year. Mom writes the days and time for Jack's soccer practice on the kitchen **calendar**. **[calendars]**

calf (kaf)

A young cow or bull is called a **calf**. Young elephants, giraffes, and whales are also called **calves**. [**calves**]

call (kawl)

1. Call means to speak in a loud voice. Bobby was listening to music with headphones and didn't hear his dad **calling** him.
2. Call also means to use the telephone to speak with someone. We **called** Grandma on her birthday.
3. Call also means to give a name to someone or something. My real name is Elizabeth, but everyone **calls** me Liz. [**calling, called**]
4. A **call** is a cry or shout. When Henry fell out of a tree, his neighbor heard his **call** and ran to help.
5. A **call** is a special sound made by a bird or other animal. We haven't seen the owl in the woods, but we have heard its **call**. [**calls**]

camcorder (kam-kord-ur)

A **camcorder** is both a television camera and a videotape recorder that is small enough to be held in the hands. Mr. McCall recorded the second-grade class play with a **camcorder** and played it back for the first graders the next day. [**camcorders**]

camel

camel (kam-uhl)

A **camel** is a large animal with one or two humps on its back, a long neck, and long legs. **Camels** live in the desert and can carry people or heavy things on their backs. [**camels**]

camera (kam-ruh)

A **camera** is a machine for taking pictures. Some **cameras** are used to take photographs and others take films for home movies or television. [**cameras**]

camp (kamp)

1. A **camp** is a place where people go to have fun and spend time outside. At **camp**, people sometimes live in cabins or tents. Most **camps** are in the country. [**camps**]
2. To **camp** means to go to a place where people spend a lot of time outdoors. Ryan and his family like to **camp** in the mountains and sleep in a large tent. A person who **camps** or goes to a **camp** is called a **camper**. [**camping, camped**]

camcorder

campground (kamp-ground)

A **campground** is a place in the country that is used for camping. At a **campground**, people sleep in tents or vans and spend a lot of time outdoors. **[campgrounds]**

can¹ (kan) or (kuhn)

When you **can** do something, it means you are able to do it. Because Chelsea **can** swim, she is allowed to go into the deep end of the pool. Before she **could** swim, she stayed in water that was not over her head. **[could]**

can² (kan)

A **can** is a metal or plastic container used to hold food, paint, and other things until we are ready to use them. When we went camping, we took **cans** of spaghetti and beans. Marla used a watering **can** to water the flowers. **[cans]**

a watering **can**

candle (kan-duhl)

A **candle** is a stick made from wax with a string inside that burns. **Candles** are used to make light. **Candles** are also used on birthday cakes. **[candles]**

candy (kan-dee)

Candy is a sweet food that has different flavors. **Candy** is usually made with sugar. Beth's favorite **candy** is made from chocolate. **[candies]**

in a **canoe**

canoe (kuh-noo)

A **canoe** is a long, narrow boat. People use paddles to move a **canoe** through water. **[canoes]**

cap (kap)

A **cap** is a small, soft, round hat with a rounded piece in the front. Each player on the baseball team wears a red **cap**. **[caps]**

capital (kap-uht-l)

1. A **capital** is a very important city in a country or state. A **capital** is a city where people make laws for everyone to follow. Washington, D.C., is the **capital** of the United States.
2. A **capital** is also a large letter of the alphabet. The **capital** letters of the alphabet are A, B, C, D, E, F, G, H, I, J, K, L, M, N, O, P, Q, R, S, T, U, V, W, X, Y, and Z. Your name begins with a **capital** letter. Sentences begin with a **capital** letter. **[capitals]**

cars and trucks

car (kahr)

1. A **car** is a machine that people drive or ride in. A **car** has an engine, a wheel for steering, and four wheels. People use **cars** to go from one place to another. Another word for **car** is **automobile**.
2. A **car** is also part of a train. **Cars** on a train are attached and move together. Maxim counted 20 **cars** in the long train that just went by. **[cars]**

card (kahrd)

A **card** is a small, thick piece of paper with words, numbers, or pictures on it. Uncle Jesse plays games of **cards** with us when we visit him. When her grandpa was sick, Dolores sent him a get-well **card**. Special **cards** made of plastic, called credit **cards** and bank **cards**, are used to buy things or to get money from bank accounts. **[cards]**

care (kair)

When you **care** about people or things, you feel good about them and want them to be treated well. Lauren feeds and hugs her dog because she **cares** about her so much. **[caring, cared]**

careful (kair-fuhl)

When people are **careful**, they think about what they are doing and try to do it well. The carpenter was **careful** not to cut his hand when he sawed the wood. Please be **careful** not to burn your hand on the hot pot on the stove.

carpenter (kahr-puhn-tuhr)

A person who builds houses, chairs, tables, and other things made of wood is called a **carpenter**. Three **carpenters** worked together to add a new room to the public library, where children can read books and listen to stories. **[carpenters]**

carrot (kair-uht)

A **carrot** is the long, orange root of a plant that grows in the ground. We eat **carrots** as a vegetable, raw or cooked. **[carrots]**

carry (kair-ee)

Carry means to hold something and move it from one place to another. We helped Mom **carry** the groceries from the elevator to our apartment.

carry

Paul likes to be **carried** on his father's shoulders. A kangaroo **carries** its baby in a pouch. **[carrying, carried]**

cart (kahrt)

A **cart** is a kind of box on wheels that is used to carry heavy things from place to place. Some **carts** have two wheels and are pulled, and some have four wheels and are pushed. **[carts]**

carton (kahrt-n)

A **carton** is a box made from thick, heavy paper. We buy juice in **cartons**. **[cartons]**

cartoon (kahr-toon)

A **cartoon** is a picture that is drawn to make people laugh. Allie likes to watch **cartoons** on television. **[cartoons]**

cash (kash)

Cash is money. Dimes, nickels, quarters, and dollar bills are **cash**.

cash machine (kash muh-sheen)

A **cash machine** is a machine with a computer that people use to take money out of their bank account or put money into it. **[cash machines]**

cash machine

cassette (kuh-set)

A **cassette** is a small, flat, plastic box with a tape inside that you can record on. A **cassette** with sounds of music or words is called an **audiocassette**. A **cassette** with sound and pictures is called a **videocassette**. Tish read the labels on the **cassettes** to find the one she wanted to play. **[cassettes]**

castle

castle (kas-uhl)

A **castle** is a large building with thick stone walls and tall towers. **Castles** were built many, many years ago to protect kings and queens. Some **castles** had water around them and a metal gate and drawbridge. **[castles]**

cat (kat)

A **cat** is an animal with four legs, a long tail, and soft fur. Some **cats** are pets. A baby **cat** is called a **kitten**.

cat

Some **cats**, like tigers and lions, live in the wild. A baby tiger or lion is called a **cub**. **[cats]**

catching a ball

catch (kach)

1. When you **catch** something, you take hold of it when it is moving. Darrell likes to **catch** the football and run with it. The spider **caught** a fly in its web.
2. Catch can also mean to become sick with something. "José, please cover your mouth when you sneeze so we won't **catch** your cold." **[catching, caught]**

caterpillar (kat-uhr-pil-uhr)

A **caterpillar** looks like a short, furry worm with tiny legs. A **caterpillar** spins a cocoon, and then grows and changes into a butterfly or moth. **[caterpillars]**

cattle (kat-l)

Cattle are cows and bulls that are raised on farms or ranches for milk and meat.

cave (kayv)

A **cave** is an open space in the side of a mountain or under the ground. Some **caves** have long tunnels, deep holes, large rooms, and rivers. Bats often live in **caves**. **[caves]**

CD (see dee)

CD is short for **compact disk**. Look under **compact disk**. **[CDs]**

CD-ROM (see dee-rahm)

A **CD-ROM** is a kind of compact disk used with a computer. It is made of plastic and is round and very thin. **CD-ROMs** store music, pictures, and other information. **[CD-ROMs]**

ceiling (see-ling)

The top of a room is called the **ceiling**. When you are in a room or hall and look up, you see the **ceiling**. **[ceilings]**

cellar (sel-uhr)

A **cellar** is a room under a building. The furnace that keeps our house warm in winter is in the **cellar**. During the winter we store our bicycles in the **cellar**. **[cellars]**

a candle in the **center** of the cake

center (sent-uhr)

When something is in the **center**, it is in the middle. On her first birthday, there was a candle in the **center** of Gwen's birthday cake. The library is in the **center** of town. **[centers]**

cereal (sir-ee-uhl)
Cereal is a food made from corn, wheat, rice, or oats, and is usually eaten for breakfast. Some **cereals** are cooked and eaten hot, and some are eaten cold with milk. [**cereals**]

chair (chair)
A **chair** is a piece of furniture to sit on. A **chair** has a seat, a back, and usually four legs. Some **chairs** also have arms. When the baby cries, we rock him gently in a rocking **chair**. [**chairs**]

chalk (chawk)
Chalk is a kind of powder made into a stick used for writing or drawing. The teacher used **chalk** to write spelling words on the board and told us to copy them. [**chalks**]

at the **chalkboard**

chalkboard (chawk-bord)
A **chalkboard** is a dark, smooth surface used for writing with chalk. A **chalkboard** is also called a **blackboard**. The word **board** is short for **chalkboard**. [**chalkboards**]

chance (chans)
1. A **chance** means that something might happen or be possible. Brian took a **chance** and tried to spell *hippopotamus*.
2. Chance also means a time to be able to do something or to be allowed to do something. At Rosa's party, each child had a **chance** to learn a magic trick from the magician. [**chances**]

change (chaynj)
When something **changes**, it becomes different from the way it was before. The gray-brown fur on an arctic fox **changes** to white in the winter. I've **changed** my mind and would like strawberries on my cereal instead of bananas. [**changing, changed**]

chapter (chap-tuhr)
A **chapter** is a large part of a book. Some books have many **chapters**. One **chapter** of the travel book tells all about zoos. [**chapters**]

chase (chays)
When you **chase** something, you run after it and try to catch it. Our cat likes to **chase** birds. Melinda **chased** after her little brother when he started running toward the street. [**chasing, chased**]

cheap (cheep)
If something is **cheap**, it costs only a little bit of money. This umbrella is very **cheap** today because it is on sale. This book for $1.00 is **cheaper** than that one for $3.00. [**cheaper, cheapest**]

check (chek)

1. Check means to look at something to see if it is right. Please **check** the grocery list to see if milk is on it. When Dad was looking for his lost keys, he **checked** in his jacket pocket. **[checking, checked]**
2. A **check** is a mark that you make to show that something has been done or is all right. Let's make a list and put a **check** next to each thing as we do it. **[checks]**

checkers (chek-uhrz)

Checkers is a game played on a board with black and red squares using round black and red pieces. Two people play **checkers** — one person plays with red pieces, and the other plays with black pieces.

cheerful (chir-fuhl)

When people are **cheerful**, they smile a lot and feel happy. Aunt Emma felt very **cheerful** after catching two small fish and one big one.

cheese (cheez)

Cheese is a food made from milk. **Cheese** can be soft or hard. Some **cheeses** melt. Joe had a **cheese** sandwich with lettuce and mustard for lunch today. **[cheeses]**

cherry (cher-ee)

A **cherry** is a small, round fruit that grows on a **cherry** tree. **Cherries** are red. Kay likes **cherry** yogurt and **cherry** pie. **[cherries]**

cherries

a **chess** set

chess (ches)

Chess is a game for two people, played on a board with rows of dark and light squares. Each player has 16 pieces. There are 6 different kinds of pieces, and each kind has a special name and special rules for being moved. Uncle Blake is going to teach Natasha and her friend Omar how to play **chess**.

chest (chest)

1. The front part of your body below your neck and above your waist is called your **chest**.
2. A **chest** is also a large, strong box for holding things. Many people keep toys and tools in **chests**. Damon was reading a story about a dragon that was guarding a **chest** full of gold coins.
3. A **chest of drawers** is a piece of furniture with drawers for keeping clothes and other things. **[chests]**

chew (choo)

Chew means to use teeth to tear food into small pieces. Giraffes **chew** leaves from the tops of trees. We watched the tiger at the zoo **chewing** a piece of meat for lunch. **[chewing, chewed]**

chicken (chik-uhn)

A **chicken** is a bird. People eat eggs and meat from **chickens**. A young **chicken** is called a **chick**. [**chickens**]

feeding a **chicken**

chief (cheef)

A **chief** is the head or leader of a group. The fire **chief** told the new firefighters that he was proud of them for doing their jobs so well. [**chiefs**]

child (childe)

A **child** is a young person who will grow up to be a man or a woman. Young boys and girls are called **children**. [**children**]

chimney (chim-nee)

A **chimney** takes smoke from a fireplace or furnace to the air outside. A **chimney** is shaped like a long box or tube made of special bricks and other materials that don't burn. [**chimneys**]

chin (chin)

Your **chin** is the part of your face below your mouth. Leah cut her **chin** when she fell from her bike. [**chins**]

chocolate (chahk-luht)

Chocolate is a food with a strong flavor. Sugar is added to **chocolate** to make it sweet. **Chocolate** is usually brown, but can also be white. **Chocolate** is used in candy, cake, and ice cream.

choose (chooz)

To **choose** means to pick the one you want from a group. After looking at all the fish, Chuck decided to **choose** two goldfish for his aquarium. [**choosing, chose, chosen**]

circle (suhr-kuhl)

A **circle** is a round line that looks like this: ○. The children held hands and danced in a **circle**. Robin drew a **circle** for the center of a flower and then drew petals all around it. [**circles**]

dancing in a **circle**

circus (suhr-kuhs)

A **circus** is a show with trained animals and clowns, and sometimes acrobats. **Circuses** travel from place to place with their show. [**circuses**]

city

city (sit-ee)

A **city** is a busy place with many buildings and many people who live and work there. Some **cities**, like New York **City**, have very tall buildings. Some **cities** have museums, theaters, orchestras, sports teams, and zoos. [**cities**]

clap (klap)

When you **clap**, you bring the front of your hands together to make a noise. The puppet show was so good that everyone began to **clap**. [**clapping, clapped**]

clarinet (klair-uh-net)

A **clarinet** is a long, narrow musical instrument that is hollow inside. You play a **clarinet** by blowing into one end of it with your mouth, while you press keys with your fingers. [**clarinets**]

class (klas)

A **class** is a group of students who are taught together in the same place. In school today, Pedro's **class** learned about whales. The room where a **class** is held is called a **classroom**. [**classes**]

claw (klaw)

A **claw** is a curved nail with a sharp point on the feet of cats, birds, reptiles, bears, and some other animals. Animals use their **claws** to hold onto things, to tear food apart, and to protect themselves. Animals like crabs and lobsters also have **claws**. Their **claws** open and close to grab things. [**claws**]

clay (klay)

Clay is a kind of earth that can be made into many different shapes when it is wet. **Clay** becomes hard as it dries. People often use **clay** to make bowls or other dishes, bricks, and sculpture. [**clays**]

clean (kleen)

1. When you **clean** something, you take dirt and dust off it. We **clean** the kitchen floor with soap and water. [**cleaning, cleaned**]
2. When there is no dirt on something, it is **clean**. Suzie's face and clothes were **clean** until she started eating that chocolate ice cream. [**cleaner, cleanest**]

Pedro's **class**

clear (klir)

1. Clear means that something is easy to see through. The airplane window was **clear** enough for Jackie to see tiny cars on the road far below.
2. Clear also means that something is easy to see, hear, or understand. The rules for the new game were **clear**, and we quickly learned how to play. **[clearer, clearest]**

click (klik)

1. To click means to make a sharp, quick noise. When the radio alarm goes on in the morning, the radio **clicks** and music starts to play.
2. To click also means to press a computer mouse to bring something onto a computer screen. When Kristin **clicks** on the picture of a castle, she opens her favorite computer game. **[clicking, clicked]**

climb (klime)

To **climb** means to move up something using your hands and feet. "Please **climb** down from there," begged Jimmy, looking up at his cat in the tree. We held the ladder for Mr. Hurley while he **climbed** up to get the cat. **[climbing, climbed]**

climbing a tree

wall clock

digital desk clock

clocks

clock (klahk)

A **clock** is a machine that shows us the time in hours, minutes, and sometimes seconds. Some **clocks** have hands that move over numbers to show the time. Others, called **digital clocks**, have numbers that change. **[clocks]**

close¹ (klohs)

Close means near. "Coretta, I want you to stay **close** to me," said Coretta's mother when they were shopping. **[closer, closest]**

close² (klohz)

When you **close** something, you shut it. We **close** our eyes when we go to sleep. Mark **closed** the screen door quickly to keep the bugs from flying in. **[closing, closed]**

closet (klahz-it)

A **closet** is a small room with a door where people keep clothes, and other things. **[closets]**

cloth (klawth)

Cloth is made from cotton, wool, or other kinds of thread. Clothes, blankets, and towels are made from **cloth**. The artist painted on **cloth** called canvas. **[cloths]**

clothes (klohz)

Clothes are the coats, shirts, pants, skirts, socks, pajamas, and other things that people wear to cover their bodies. Tom packed his warm **clothes** when he went to the mountains to ski. Another word for **clothes** is **clothing**. **[clothes]**

cloud (kloud)

A **cloud** looks like a white or gray shape floating in the sky. A **cloud** is made of many tiny drops of water or ice. Rain and snow fall to the earth from the **clouds**. **[clouds]**

clown (kloun)

A **clown** is a person who wears bright, funny clothes and does tricks and other things to make people laugh. Two **clowns** at the circus did somersaults and then did tricks with dogs and elephants. **[clowns]**

clown

club (kluhb)

A **club** is a group of people who meet to do something together that they all like. Helene joined a hiking **club**. Joe belongs to a camera **club**. **[clubs]**

coast

coast (kohst)

The **coast** is the land at the edge of the sea or the ocean. If you look at a map of the United States, the East **Coast** is on the right side and touches the Atlantic Ocean. The West **Coast** is on the left side and touches the Pacific Ocean. **[coasts]**

coat (koht)

A **coat** is clothing that you wear to keep warm or dry. A **coat** is worn over other clothes. A **coat** that is made to protect you from the rain is called a **raincoat**. **[coats]**

cocoon (kuh-koon)

A **cocoon** is the small covering that a caterpillar spins around itself to live in before it becomes a butterfly or moth. **[cocoons]**

coin (koin)
A **coin** is a piece of metal with a picture and number on it that is used as money. Pennies, nickels, dimes, and quarters are **coins**. **[coins]**

cold (kohld)
1. Something that is **cold** has a very low temperature, and is not warm or hot. When water is very **cold**, it freezes and turns to ice. The **coldest** state of the United States is Alaska. **[colder, coldest]**
2. A **cold** is also a kind of sickness. A person who has a **cold** often coughs and sneezes and does not feel well. **[colds]**

collect (kuh-lekt)
Collect means to put things together in one place. Mr. and Mrs. Walter **collect** water when it rains and use it to water their flowers. When Uncle Morris taught writing, he **collected** books by many different authors. **[collecting, collected]**

color (kuhl-uhr)
Red, yellow, and blue are **colors**. They are the **colors** that make other **colors** and are called primary **colors**. The dancers wore costumes of different colors. **[colors]**

color

comb (kohm)
A **comb** is a straight piece of plastic or metal with small pieces, called teeth, attached to it. You hold a **comb** in your hand. People use **combs** to smooth their hair or an animal's fur. **[combs]**

compact disk (kahm-pakt disk)
A **compact disk** is round and very thin. It is made of plastic. A **compact disk** stores music, pictures, and other information that can be played back on a special player called a **CD player**. **CD** is short for **compact disk**. The kindergarten class listened to a **CD** with many different kinds of songs on it. **[compact disks]**

compass (kuhm-puhs)
A **compass** is a round instrument that shows directions with an arrow or needle that moves and points to the north. The hikers used a **compass** to find their way out of the woods. The **compass** on the ferry showed that it was going in the right direction. **[compasses]**

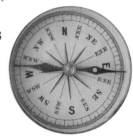
compass

complete (kuhm-pleet)
Something is **complete** when all of its parts are there together. The **complete** alphabet has 26 letters. Nina has to **complete** her homework before she is allowed to watch television after dinner. **[completing, completed]**

computer

computer (kuhm-**pyoot**-uhr)

A **computer** is a machine that people use for writing stories, sending messages to other people, drawing pictures, solving number problems, playing games, and storing information that can be used over and over again. A **computer** works very fast. [**computers**]

concert (**kahn**-suhrt)

When singers sing or musicians play instruments before an audience, they are giving a **concert**. The musicians played their guitars and sang songs at the **concert** at school yesterday. [**concerts**]

cone (kohn)

A **cone** is something that is flat and round at one end and has a point at the other end. Tony's favorite kind of **cone** is an ice-cream **cone**. Bright orange **cones** were placed around a large hole in the street until the street could be fixed. [**cones**]

confuse (kuhn-**fyooz**)

Confuse means to mix up so that something is not clear. That game used to **confuse** us. It became less **confusing** after we read the directions a few times. The story **confused** me at first, but by the second chapter I thought it was exciting and fun. [**confusing, confused**]

container (kuhn-**tayn**-uhr)

A **container** holds or stores things. Boxes, jars, and cans are **containers**. In the cafeteria at school, there are special **containers** for bottles and paper to be recycled. [**containers**]

contest (**kahn**-test)

In a **contest**, people play a game or race against each other to see who is best at it. The winner is the one who does best in the **contest**. Paul won the spelling **contest** when he spelled more words right than anyone else. [**contests**]

a running **contest**

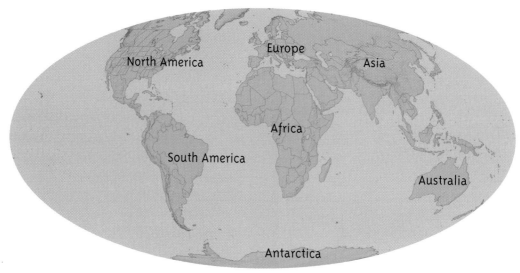

continents of the world

continent (kahnt-n-uhnt)

A **continent** is one of the large pieces of land that make up the earth. There are seven **continents**. The names of the **continents** are North America, South America, Europe, Asia, Africa, Australia, and Antarctica. The United States is on the **continent** of North America. [**continents**]

continue (kuhn-tin-yoo)

Continue means to keep doing something. Let's **continue** this story tomorrow. It **continued** to rain all afternoon. They **continued** to train the elephant at the circus until it had learned the new trick. [**continuing, continued**]

control (kuhn-trohl)

When you **control** something, you decide what is to be done and when it is to be done. When the traffic light is broken, a police officer **controls** the traffic by deciding which cars should stop or go. [**controlling, controlled**]

learning to **cook**

cook (kuk)

When you **cook**, you heat up food until it is hot and ready for eating. When food is being fried, baked, or boiled, it is being **cooked**. A person who **cooks** is called a **cook**. A **cook** who makes special foods is also called a **chef**. [**cooking, cooked**]

cookie (kuk-ee)

A **cookie** is a kind of food that is small, flat, and sweet. Most **cookies** are baked. Josh likes sandwich **cookies** with vanilla cream in the middle. [**cookies**]

cool (kool)

Something that is **cool** is warmer than something that is cold. **Cool** means a little cold. The flowers in the shop are kept **cool** so they will stay fresh. [**cooler, coolest**]

cooperate (koh-**ahp**-uh-rayt)

When people **cooperate**, they work together. The neighbors **cooperated** and cleaned up the park last May. [**cooperating, cooperated**]

copy (kahp-ee)

1. To **copy** is to act like someone else or to make something look just like something else. Christopher **copies** the names of the states to try to learn how to spell them. Becky drew a giraffe by **copying** a giraffe from a picture her father took with his new camera. [**copying, copied**]
2. A **copy** is something that looks just like something else. Aunt Maria wanted a **copy** of the picture of us when we were babies. The artist made 25 **copies** of his picture to sell at the fair. [**copies**]

corn

corn (korn)

Corn is a vegetable that grows on a tall green plant. The seeds of **corn** are yellow or white and grow in small rows. People and animals eat **corn**. On the farm, we picked **corn** and ate it the same day.

corner (kor-nuhr)

A **corner** is the place where two lines or two sides of something meet. Let's put this big plant in the **corner** by the window. [**corners**]

correct (kuh-rekt)

1. To **correct** something is to make sure it has no mistakes. Miranda had to **correct** her spelling before giving her story to her teacher. [**correcting, corrected**]
2. When something is **correct**, it is right. We counted our money to see if we had the **correct** amount.

cost (kawst)

1. The **cost** of something is the amount of money you have to pay to buy it. What is the **cost** of a ride on the subway? [**costs**]
2. To **cost** means to have a price that you can buy something for. How much does that rug **cost**? The big panda we bought at the yard sale **cost** $2.00. [**costing, cost**]

costume (kahs-toom)

A **costume** is special clothing that you put on so that you look like someone else. We wore **costumes** to the Halloween party. [**costumes**]

wearing **costumes**

cotton (kaht-n)

Cotton is the part of the cotton plant that grows in small white balls. The cloth made from **cotton** threads is also called **cotton**. I have pants and a jacket made of **cotton**.

count (kount)

1. When you **count**, you say the numbers in order. Patti was proud when she learned to **count** to 100. The race begins when Ms. Rivers **counts** to 3 — 1, 2, 3, go!
2. Count also means to add up how many there are. Please **count** the pencils to see if there are enough for everyone. [**counting, counted**]

the **country**

country (kuhn-tree)

1. A **country** is the area on a continent where people live and have the same laws and leaders. China and India are two large **countries** on the continent of Asia.
2. The **country** is also land that is away from cities and that has woods, farms, and fields on it. Dorrie, Carl, and Rosa live in the city and visit a farm in the **country** every summer. Megan goes to camp in the **country** in July. [**countries**]

cousin (kuhz-uhn)

A **cousin** is the child of an uncle or an aunt. In Karen's family, Aunt Tess has one daughter and Uncle Harper has three sons. Karen has four **cousins**. [**cousins**]

cover (kuhv-uhr)

1. To **cover** means to put something on top of something else. Lucy **covers** the table with paper so she won't get paste on it. The field was **covered** with tall ears of corn.
2. To **cover** also means to put something on top of something else to keep it warm or to protect it. When we camp out, we **cover** ourselves with extra blankets. [**covering, covered**]
3. A **cover** is something you put on something else. That **cover** belongs on top of the garbage can. [**covers**]

cow (kou)

A **cow** is a large female animal that gives milk. A young **cow** is called a **calf**. [**cows**]

crab (krab)

A **crab** is an animal that has a hard shell and lives in water. **Crabs** have four pairs of legs and two claws. [**crabs**]

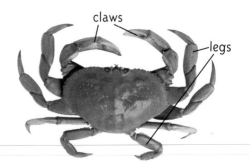

claws

legs

crab

crack (krak)

A **crack** is a very thin break in something. If something has a **crack** in it, it looks almost whole, but it is broken. The window with a **crack** in it has to be fixed because it lets in cold air. [**cracks**]

cracker (krak-uhr)

A **cracker** is a small, flat, baked food that is like a cookie but is not sweet. Janette likes peanut butter on **crackers**. Max likes **crackers** with his soup. [**crackers**]

cranes in the harbor

crane (krayn)

A **crane** is a large machine with a long arm that is used for lifting and moving heavy things. [**cranes**]

crash (krash)

1. When something **crashes**, it makes a loud sound and sometimes breaks. During a storm at sea, huge waves **crash** against the side of the boat. [**crashing, crashed**]
2. A **crash** is a loud sound. There was a loud **crash** in the kitchen when Billy dropped the dishes he was carrying. [**crashes**]

crawl (krawl)

crawling

1. Crawl means to move along the floor or ground on your hands and knees. Most babies can **crawl** when they are nine months old.
2. Crawl also means to move very slowly. When the road is icy, the cars **crawl**. [**crawling, crawled**]

crayon (kray-uhn)

A **crayon** is a piece of wax shaped like a short pencil. **Crayons** come in many colors and are used for coloring, drawing, and writing. Amy drew a picture of a farm with a pencil and colored it in with **crayons**. [**crayons**]

create (kree-ayt)

To **create** is to make something new or to make something in a new way. Let's **create** a story about a child who falls asleep and wakes up in a castle. Kevin is **creating** a drink by mixing all the leftover juices together. [**creating, created**]

crocodile (krahk-uh-dile)

A **crocodile** is a reptile that lives in the water in warm places. **Crocodiles** have long, low bodies and short legs. Do you know how a **crocodile** is different from an alligator? A **crocodile**'s head is more pointed in front and has two teeth that stick out when its mouth is closed. [**crocodiles**]

crooked (kruk-id)

Something that is **crooked** is bent or curved. It is not straight. Lucas drew **crooked** lines on the paper to look like lightning. The picture on the wall looks **crooked** because one side is higher than the other.

crop (krahp)

A **crop** is a plant that is grown in large amounts and often sold as food. Farmers grow wheat, corn, potatoes, tomatoes, and many other kinds of **crops**. [**crops**]

cross (kraws)

When you **cross** something, you move from one side to the other. The school guard stopped the traffic to let the children **cross** the street. If we want to get to the other side of the river, we'll have to **cross** the bridge. [**crossing, crossed**]

crossing the street

crowd (kroud)

A **crowd** is a large group of people who are together in the same place. A large **crowd** gathered to watch the fireworks. [**crowds**]

wearing a paper **crown**

crown (kroun)

A **crown** is a round band often made of gold and jewels, worn on the head by kings and queens. Sarah wears a paper **crown** when she pretends to be a queen. [**crowns**]

crutch (kruhch)

A **crutch** is a pole with a pad at the top to lean on. **Crutches** are placed under the arms to help a person walk or stay balanced. Mai learned to move on **crutches** when she broke her leg. [**crutches**]

cry (krie)

To **cry** means to have tears coming from your eyes. People often **cry** when they are sad, hurt, or frightened. Jack **cried** when his dog, Pluto, was hit by a car. [**crying, cried**]

lion **cub**

cub (kuhb)

A **cub** is a young bear or a young lion. Young tigers, wolves, and sharks are also called **cubs**. [**cubs**]

cube (kyoob)

A **cube** is like a block that has six sides. The sides of a **cube** are usually straight. How many ice **cubes** do you want in your lemonade? [**cubes**]

cup (kuhp)

1. A **cup** is a small, round container that is open on the top and has a handle. People often drink liquids from **cups**.
2. A **cup** is also an amount used for measuring. The baker measured four **cups** of flour for the cake she was baking. [**cups**]

curious (kyur-ee-uhs)

A person who is **curious** is very interested in knowing or learning about things. People who are **curious** often ask questions. "What do monkeys eat?" asked Brittany, **curious** about the animals at the zoo. Neil and Tara are **curious** about how to become an astronaut.

curl (kuhrl)

1. A **curl** is a round shape like a circle. Matt's hair was full of **curls**. [**curls**]
2. To **curl** means to shape something like a **curl**. Bobbie likes to **curl** the hair on her new doll. Mikele wrapped the gift with a blue ribbon and **curled** the ends of the ribbon. [**curling, curled**]

curve (kuhrv)

1. A **curve** is a line that bends into a rounded shape. A **curve** is not straight. We could not see past the **curve** in the road. [**curves**]
2. To **curve** means to bend. The line for the movie is so long that it goes down the block and **curves** around the corner. [**curving, curved**]

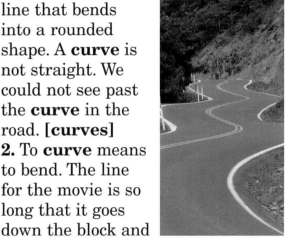
curves in a road

cut (kuht)

1. To **cut** something means to use scissors or a knife to divide it into pieces. If we **cut** the paper in half, we can each have a piece. Dale **cut** a slice of cake for everyone and put each slice on a paper plate.
2. To **cut** also means to take part of something away. Sal **cuts** the grass every week during the summer. [**cutting, cut**]
3. A **cut** is a thin break in the skin made by something sharp. Penny got a **cut** in her finger when she picked up the broken glass. [**cuts**]

Dd

dad (dad) and
daddy (dad-ee)
Dad and **daddy** are names for a father. "**Daddy**, are we going to the zoo tomorrow?" asked Max. [**dads, daddies**]

milk
cheese
ice cream
yogurt

foods from a **dairy**

dairy (dair-ee)
A **dairy** is a place where milk is kept and where foods like cheese, butter, and ice cream are made from milk. [**dairies**]

daisy (day-zee)
A **daisy** is a flower that has a round yellow center and whose petals are often white, yellow, or pink. Most **daisies** grow wild in fields. [**daisies**]

dam (dam)
A **dam** is a wall that is built across a river or other moving water to hold back the flow of water. A lake forms where a **dam** has been built. Water from **dams** is used on farms and to make electricity. [**dams**]

damp (damp)
Damp means a little wet. Ilse's wet bathing suit still felt **damp** after hanging on the clothesline for an hour.

dance (dans)
1. When people **dance**, they move their bodies to music. At parties, we like to **dance** in a long line following the leader. A person who **dances** is called a **dancer**. [**dancing, danced**]
2. The way people move to music is called a **dance**. We practiced two new **dances**. [**dances**]

a ballet **dancer**

dandelion (dan-duh-lie-uhn)
A **dandelion** is a small plant with a yellow flower and green leaves. **Dandelions** often grow as weeds in grass. The **dandelion** flower turns into a soft white ball with tiny parts that float in the air. [**dandelions**]

danger (dayn-juhr)
When there is **danger**, something might happen that could hurt you. The big hole in the road is a **danger** to cars. When something is a **danger**, we say it is **dangerous**. Running into the street is **dangerous**. [**dangers**]

dark (dahrk)

1. Dark means that there is no light at all or that there is only a little bit of light. At night it is **dark** outside.
2. Dark also means that a color has less light in it. The white stars on the flag are on a **dark** blue background. **[darker, darkest]**

date (dayt)

A **date** is a day of the month or the year. A **date** is also the day when something happens or happened. What is the **date** of your birthday? **[dates]**

daughter (dawt-uhr)

A **daughter** is the female child of a man or woman. Mom is Grandma's **daughter**. My cousin Liz is my aunt and uncle's **daughter**. **[daughters]**

day (day)

1. Day is the time that starts when the sun comes up and ends when the sun goes down.
2. A **day** is also the period of time equal to 24 hours. A **day** starts at 12 o'clock midnight and goes to the next 12 o'clock midnight. There are seven **days** in a week. The names of the **days** of the week are Sunday, Monday, Tuesday, Wednesday, Thursday, Friday, and Saturday. **[days]**

day care (day kair)

Day care is the care given to young children away from their home while their parents or others who take care of them are at work. Carlo and Meg like free play and story hour at **day care**.

dead (ded)

Something that is **dead** is not living any longer. We saw a **dead** animal by the side of the road. After the long winter some branches on the trees in the park were **dead**.

deaf (def)

When people are **deaf**, they cannot hear sounds. Some **deaf** people are able to hear sounds by using a hearing aid. Some people who are **deaf** also speak with their hands in a language called **sign language**. **[deafer, deafest]**

dear (dir)

1. When writing a letter, people often begin with the word **dear**.
2. The word **dear** is also used for someone or something very special to you. Mrs. Green is Grandmother's oldest and **dearest** friend. **[dearer, dearest]**

decide (di-side)

When you **decide**, you make up your mind and choose. Ginny is trying to **decide** which mystery story to read today. **[deciding, decided]**

at **day care**

deep (deep)

If something is **deep**, it goes down very far. Workers dug a **deep** hole on our block and planted a new tree. The town pool is **deeper** at one end than the other.
[deeper, deepest]

deer

deer (dir)

A **deer** is an animal with four long legs and short, brown fur. A **deer** is a mammal and can run very fast.
[deer]

define (di-fine)

When you **define** something, you say what it means. Dictionaries **define** words. The word *delicious* is defined on this page.
[defining, defined]

delicious (di-lish-uhs)

When food tastes very good, we say it is **delicious**. Dani thinks peanut butter and jelly are **delicious** together.

deliver (di-liv-uhr)

Deliver means to take something to a place it is supposed to go and then leave it there. Ashley gets up early to **deliver** newspapers in her neighborhood.
[delivering, delivered]

deliver

dentist (dent-uhst)

A **dentist** is a doctor who takes care of people's teeth and gums and helps to keep them healthy. **[dentists]**

describe (di-skribe)

When you **describe** something, you tell about it, so that someone else will know what it is like. "Mattie," said the art teacher, "will you please **describe** your drawing to the class?" **[describing, described]**

desert (dez-uhrt)

A **desert** is a very dry place with little rain, where few plants and animals can live. Many **deserts** are hot and sandy. Cactus plants can grow in **deserts**, and camels can live there. **[deserts]**

desert

design (di-zine)
1. When you **design** something, you put shapes and colors together in a special way. Ingrid is **designing** a card on the computer. Stuart **designed** and painted a card with a tiger chasing an elephant. **[designing, designed]**
2. The special shapes and colors of things are called a **design**. I like the **design** on your shirt. **[designs]**

desk (desk)
A **desk** is a table that is often used for writing and other kinds of work. Many **desks** have drawers. Mom's computer is on the **desk** in her office at home. **[desks]**

sundae

cookies

desserts

dessert (di-zuhrt)
Dessert is sweet food eaten at the end of a meal. After dinner, would you like fruit, cake, or ice cream for **dessert**? **[desserts]**

detective (di-tek-tiv)
A **detective** is a person who tries to solve mysteries by discovering how something was done or who did it. Some **detectives** are police officers. **Detectives** caught the people who robbed the bank. **[detectives]**

diamond (die-muhnd)
1. A **diamond** is a very hard, clear stone that comes from inside the earth. **Diamonds** are shiny and are used in rings and other jewelry.
2. A **diamond** is also a shape with four sides and four corners. A **diamond** looks like this: ♦. **[diamonds]**

dictionary (dik-shuh-ner-ee)
People use a **dictionary** to find out what words mean, how to spell them, and how to say them. Most **dictionaries** are books. Some **dictionaries** can also be found on a computer or a CD-ROM. You are reading a **dictionary** now. If you do not know what a tugboat is, you can look it up in this **dictionary**. **[dictionaries]**

die (die)
To **die** means not to be alive anymore. We water the plants in our house every week so they will not **die**. **[dying, died]**

different (dif-ruhnt)
Something that is **different** is not like something else. A rabbit is **different** from a cat. We wear **different** clothes when it is warm outdoors than we do when it is cold.

difficult (dif-uh-kuhlt)
When something is **difficult**, it is hard to understand or to do. Mel thought it was **difficult** to spell new words until he started using a dictionary. Sara's hair had so many knots in it that it was **difficult** to comb.

dig (dig)

Dig means to go down into something to make a hole in it. Squirrels **dig** holes in the ground to store food for the winter. **[digging, dug]**

dime (dime)

A **dime** is a coin that is an amount of money equal to ten pennies or two nickels. Two **dimes** plus one nickel are equal to one quarter. Do you know how many **dimes** there are in a dollar? **[dimes]**

dime

dinner (din-uhr)

Dinner is often eaten early in the evening. It is usually the biggest meal of the day. On Sundays, Hank's family has **dinner** early in the afternoon. **[dinners]**

dinosaur (die-nuh-sor)

A **dinosaur** is a reptile that lived millions of years ago. **Dinosaurs** were different shapes and sizes. A **dinosaur** that ate only plants is called a **herbivore**. A **dinosaur** that ate plants and meat from animals is called a **carnivore**. No **dinosaurs** are alive today. **[dinosaurs]**

dinosaur

dip (dip)

When you **dip** something, you put it into a liquid and take it out quickly. The painters **dipped** their brushes into the paint and started painting the fence. **[dipping, dipped]**

direction (duh-rek-shuhn)

1. A **direction** is somewhere you look at or point to, or where a sign or compass points to. Pointing to her left, Cleo said, "The school I go to is in that **direction**." *North, south, east,* and *west* are **directions**.
2. Directions tell the way to get to a place or the way to do something. We stopped and asked for **directions** to the shoe store. **[directions]**

dirt (duhrt)

Dirt is another word for earth. Trees, flowers, and weeds grow in **dirt**. Lil's dog loves to roll in **dirt**. When something has **dirt** on it, we say it is **dirty**. These **dirty** clothes need to be washed.

disappear (dis-uh-pir)

When something **disappears**, you are not able to see it any longer. Magicians are very good at making things **disappear**. **[disappearing, disappeared]**

disappoint (dis-uh-point)

To **disappoint** means to make someone feel unhappy because something didn't happen or because something went wrong. Carlita was **disappointed** when she got sick and had to stay home from school. **[disappointing, disappointed]**

discover (dis-kuh-vuhr)
When you **discover** something, you see it or learn about it for the first time. Did the birds **discover** the new feeder on the tree? **[discovering, discovered]**

dish (dish)
A **dish** is a plate or other container to hold food. Let's heat up a **dish** of spaghetti for lunch. **[dishes]**

floppy disk   compact disk

disks

disk (disk)
1. A **disk** is thin, flat, and round like a coin or a plate.
2. A **disk** is also a thin, flat piece of plastic or metal that stores music or information for use on a disk player of a computer. Another spelling of a **disk** for a computer is **disc**. **[disks]**

distance (dis-tuhns)
Distance means how far one thing is from another or the space between two things. It is a very long **distance** from Earth to the moon. **[distances]**

dive (dive)
To **dive** is to go into water with your head and arms first. A person who **dives** is called a **diver**. A board used for **diving** is called a **diving board**. **[diving, dived** or **dove]**

divide (duh-vide)
When you **divide** something, you break it into smaller pieces. Jonah **divided** his time between doing his homework and practicing the piano. **[dividing, divided]**

do (doo)
To **do** something means to work on it or make it happen. When Carlton **does** gardening, he pulls out weeds and waters the plants. Anita likes to **do** jigsaw puzzles. What are you **doing** tomorrow? **[doing, did]**

dock (dahk)
A **dock** is a place on the water where boats can be tied up or where ships can rest. At the end of its trip, the ferry pulled up to the **dock** to let the passengers off. **[docks]**

boats at a **dock**

doctor (dahk-tuhr)
A **doctor** is a person who is trained to help sick people get well. The **doctor** gave Ronald medicine for his sore throat. **[doctors]**

English bulldog

golden retriever

sheepdog

chihuahua

poodle

dogs

dog (dawg)

A **dog** is an animal that has four legs, a tail, and fur. Some **dogs** are pets and some are trained to work on ranches or to help police officers. A **dog** that is trained to help someone who is blind is called a **guide dog**. [**dogs**]

doll (dahl)

A **doll** is a toy that looks like a person. **Dolls** can look like children or grown-ups. Samantha likes to change the clothes on her new **doll**. [**dolls**]

dollar (dahl-uhr)

A **dollar** is an amount of money equal to 100 pennies. In the United States, a **dollar** is made of paper. Four quarters are equal to one **dollar**. Ten dimes are also equal to one **dollar**. [**dollars**]

dollhouse (dahl-hous)

A **dollhouse** is a toy house with rooms and furniture. Some **dollhouses** are open in the back so children can reach into the rooms and play with the small dolls and furniture. [**dollhouses**]

dolphin (dahl-fin)

A **dolphin** is a kind of small whale. **Dolphins** are mammals that are strong swimmers and good divers. **Dolphins** are very intelligent and friendly to people. [**dolphins**]

dolphins

donkey (dahng-kee)

A **donkey** is a mammal that looks like a small horse with a large head and long ears. **Donkeys** are able to carry heavy things on their backs. [**donkeys**]

door (dor)

A **door** opens and closes to let people and things go in and out of a room or a building. The **door** to the kitchen swings back and forth. Our garage **door** opens from the bottom. [**doors**]

dot (daht)

A **dot** is a round spot. Elena's raincoat and matching hat have red **dots** on them. The **dot** at the end of a sentence is called a **period**. [**dots**]

down (doun)

When something goes **down**, it goes from a higher place to a lower one. Let's take the escalator **down** to the first floor, so we can see all of the shops on the way. The librarian took **down** a book from the shelf.

dozen (duhz-uhn)

A **dozen** means there are 12 of something. A **dozen** children and two teachers went on a trip to the aquarium. If we pick two **dozen** strawberries, how many strawberries will we have? [**dozens**]

a **dozen** muffins

dragon (drag-uhn)

A **dragon** is an imaginary monster that usually has wings and breathes fire. **Dragons** are not real. **Dragons** are often shown with long, pointed tails and big feet with long claws. Lukas likes to play a computer game where he tries to catch **dragons**. [**dragons**]

draw (draw)

When you **draw**, you make a picture using lines. Tamika likes to **draw** on paper with a pencil and crayons. After visiting the aquarium, she **drew** a picture of a dolphin jumping out of the water. [**drawing, drew**]

drawing a picture

drawbridge (draw-brij)

A **drawbridge** is a bridge that opens up so that boats can go past it. The cars had to wait in line until all the ships had passed and the **drawbridge** was closed. [**drawbridges**]

drawer (dror)

A **drawer** is an open box that moves in and out of a piece of furniture. People store things in **drawers**. I keep my shirts in one **drawer** and my pajamas in another **drawer**. [**drawers**]

drawing (draw-ing)

When a person makes a picture by drawing lines, the picture is called a **drawing**. The first-grade children made **drawings** to decorate their classroom. [**drawings**]

dream (dreem)

1. A **dream** is a story or a picture that is in your mind when you are sleeping. Letitia had a funny **dream** last night about flying bears and dancing dolphins. **[dreams]**

2. To **dream** is to have stories or pictures in your mind when you are sleeping or awake. Miguel **dreams** of becoming a famous basketball star. **[dreaming, dreamed]**

dress (dres)

1. A **dress** is clothing that girls and women wear. A **dress** looks like a blouse and a skirt sewn together. In the play, Jessie wore a **dress** with a long, wide skirt and a large bow. **[dresses]**

2. To **dress** means to put on clothes. Michael **dresses** for school in the morning and then eats his breakfast. **[dressing, dressed]**

dressed for a Halloween party

using a **drill**

drill (dril)

1. A **drill** is a tool for making holes. The carpenter uses a **drill** to make holes in the wood before hammering in the nails.

2. A **drill** is also an activity that is practiced over and over again so it is learned well. Once a month we have a fire **drill** at school to practice how to act and where to go if there is a fire. **[drills]**

3. To **drill** means to make a hole in something with a tool called a **drill**. Boats off the shore were **drilling** for oil. **[drilling, drilled]**

drink (dringk)

1. When you **drink**, you put liquid into your mouth and swallow it. At lunch, Allen **drinks** milk with his sandwich. **[drinking, drank, drunk]**

2. A **drink** is liquid that you can put into your mouth and swallow. Would you like a cold drink? **[drinks]**

drip (drip)

When something **drips**, liquid falls from it in drops. Water **drips** from melting icicles. The soup **dripped** on Ty's shirt. **[dripping, dripped]**

drive (drive)

To **drive** means to steer a car, truck, bus, train, or tractor and make it move. The person who **drives** a car, truck, or bus is called the **driver**. The person who **drives** a train is called an **engineer**. [**driving, drove**]

drop (drahp)

1. A **drop** is a tiny amount of liquid. Early in the morning, we saw **drops** of water on the flowers. [**drops**]
2. To **drop** means to move from someplace higher to someplace lower. When something **drops**, it falls. Ripe apples **drop** from the trees in autumn. The baby-sitter bent down to pick up the toy the baby had **dropped**. [**dropping, dropped**]

drums

drum (druhm)

A **drum** is a round, hollow musical instrument, with a kind of skin stretched over it on the top and bottom. A **drum** makes sounds when it is hit with a stick or with hands. A person who plays **drums** is called a **drummer**. [**drums**]

dry (drie)

1. Something that is **dry** does not have liquid in it or on it. Are your hands **dry**? After the flood there wasn't a **dry** basement on our street. [**drier, driest**]
2. To **dry** something means to make the water go out of it. We hung the beach towels out on a line to **dry**. Holly **dried** herself after her bath. A machine that **dries** things is called a **dryer**. [**drying, dried**]

duck (duhk)

A **duck** is a bird that swims and lives in water. A **duck** has a short neck and short legs. The feathers of male and female **ducks** are different colors. [**ducks**]

mallard **duck**

dug (duhg)

Dug comes from **dig**. The dog **dug** a hole in the ground and buried its bone.

dull (duhl)

1. Something that is **dull** is not sharp. This pair of scissors is so **dull** that it won't even cut string.
2. Dull also means that something is not interesting. The movie was so **dull** that I fell asleep watching it. [**duller, dullest**]

dust (duhst)

Very small pieces of dirt are called **dust**. We used a cloth to remove the **dust** from the furniture.

Ee

each (eech)

Each means every one, not just some or most. **Each** winner was given a prize.

eagle (ee-guhl)

An **eagle** is a big bird that has long wings and a curved beak. **Eagles** build their nests in high places. **[eagles]**

eagle

ear (ir)

An **ear** is the part of the body used to hear and to keep balance. You have two **ears**, one on each side of your head. **Ears** can be on the top of the head like a giraffe's, large like an elephant's, or long like a rabbit's. **[ears]**

early (uhr-lee)

1. Early means close to the time that something begins. Farmers get up **early** in the morning to feed their animals and milk their cows.
2. Early also means before the usual time. Kate woke up **early** today. **[earlier, earliest]**

earn (uhrn)

Earn means to get something for working at a job or for working in some other way. Henry's brother **earns** money by working in a store after school. **[earning, earned]**

wearing **earrings**

earring (ir-ing)

An **earring** is jewelry that is worn on the ear. Keri likes her **earrings** made from beads. **[earrings]**

earth (uhrth)

1. Earth is the name of the planet where we live. **Earth** is shaped like a ball and has land and oceans on its surface.
2. Earth also means the dirt on the ground that plants grow in.

earthquake (uhrth-kwayk)

An **earthquake** happens when huge layers of the earth move and make the ground shake. In a big **earthquake**, buildings, roads, and bridges can crack and sometimes fall down. **[earthquakes]**

east (eest)

East is a direction on a compass opposite of west. When the sun rises in the morning, it rises in the **east**. The Atlantic Ocean is on the **east** coast of the United States.

easy (ee-zee)

Easy means not difficult. When something is **easy** for you, you do not have to try hard to do it. Milton finds it **easier** to play the new song on his violin now that he has practiced it a few times. **[easier, easiest]**

eating lunch in the school cafeteria

eat (eet)

Eat means to take food into your body through your mouth and then chew it and swallow it. Let's **eat** lunch soon. **[eating, ate, eaten]**

echo (ek-oh)

An **echo** is a sound that gets repeated after it is first made. For a sound to **echo**, it travels through open space, hits a flat surface, and bounces back. When Arthur shouted "Hi there" across the canyon, we heard the **echo** "Hi there, hi there, hi there." **[echoes]**

edge (ej)

An **edge** is a line or place where a surface ends. The pencil was too close to the **edge** of the desk and rolled off. **[edges]**

egg (eg)

An **egg** has a hard shell on the outside and can hold a baby bird or other animal on the inside. Birds, turtles, and most snakes lay **eggs**. **[eggs]**

a carton of **eggs**

eight (ayt)

Eight is the number that is one more than seven and one less than nine. An octopus has **eight** arms. If you have a nickel and three pennies, you have **eight** cents.

elbow (el-boh)

Your **elbow** is the middle part of your arm that bends. When Tanya lies on the floor to watch television, she bends her **elbows** and rests her head on her hands. **[elbows]**

leaning on their **elbows**

electricity (i-lek-**tris**-uht-ee)
Electricity is a kind of energy that is used in many ways. **Electricity** can make light and heat, and it can make machines work. Lamps, refrigerators, computers, television sets, and trains are some of the things that use **electricity**.

elephant (**el**-uh-fuhnt)
An **elephant** is a very big mammal with a large head, big ears, and a long nose called a trunk. **Elephants** are the largest animals on land. Most **elephants** live in Africa and Asia. The **elephant** at the zoo flapped its ears to cool itself. [**elephants**]

elephant

elevator (**el**-uh-vayt-uhr)
An **elevator** is a small room that moves up and down in a building to take people and things to different floors. [**elevators**]

emergency (i-**muhr**-juhn-see)
An **emergency** is something that happens suddenly and needs to be taken care of right away. Fires, floods, and airplane accidents are **emergencies**. [**emergencies**]

an **empty** room

empty (**emp**-tee)
When something is **empty**, it has nothing inside of it. This glass is almost **empty**. [**emptier, emptiest**]

encyclopedia (en-sie-kluh-**peed**-ee-uh)
An **encyclopedia** is a book with information about many things. The librarian asked Amanda if she wanted to read the **encyclopedia** as a book or look at it on a computer. [**encyclopedias**]

end (end)
1. The **end** of something is the last part of it. There is a lake at the **end** of the trail in the woods. Dessert is served at the **end** of a meal. [**ends**]
2. To **end** means to finish or come to the last part. [**ending, ended**]

enemy (**en**-uh-mee)
1. An **enemy** is someone who is not a friend, especially a person fighting against another person in a war. When people fight wars, they are **enemies.**
2. An **enemy** is also something that is a danger to something else. Polluted water is an **enemy** to fish and people. [**enemies**]

energy (en-uhr-jee)

Energy is what makes things move. People eat food to get **energy**. The heat from the sun and electricity are different kinds of **energy**. The dancer needed a lot of **energy** to lift the other dancer into the air.

engine (en-juhn)

An **engine** is a machine that uses one kind of energy to make another kind of energy. The **engine** in a car, airplane, train, or ship creates the power that makes it move. **[engines]**

checking the **engine**

enough (i-nuhf)

When there is **enough**, no more is needed or wanted. There are **enough** chairs for everyone.

enter (ent-uhr)

To **enter** is to go into a place. The firefighter **entered** the burning building through a window on the second floor. **[entering, entered]**

envelope (en-vuh-lohp)

An **envelope** holds cards and letters, and is made of paper that has been folded and has glue on it to close it. Don't forget to write the address and put a stamp on the **envelope** before mailing your letter. **[envelopes]**

environment (en-vie-ruhn-muhnt)

The **environment** is the air, the land, and the water that make up our world. When people protect the **environment**, they try to keep dirt and other things from polluting the air we breathe, the water we drink, and the soil that plants use. **[environments]**

equal (ee-kwuhl)

Equal means the same amount or size. An **equal** sign is written =. The recipe called for **equal** amounts of sugar and lemon juice. Four nickels and three dimes **equal** two quarters or fifty cents. **[equaling, equaled]**

equal

erase (i-rays)

When you **erase** something you have written or drawn, you rub it with something to make it disappear. Ivy is going to **erase** the mistake on her paper and try to write the sentence again. Something that is used for **erasing** is called an **eraser.** Is there an **eraser** at the end of your pencil? **[erasing, erased]**

escalator (es-kuh-layt-uhr)
An **escalator** is a machine made of moving stairs. In buildings with stores and offices, people often use **escalators** to go from one floor to another floor. [**escalators**]

escape (is-kayp)
To **escape** means to get away from something that is keeping you in or that is dangerous. When the gate was left open, the baby goat was able to **escape** from the yard. [**escaping, escaped**]

evening

evening (eev-ning)
The **evening** is the part of the day that comes after the afternoon but before night. In the summer it is still light in the **evening**. In the winter it is dark outside when we have our **evening** meal. [**evenings**]

everyone (ev-ree-wuhn)
Everyone means every person. **Everyone** playing in the baseball game was given a chance to bat. Another word for **everyone** is **everybody**. **Everybody** was told to stay in line when we entered the museum.

evil (ee-vuhl)
Evil means very bad and wanting to hurt people. Tad and his sister sometimes pretend to be heroes who stop **evil** monsters from hurting people.

excellent (ek-suh-luhnt)
Excellent means very good. Dogs have **excellent** hearing and can hear sounds that people cannot hear. The Bigg twins are both **excellent** at jigsaw puzzles.

except (ik-sept)
Except means that something or someone is left out or different from something else. All of the children were tall enough to go on the ride at the fair **except** Joshua's baby brother.

exciting (ik-site-ing)
When something is **exciting**, it makes you feel very good when you do it or think about it. Amy finds learning new things about animals **exciting.** The bicycle race was an **exciting** one for Tony, the winner.

an **exciting** race

excuse

1. (ik-**skyooz**) When **excuse** is pronounced ik-**skyooz**, it means to allow someone not to do something. The teacher agreed to **excuse** three children from taking the test today because they had been out sick all week. **[excusing, excused]**

2. (ik-**skyoos**) When **excuse** is pronounced ik-**skyoos**, it is the reason someone gives to try to explain something. The baby-sitter's **excuse** for arriving late was that her car had a flat tire. **[excuses]**

exercise (ek-**suhr**-size)

1. Exercise means to move your body in a way that makes you stay strong and healthy. Playing sports, dancing, swimming, and doing gymnastics are good ways to **exercise**. **[exercising, exercised]**

2. An **exercise** is something you do as a way to practice. Alison practices **exercises** on the piano every day. **[exercises]**

exercising

exit (eg-zit) or (ek-sit)

An **exit** is the way out of a building. Each **exit** in the movie theater has a red light over it and a bar you press to open the door. **[exits]**

expensive (ik-**spen**-siv)

If something is **expensive**, it costs a lot of money. Cara loves borrowing books from the library for free, because buying so many books would be much too **expensive**.

explain (ik-**splayn**)

When you **explain** something, you say something to help someone understand. Please **explain** to me how this box opens. **[explaining, explained]**

explode (ik-**splohd**)

When something **explodes**, it breaks apart into pieces with a loud noise. When the fireworks **explode**, the sky at night will be filled with bright lights. **[exploding, exploded]**

exploding fireworks

explore (ik-**splor**)

Explore means to go to new places and find out about them. A person who **explores** is called an **explorer**. **[exploring, explored]**

extra (ek-struh)

If something is **extra**, it is more than may be needed. Ariel always carries **extra** pencils in her backpack. Jason asked Donald if he had an **extra** sweater he could borrow.

eye (ie)

An **eye** is the part of the body used to see. Mammals, fish, and birds have **eyes**. People have two **eyes** on the front of the face. Some animals, like fish and crocodiles, have **eyes** on the sides of the head. **[eyes]**

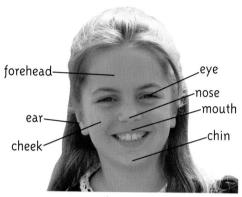

forehead — eye
— nose
— mouth
ear —
cheek — chin

face

face (fays)

The **face** is the front part of the head. The eyes, nose, and mouth are part of the **face**. **[faces]**

fact (fakt)

A **fact** is information that is true. It is a **fact** that insects have six legs. It is also a **fact** that the blue whale is the largest living animal. **[facts]**

factory (fak-tuh-ree)

A **factory** is a building where people and machines make a large number of things. Toys and many kinds of clothing are made in **factories**. **[factories]**

inside a **factory**

fair (fair)

1. When people are **fair**, they treat everyone the same way. To be **fair** we will cut the pizza so all the slices are the same size.
2. A **fair** is a place where people go to play games, go on rides, and have fun. At some **fairs** people show animals they have raised and sell things they have made. **[fairs]**

fairy (fair-ee)

A **fairy** is a tiny, imaginary person with wings. Stories about **fairies** and their magic are called **fairy tales**. In one **fairy tale**, a **fairy** flew from house to house leaving gifts for people. **[fairies]**

fall (fawl)

1. Fall is a season of the year. **Fall** comes after summer and before winter. Another word for **fall** is **autumn**. In **fall**, the leaves of some trees change color from green to yellow and red. **[falls]**
2. To **fall** means to go from a higher place to a lower place. Your helmet will protect you if you **fall** while skating. **[falling, fell, fallen]**

false (fawls)

If something is **false**, it is not true. Because there are some birds that cannot fly, it would be **false** to say that all birds fly.

family (fam-uh-lee)

1. You and your parents and any brothers and sisters you have are a **family**. Your grandparents and aunts, uncles, and cousins are also part of your **family**.

2. A **family** is also a group of animals whose bodies are alike or a group of plants that are alike in some ways. Pet cats and wild cats belong to the cat **family**. **[families]**

famous sculpture

famous (fay-muhs)

For people or things to be **famous**, many people have to know about them. Thomas Edison is **famous** for inventing the light bulb. Mount Rushmore is **famous** for its sculpture of four American presidents.

far (far)

1. **Far** means away from or not close. It is too **far** for Michele to walk to my house.

2. When you talk about how **far** something is from something else, you mean the distance between the two places. How **far** is your house from the nearest grocery store? **[farther, farthest]**

farm

farm (fahrm)

A **farm** is a place with land that is used to grow plants and raise animals for food. We grow corn and other vegetables on our **farm**. A person who works on a **farm** is called a **farmer**. **[farms]**

fast (fast)

Fast means quick or moving quickly. Jan is **fast** in the morning and can take a bath and dress in 15 minutes. **[faster, fastest]**

fat (fat)

1. **Fat** means weighing a lot for a person's or animal's size. The vet told us our cat is too **fat**.

2. **Fat** is also a kind of oil that is found in plants and meats and in things made from milk. We buy cheese without **fat** for Grandpa.

father (fahᴛʜ-uhr)

A **father** is a man who has a child or children. Your **father** is your male parent. Tim made a card for his **father** for **Father's** Day. **[fathers]**

favorite (fay-vuh-rit)

Favorite means being liked the best. Do you have a **favorite** sport?

fear (fir)

Fear is a feeling you have when you think something bad is going to happen. **[fears]**

feast (feest)

A **feast** is a special meal made for many people. There will be a **feast** when the king visits. **[feasts]**

feather (feтн-uhr)

A **feather** is the part of a bird's body that keeps it warm and helps it fly. A **feather** is light and strong. **[feathers]**

feed

feed (feed)

To **feed** is to give food to a person or an animal. Sara **feeds** the fish in her aquarium once a day. Tim is **feeding** a horse. **[feeding, fed]**

feel (feel)

1. To **feel** is to touch something. One of the ways you learn about things in the world is to **feel** them. Does cotton **feel** different from wool? **2.** How you **feel** also lets you know how you are. People **feel** different ways at different times. Sasha **felt** happy when her friend came to visit and sad when she left. **[feeling, felt]**

feeling (fee-ling)

When you have a **feeling**, you know how you are. Allie remembers her **feelings** of fear and excitement when she first jumped off a diving board. **[feelings]**

female (fee-mayl)

People and animals are either **female** or male. Girls and women are **female**. Mothers, grandmothers, aunts, and sisters are **female**. **Female** grown-ups can give birth to babies.

fence (fens)

A **fence** is a kind of wall usually made of pieces of wood or wire. A **fence** around our garden keeps animals from eating our plants. **[fences]**

ferry (fer-ee)

A **ferry** is a boat that carries passengers, cars, and other things across water. When we visited the state of Washington, we took a **ferry** to the islands. **[ferries]**

ferry

few (fyoo)

Few means not many. Samantha had a **few** tissues in her pocket and gave one to Alex when he started to sneeze. **[fewer, fewest]**

field (feeld)

A **field** is a flat, open area of land without trees or buildings. Some **fields** are used by farmers to grow plants. Other **fields** are used to play sports such as football. **[fields]**

fight (fite)

1. Sometimes when people are angry, they **fight**. A person sometimes **fights** by yelling or shouting or even hitting. **[fighting, fought]**
2. A **fight** is what happens when people fight each other. **[fights]**

fill (fil)

Fill means to add to something until nothing else will fit in. Nita **filled** her bowl with vegetable and noodle soup. **[filling, filled]**

find (finde)

Find means to come across something by accident or to see it after you had been looking for it. Can you **find** the word *fox* in the dictionary? **[finding, found]**

finger (fing-guhr)

A **finger** is one of the five pointed parts of the hand. Each **finger** has a nail at the end. The thumb is the **finger** on the side of the hand. **[fingers]**

fingers

fingerprint (fing-guhr-print)

A **fingerprint** is the mark that the tip of a finger leaves on a surface. Everyone's **fingerprints** are different. Oliver had strawberry jelly on his hand and left red **fingerprints** on the refrigerator door. **[fingerprints]**

finish (fin-ish)

To **finish** something is to come to the end of it. Let's play a game after we **finish** dinner. **[finishing, finished]**

firefighter at a **fire**

fire (fire)

Fire is the heat, flames, and light that are created when something burns. **Fires** are used to heat and cook things. **Fires** can also burn buildings or forests. **[fires]**

fire engine (fire en-juhn)

A **fire engine** is a truck that carries hoses, hooks, and ladders for firefighters to use. **[fire engines]**

firefighter (fire-fite-uhr)

A **firefighter** is a person who works to put out fires. **Firefighters** fight fires in buildings, on boats, and in forests.

fireplace (fire-plays)

A **fireplace** is a place in a house where it is safe to build a fire. **Fireplaces** are usually made of bricks or stone and have a chimney. [**fireplaces**]

fireworks (fire-wuhrks)

When **fireworks** are set off, they make a loud noise and create bright lights in different shapes and colors in the air or sky. We watched **fireworks** last July 4th.

first (fuhrst)

When something is **first**, there is nothing that comes before it. Rob's parents have a photograph of Rob taking his **first** steps.

first aid (fuhrst ayd)

First aid is the care given to someone who is sick or has been hurt in an accident and needs help.

fish (fish)

A **fish** is an animal that lives in water. A **fish** has a bone down its back and fins that help it swim. A **fish** also has gills that help it breathe in water. A person who catches **fish** for work or as a sport is called a **fisherman**. [**fish** or **fishes**]

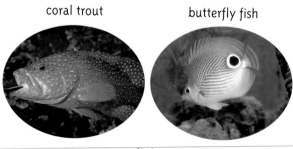

coral trout   butterfly fish

fish

fit (fit)

Fit means to be the right size and the right shape. Nan was going to borrow her friend's jacket, but it didn't **fit**. [**fitting, fitted**]

five (five)

Five is the number that comes after four and before six. **Five** is written **5.** You have **five** fingers on your hand and **five** toes on your foot.

fix (fiks)

If something is broken and you **fix** it, you make it work again. Denise is learning how to **fix** a flat tire. [**fixing, fixed**]

American flag

Mexican flag

Canadian flag

flags

flag (flag)

A **flag** is a piece of cloth that has different shapes and colors on it. Every country has its own **flag** with its own design. [**flags**]

flame (flaym)

A **flame** is the part of a fire that moves in the air. When Mr. Fox's barn was on fire, the **flames** shot up into the sky. [**flames**]

flashlight

flashlight (flash-lite)

A **flashlight** is a small light that you can hold in your hand. **Flashlights** make light using a battery and a bulb. **[flashlights]**

flat (flat)

When something is **flat**, it is smooth and does not have bumps. We looked for a **flat** place to put up the tent. **[flatter, flattest]**

flavor (flay-vuhr)

The **flavor** of something is how it tastes. Tess's favorite frozen yogurt **flavor** is vanilla. **[flavors]**

float (floht)

When something **floats** in water, it does not sink to the bottom. When something **floats** in air, it does not fall to the ground. The toy sailboats **floated** across the pool in the park. **[floating, floated]**

flood (fluhd)

When water spills into an area that is usually dry or that should be dry, it is called a **flood**. There was a **flood** in the town when the dam broke. **[floods]**

floor (flor)

The **floor** is the bottom part of a room opposite the ceiling. You walk on the **floor** and put furniture on it. Umberto sat on the **floor** watching television. **[floors]**

flour (flour)

Flour is a powder that you bake or cook with. It is usually made from wheat. Aunt Fran measured **flour** for a banana cake. **[flours]**

flow (floh)

To **flow** means to move along or through something. Water **flows** through pipes and electricity **flows** through wires. **[flowing, flowed]**

flower (flou-uhr)

A **flower** is the part of a plant that makes seeds or fruit. **Flowers** often have brightly colored parts called petals. Some **flowers**, like roses, smell good. **[flowers]**

flower

playing the **flute**

flute (floot)

A **flute** is a musical instrument that is shaped like a long tube. Tracy practices blowing into her **flute** and pressing the keys. [**flutes**]

fly¹ (flie)

A **fly** is an insect that has one pair of clear wings and that eats wet food. At the picnic we put plastic over the food to keep the **flies** away. [**flies**]

fly² (flie)

To **fly** is to move through or in the air, often using wings. Birds and insects **fly**. People **fly** in airplanes and helicopters. Flags, balloons, and kites also **fly**. [**flying, flew, flown**]

fold (fohld)

To **fold** means to bend so that one part goes under another. Birds and insects **fold** their wings down when they are not flying. When the clothes and towels dried, Sal **folded** them. [**folding, folded**]

a **folding** ruler

follow (fahl-oh)

To **follow** means to go behind or come after. The chicks **follow** their mother wherever she goes. If you **follow** those signs, you will get to the state fair. [**following, followed**]

food (food)

Food is what living things eat to get energy and stay alive. **Food** helps people and animals grow and be healthy. People eat fruits, vegetables, meat, and fish as **food**. In the wild, animals eat plants and smaller animals as **food**. [**foods**]

1. The **foot** is the flat part of the body at the end of the leg, used to stand, walk, and run. A person has two **feet**, and each **foot** has five toes at one end and a heel at the other end.

2. A **foot** is also used to measure the length or height of something. There are 12 inches in 1 **foot**. Sofia is 3 **feet** tall. [**feet**]

football (fut-bawl)

1. Football is a game played on a large field by two teams with 11 players each. The team with the ball throws, carries, or kicks the ball down the field. The team without the ball tries to stop the other team or get the ball.

football

2. Football is also the name of the ball used in the game of football. A **football** is oval in shape and comes to a point at each end. [**footballs**]

footprint (fut-print)

A **footprint** is the mark a foot makes. You can make a **footprint** with your bare foot or with shoes on. We tried to guess which birds had been on the beach by looking at their different **footprints**. **[footprints]**

forest (for-ist) or (fahr-uhst)

A **forest** is a large area where many trees and other plants grow close together. Many plants and animals live in **forests**. The trees in **forests** help make air, store water, and keep the soil from washing away. The wood we use for building comes from trees in **forests**. **[forests]**

forget (fuhr-get)

When you **forget** something, you do not remember it or cannot remember it. If you **forget** my phone number, you can find it in the telephone book. **[forgetting, forgot]**

forgive (fur-giv)

When you **forgive** someone who has done something wrong, you are not angry at that person anymore. When Josh borrowed Mike's ball and lost it, Mike **forgave** Josh. **[forgiving, forgave, forgiven]**

fork (fork)

A **fork** is a tool with a row of thin, pointed parts that are attached to a handle. Metal and plastic **forks** are used for eating. Some **forks** are large tools used for digging up the ground or for lifting hay. **[forks]**

forward (for-wuhrd)

Forward means toward what is ahead or in front. The line of people waiting to get on the bus moved **forward** slowly. Brigit looks **forward** to going to the museum with her class next week.

fossil of a fish

fossil (fahs-uhl)

A **fossil** is the part of a plant or animal that has been left behind in the earth after the plant or animal died many, many years ago. We know about dinosaurs because of **fossils** of their footprints and bones. **[fossils]**

fought (fawt)

Fought comes from **fight**. The brothers **fought** over who would use the new skateboard first.

found (found)

Found comes from **find**. At the video store, Erica **found** a tape she wanted to watch. After looking in two closets, Burt **found** his other boot.

four (for)

Four is the number that comes after three and before five. **Four** is written 4.

four-leaf clover

fox

fox (fahks)

A **fox** is a wild animal with a pointed nose, a very long tail, and long, thick fur. Many **foxes** have reddish-brown fur. **Foxes** are smart and hard to catch. **[foxes]**

free (free)

1. When something is **free**, you do not have to pay anything for it. This week at the store, if you buy two shirts, you get a third one **free**.
2. Free also means going where you want or doing what you want. In the city park, there is a large area with a fence around it where people can let their dogs run **free** without a leash. **[freer, freest]**

freeze (freez)

1. To **freeze** means to change from a liquid to a solid. Water becomes ice when it **freezes**. We can't skate on the lake until it **freezes**.
2. To **freeze** also means to lower the temperature of something so that it becomes very cold. Let's **freeze** the cooked chicken we can't eat now so we can have it another time. **[freezing, froze, frozen]**

fresh (fresh)

1. When food is **fresh**, it is good for eating, and only a little time has passed since it was made, picked, or caught. The bakery makes **fresh** bread every day.
2. Fresh also means clean or new. Jody put on **fresh** pajamas after her bath. Marcus put a **fresh** coat of paint on his boat.
3. When water is **fresh**, it has no salt. Some fish live in **fresh** water and some live in salt water.
4. When air is **fresh**, it is clean and good for breathing.
[fresher, freshest]

friend (frend)

A **friend** is someone you like and have fun with. A **friend** is also someone who helps you when you need help. Sam, Jon, and Al have been **friends** for two years. **[friends]**

friends

friendly (frend-lee)

Friendly means acting as if you like someone. When people are **friendly** they are nice and try to help you. Meli said hello and was **friendly** to the new girl in her class. **[friendlier, friendliest]**

frighten (frite-n)

To **frighten** means to make someone or something afraid. Loud noise **frightens** the puppy so much that it starts to make crying sounds. Do you ever get **frightened**? [**frightening, frightened**]

frog (frawg) or (frahg)

A **frog** is an animal with smooth skin that is usually green or brown with spots. **Frogs** have eyes that stick out and long back legs with strong muscles for jumping. **Frogs** need a wet place and often live in water. [**frogs**]

tree **frog**

front (fruhnt)

The **front** of something is the part that comes first or faces forward. Gillian has pockets on the **front** of her shirt. The city bus stops in **front** of the school.

frost (frawst)

Frost is a very thin layer of ice. We scratched the **frost** off the window so we could look outside.

frown (froun)

1. A **frown** is a look on your face when your mouth turns down at each end. Jack's smile turned to a **frown** when his toy car suddenly stopped working. [**frowns**]
2. When you **frown**, your mouth turns down at each end. People **frown** when they are unhappy or angry or thinking very hard about something. [**frowning, frowned**]

frozen (froh-zuhn)

Frozen comes from **freeze**. Ice is **frozen** water. The ice fishermen walked on the surface of the **frozen** lake and cut a hole in the ice to fish. **Frozen** yogurt is almost like ice cream.

fruit (froot)

The **fruit** of a plant is the part that holds the seeds. We eat the skin of some **fruit**, such as grapes, apples, and berries. We peel off the skin of other **fruit**, such as oranges, pineapples, and bananas, before eating the **fruit**. [**fruit** or **fruits**]

peaches

pineapple

limes

bananas

pear

oranges

fruit

fry (frie)

To **fry** means to cook in a pan with hot oil. At the restaurant we watched the cook **fry** onions and potatoes. [**frying, fried**]

full (ful)

When something is **full**, there is no room left to hold anything else. When the garbage bag in the kitchen was **full**, Greer tied it up and put it in a large can outside. **[fuller, fullest]**

full bag

fun (fuhn)

When something is **fun**, it makes you feel good and you like to do it. Mei and Eric always have **fun** on the swings in the playground.

having **fun** on a sled

funny (fuhn-ee)

1. If something is **funny**, it makes you laugh or smile. When Terry was sick, his friends sent him **funny** cards that made him feel better.
2. Funny also means strange or not usual. In the spring, Cynthia heard **funny** noises in the chimney and discovered that birds had built a nest there. **[funnier, funniest]**

fur (fuhr)

Fur is the soft, thick hair that covers the body of some animals. **Fur** helps to keep animals warm. In the summer Otto's dog loses big balls of **fur**. When something has **fur** or has something that looks or feels like **fur**, we say it is **furry**. Lara has pink, **furry** mittens.

brown and white **fur**

furnace (fuhr-nuhs)

A **furnace** is a machine that makes heat. Some **furnaces** burn things like oil and gas to heat buildings and keep people warm. Other **furnaces** can reach very high temperatures and are used to make different kinds of metal. **[furnaces]**

furniture (fuhr-nuh-chuhr)

Things like chairs, sofas, tables, beds, and desks are **furniture**. **Furniture** is used for activities like sitting, eating, sleeping, and studying and to hold things.

future (fyoo-chuhr)

The **future** is the time that comes later. The **future** has not happened yet. Luke wants to be a policeman in the **future** when he grows up. Olga's parents are saving money so they can start a business in the **future**. **[future]**

Gg

gallon (gal-uhn)

A **gallon** is an amount of liquid. There are four quarts in one **gallon**. A half **gallon** has two quarts of liquid. Mom took a half **gallon** of milk out of the refrigerator. Mr. Woods bought a **gallon** of red paint to paint his barn. [**gallons**]

gallop (gal-uhp)

To **gallop** is to run very fast. Horses and many other animals with four feet can **gallop**. The zebras **galloped** across the plains to escape from the lion chasing them. [**galloping, galloped**]

game (gaym)

A **game** is something that has special rules and that you do for fun. Some **games**, like checkers and chess, are played on a special board. Basketball, baseball, soccer, and tennis are **games** played with a ball. Miguel likes card **games** and computer **games**. [**games**]

playing a **game** of checkers

garage (guh-rahzh)

1. A **garage** is a building where one car or many are kept.
2. A **garage** is also a business where cars are repaired. [**garages**]

garbage (gahr-bij)

Garbage is food or other things that people have thrown away. A large truck picks up **garbage** in Nicole's neighborhood on Mondays and Thursdays.

garden (gahrd-n)

A **garden** is a place outdoors where people grow plants. Toni's family has a large vegetable **garden** with a fence around it. [**gardens**]

working in a **garden**

gas (gas)

1. A **gas** is something that fills up space, but usually cannot be seen. The air we breathe is made of different kinds of **gases**. **Gas** is sometimes stored in pipes and is used for heating homes and businesses and for cooking.
2. The word **gas** is also short for **gasoline**. This kind of **gas** is a liquid made from oil. **Gas** is used in cars, trucks, and motorcycles. [**gases**]

gate (gayt)

A **gate** is a kind of door in a fence or a wall. It is often made of pieces of metal or wood. Please close the **gate**, so our new puppy will not run away. **[gates]**

gather (GATH-ur)

Gather means to bring things together or to come together. At the end of the day, I **gather** up my toys and put them away. People **gathered** to watch the parade. **[gathering, gathered]**

gentle (jent-l)

A **gentle** person or animal is kind and very careful with other people or things. Hugo is **gentle** when he touches his cat Tango. **[gentler, gentlest]**

gentle

get (get)

1. To **get** is to have something by buying, borrowing, or receiving it from someone else. We need to **get** some paper towels at the store. Shana is **getting** her hair cut.
2. To **get** also means to go after something and bring it back. Let's **get** our bicycles and go for a ride.
3. To **get** also means to arrive. How long will it take you to **get** here? **[getting, got, gotten]**

ghost (gohst)

A **ghost** is what some people imagine a dead person might be like if the person came back to Earth. The movie about **ghosts** was mostly silly, but also a little scary. **[ghosts]**

giant (jie-uhnt)

1. A **giant** is a very large person. The **giant** in the fairy tale could crush a whole village with one step. **[giants]**
2. Something that is **giant** is very big. Lauren won a prize at the fair for growing a **giant** pumpkin.

giggle (gig-uhl)

When you **giggle**, you laugh with short, quick sounds. At the movie, all the kids were **giggling** and moving around in their seats. **[giggling, giggled]**

giraffe (juh-raf)

A **giraffe** is a very tall animal with long, thin legs and a very long neck. **Giraffes** are the tallest living animals. **Giraffes** come from Africa. **[giraffes]**

giraffes

girl (guhrl)

A **girl** is a young female person who is still a child. When **girls** grow up, they become women. There are ten **girls** in Amanda's class and twelve boys. **[girls]**

give (giv)

When you **give** something to someone, you let the person have it. For Mother's Day, Tom is **giving** his mother a card he made for her. Last year, he **gave** her a plant he grew from seeds. **[giving, gave, given]**

glad (glad)

If you are **glad**, you are happy about something. We were **glad** to see our cousins when they came to visit. I'm **glad** that summer is almost here. **[gladder, gladdest]**

glass (glas)

1. Glass is a material that is hard and smooth and easy to break. You can see through most **glass**. **Glass** is used for windows and mirrors.
2. A **glass** is also a round container made of **glass** or plastic that you drink out of. My little brother drinks his juice from a cup, but I use a **glass**. **[glasses]**

glasses (glas-iz)

Glasses are small pieces of glass or plastic that some people wear in front of their eyes to help them see better. Letitia wears **glasses** and can now see the blackboard at school much better. Dark **glasses** that protect your eyes from the sun are called **sunglasses**.

globes

globe (glohb)

A **globe** is a map of the world in the shape of a ball. Can you find Mexico on the **globe**? **[globes]**

glove (gluhv)

1. A **glove** is a kind of clothing worn on the hand to keep it warm. A **glove** covers each finger separately. Ceci bought a new pair of **gloves** that match her coat.
2. Another kind of **glove** is very thick and has one place for the thumb and one place for the rest of the fingers. This kind of **glove** is used for sports like baseball and boxing. **[gloves]**

a baseball **glove**

glue (gloo)

1. Glue is a thick, sticky liquid used to hold things together. Lily is using pieces of paper and **glue** to make a picture. **[glues]**

2. If you **glue** something, you use a thick, sticky liquid to make it stick to something else. After **gluing** the handle back onto the cup, we waited until the next day before using it. **[gluing, glued]**

using **glue**

go (goh)

To **go** means to move from one place to another place. Emily wants to **go** to the zoo on Saturday. "It's your turn to **go**," said Elana during the game of checkers with Tiesha. **[going, went, gone]**

goal (gohl)

1. A **goal** is something you want to work hard to get or something you want to do or become. My sister's **goal** is to become a doctor. My **goal** is to save money for a dollhouse.

2. In some games, like soccer and football, a **goal** is a place where you try to make the ball go to get points. **[goals]**

goat

goat (goht)

A **goat** is an animal with four legs, horns, and sometimes a beard. Some **goats** are wild and live in the mountains. People also raise **goats** for their milk and wool. **[goats]**

goggles (gahg-uhlz)

Goggles are a kind of big glasses that people wear to protect their eyes or to see under water. People who work with dangerous tools or big machines wear **goggles** to protect their eyes from dust and dirt. Efie wears **goggles** over her glasses when she skis.

wearing **goggles** for swimming

gold (gohld)

Gold is a yellow metal that is often found underground. **Gold** is mixed with other metals to make jewelry, coins, and parts for machines. Frank's parents wear **gold** wedding rings.

goldfish (gohld-fish)

A **goldfish** is a kind of small yellow or orange fish that many people keep in a bowl or a small aquarium. Some **goldfish** live outdoors in ponds and grow quite large. [**goldfish** or **goldfishes**]

good (gud)

1. When you like something, you say that it is **good**. I'm reading a **good** book. That pizza was really **good**.
2. Good can also mean that you do something well. Daryl is a **good** skater, but Karla is a **better** one.
3. Good also means acting in a way that you should be acting. Lie down, Buster — that's a **good** dog.
4. Something that is **good** for you helps to make you healthy. Exercise and eating fruit and vegetables are **good** for you. [**better, best**]

good-bye (gud-bie)

You say **good-bye** when you or someone else leaves a place or when you finish talking on the telephone. I was sad at the end of the summer when I had to say **good-bye** to my friends at camp.

goose (goos)

A **goose** is a large bird with a long neck that lives near water and is a good swimmer. Groups of **geese** fly south in the fall and spend the winter in a warmer place. [**geese**]

goose

gorilla

gorilla (guh-ril-uh)

A **gorilla** is a very large wild animal that comes from the jungles of Africa. **Gorillas** have long arms and short legs and are very strong. **Gorillas** are mammals. [**gorillas**]

grade (grayd)

1. A **grade** is a group of children about the same age who do the same kind of work together at school for a school year. Jane is in the second **grade**.
2. A **grade** is also a letter or a number that shows how well you have done some work or how much you learned in a class. Sarah smiled when she saw that her **grade** in spelling went from a C to a B. [**grades**]

grain (grayn)

A **grain** is a tiny seed of rice, corn, wheat, or other plants that is used for growing new plants or is eaten. **Grain** is used to make breakfast cereal and flour. This loaf of bread is made with seven different kinds of **grains**. [**grains**]

grandchild (gran-childe)

You are the **grandchild** of your grandmother and grandfather. A **granddaughter** is a female **grandchild**. A **grandson** is a male **grandchild**. [**grandchildren**]

grandparent (grand-par-uhnt)

Your **grandparent** is the mother or the father of your mother and father. Your **grandmother** is the mother of your mother or father. Your **grandfather** is the father of your mother or father. [**grandparents**]

grape (grayp)

A **grape** is a small, round fruit that can be green, red, or purple. **Grapes** grow in bunches and sometimes have seeds in them. Kenny likes **grape** juice and **grape** jelly. [**grapes**]

grapes

grapefruit (grayp-froot)

A **grapefruit** is a large, round, sour fruit that has yellow skin and is white or pink inside. Stephanie likes to drink orange juice or eat half a **grapefruit** for breakfast. [**grapefruits** or **grapefruit**]

grapefruit

grass (gras)

Grass is a green plant that grows in yards and parks. Our **grass** should be cut soon. Cows eat a kind of tall **grass** that grows in fields. [**grasses**]

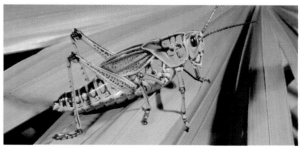

grasshopper

grasshopper (gras-hahp-uhr)

A **grasshopper** is a large insect with strong back legs for jumping. Some **grasshoppers** make sounds by rubbing their legs or wings together. [**grasshoppers**]

gray (gray)

Gray is a color made by mixing black and white together. The sky is **gray** on a rainy day. **Gray** is also spelled **grey**.

great (grayt)

1. Great means very important and well known. We learned about Beethoven and other **great** musicians in school today.
2. Great also means large in size or number. A very long, tall wall in China is called the **Great** Wall of China. A **great** many people visited the national parks last summer.
3. If something is **great**, it is very good. This would be a **great** afternoon to go swimming. Kisha is a **great** ice-skater. [**greater, greatest**]

great grandparent (grayt grand-par-uhnt)

A **great grandparent** is the mother or father of your grandmother or grandfather. Your **great grandmother** is the mother of your grandmother. Your **great grandfather** is the father of your grandfather. Ian's **great grandmother** lives with his grandmother in Minnesota. **[great grandparents]**

green (green)

Green is a color you get by mixing blue and yellow. Grass, leaves, and dollar bills are **green**. Marcy eats **green** beans, lettuce, and other **green** vegetables.

greenhouse (green-hous)

A **greenhouse** is a building that is made mostly of glass or plastic and is used for growing plants. The gardeners grew tiny tomato plants from seeds in their **greenhouse** and then planted them outdoors when it got warm. **[greenhouses]**

greenhouse

grocery

grocery (groh-suh-ree)

A **grocery** is a store where you can buy food, soap, and other things you use at home. The things that you buy in a **grocery** store are called **groceries**. A very large store that sells **groceries** is called a **supermarket**. **[groceries]**

ground (ground)

The **ground** is the earth under your feet when you are outdoors. We dug a hole in the **ground** to plant a rosebush.

group (groop)

A **group** is more than two people or things together. A **group** of us will be going to the soccer game tomorrow. At the park, Fred saw someone walking a **group** of dogs. **[groups]**

grow (groh)

When plants, animals, or people get bigger or taller, we say that they **grow**. We're **growing** sunflowers in our backyard. When children **grow** up, they become adults. **[growing, grown]**

grown-up (groh-nuhp)

A **grown-up** is a person who is no longer a child. Men and women are **grown-ups**. [grown-ups]

guard (gahrd)

1. If you **guard** something, you watch it all the time so that nothing bad happens to it or no one takes it. The dog **guards** its bone and barks when anyone comes near it. **[guarding, guarded]**
2. A **guard** is someone who watches or protects something or someone. There are crossing **guards** at each corner near the school to control traffic before and after school. **[guards]**

guess (ges)

To **guess** is to answer a question or to try to find the answer to a problem without knowing that the answer is right. Dad **guessed** it would take him between one and two hours to fix the car. **[guessing, guessed]**

guitar (gi-tahr)

A **guitar** is a musical instrument with strings attached to a long, narrow piece at one end. At the other end of a **guitar** is a large, curved box with a round opening. A **guitar** is played by moving your fingers on the strings. Ronnie taught us a new song, and we all sang while she played the **guitar**. [guitars]

guitar

gun (guhn)

A **gun** is held in the hand and used for shooting at something. The hunter shot the deer with a long **gun** called a rifle. Police officers and soldiers carry **guns**. [guns]

gym (jim)

A **gym** is a room or building where people play sports like basketball or do different kinds of exercises. Our school is building a new **gym** that will have a large swimming pool. [gyms]

doing **gymnastics**

gymnastics (jim-nas-tiks)

Gymnastics is a group of exercises in which a person bends and turns the body in special ways while moving along the ground or in the air. To do **gymnastics** a person must be strong and have good balance. In **gymnastics** class, the children are practicing doing forward and backward somersaults on mats and are learning to stand on their hands.

Hh

habit (hab-it)

A **habit** is something that you do often without thinking about it. **Habits** can be good or bad. Maxie has a **habit** of biting her nails. Mom wants us to get into the **habit** of cleaning our room. **[habits]**

habitat (hab-uh-tat)

The **habitat** of an animal or plant is the place where it lives and grows best. A polar bear's natural **habitat** is the far north, although some polar bears live in zoos. The **habitat** of a cactus is the desert. **[habitats]**

hair (hair)

Your **hair** grows on your head. Raymond has straight black **hair**, and Carol's brown **hair** curls. Animals have **hair** called fur on their bodies. **[hairs]**

half (haf)

Half is one of two equal parts of something. When something has been divided into two equal parts, it has been divided in **half**. Blossom cut her sandwich in **half**. **Half** the class put on a play, while the other **half** watched. **[halves]**

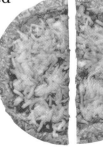

cut in **half**

hall (hawl)

A **hall** is a place in a building that people walk through to get from one room to another. **[halls]**

hamburger (ham-buhr-guhr)

A **hamburger** is beef that has been cut into tiny pieces and made into a round, flat shape and cooked. **[hamburgers]**

hammering a nail into a fence

hammer (ham-uhr)

1. A **hammer** is a tool used for hitting nails into wood or walls. A **hammer** has a long handle with a heavy metal piece at one end. **[hammers]**
2. If you **hammer** something, you hit it with a tool called a hammer. **[hammering, hammered]**

hamster (ham-stuhr)

A **hamster** is a small animal with short fur and a short tail. Henry's pet **hamster** lives in a cage. **[hamsters]**

hand (hand)

1. A **hand** is the part of your body at the end of your arm. Your fingers and thumbs are part of your **hands**. We pick things up and hold them with our **hands**. I held Joey's **hand** when we crossed the street.
2. A **hand** is also one of the long pieces on some watches and clocks that move around the numbers so that we can tell time. My watch has an hour **hand** and a minute **hand**. **[hands]**
3. If you **hand** something to someone, you give it to that person. Will you **hand** me that book, please? **[handing, handed]**

handle (han-duhl)

A **handle** is a piece that you can hold onto when you want to lift or move something. Cups, knives, suitcases, and many other things have **handles**. **[handles]**

hang (hang)

To **hang** means to be held at the top but not at the bottom. Please **hang** your coats on those hooks by the door. **[hanging, hung]**

hanging on

happen (hap-uhn)

To **happen** means to take place. Look at what **happens** to corn when insects eat it. When Mom read a story about a castle burning down, Kristin asked, "Did that really **happen**?" **[happening, happened]**

happy (hap-ee)

To be **happy** means to feel good about something. People often smile when they are **happy**. I was very **happy** to see my friend Susie on the first day of school. **[happier, happiest]**

harbor (hahr-buhr)

A **harbor** is a place along the shore where ships and boats can come into shore and be safe. Some **harbors** have docks. **[harbors]**

harbor

hard (hahrd)

1. Something that is **hard** doesn't bend or change its shape when you touch it. It is not easy to cut into or break something that is **hard**. Rocks and metal are **hard**.
2. **Hard** also means not easy to do. Something that is **hard** takes a lot of time or energy. It's **hard** to run backward. **[harder, hardest]**

harmonica (har-**mahn**-i-kuh)

A **harmonica** is a small musical instrument with a row of tiny square holes. The notes on a **harmonica** are played by blowing into the holes or pulling air back through the holes. [**harmonicas**]

harmonica

harvest (**hahr**-vuhst)

1. Harvest is the time or season when large amounts of fruit, vegetables, grains, or other plants become ripe and are picked or gathered. The **harvest** season is usually in late summer or autumn. We had a good **harvest** of peas and tomatoes this year. [**harvests**]

2. To **harvest** is to pick or gather plants. My uncle has big machines to help him **harvest** his wheat. It takes many people to help **harvest** the potatoes, squash, and corn. [**harvesting, harvested**]

wheat **harvest**

hat (hat)

A **hat** is a piece of clothing worn on the head. A **hat** is usually worn to protect a person from the cold, sun, rain, or wind. [**hats**]

hatch (hach)

To **hatch** means to break the shell of an egg and come out of it. Chickens, ducks, alligators, and turtles **hatch** from eggs. [**hatching, hatched**]

hate (hayt)

Hate is the opposite of love. To **hate** means to have a very strong feeling that you don't like something or someone. Gayle **hates** squash and cauliflower, but she loves spinach and carrots. [**hating, hated**]

haunted (**hawnt**-id)

If you say that a place is **haunted**, you act as if there are ghosts there. Yolanda is reading a mystery story about a **haunted** house with lots of scary things in it.

have (hav)

If you **have** something, it is with you or part of you, or you own it or feel it. Felipe and Rob **have** blue bikes. We **have** three computers in the library at school. [**having, had**]

hay (hay)

Hay is a kind of dried grass that is used to feed cows and horses and other animals. Farmers cut **hay** in the autumn for animals in winter.

head (hed)

Your **head** is the part of your body above your neck. Your eyes, nose, mouth, and ears are part of your **head**. Uncle Sal has very little hair on his **head**. [**heads**]

headphones (hed-fohnz)

Headphones are something to put over the ears to listen to tapes, CDs, or other things. Some **headphones** are worn to protect the ears from loud noise.

headphones

heal (heel)

To **heal** is to get well after you have been hurt or sick. It took six weeks for Gila's broken arm to **heal**. The cut on my dog's leg **healed** in a few days. [**healing, healed**]

healthy (hel-thee)

To be **healthy** is to feel well and not be sick. Eating the right food and getting enough sleep and exercise help people to stay **healthy**. [**healthier, healthiest**]

hear (hir)

To **hear** is to have sounds come into your ears. Last summer, when the windows were open, we could **hear** our neighbor practicing his violin. [**hearing, heard**]

heart (hahrt)

1. Your **heart** is an important part of your body that is in your chest. When your **heart** beats, it sends out blood through your whole body.
2. A **heart** is also a shape like this: ♥. Stacey made a valentine with a big red **heart** on it for her friend. [**hearts**]

heat (heet)

1. **Heat** is what makes someone or something feel warm or hot. **Heat** from the sun warms the earth and helps to make things grow. **Heat** is used to cook food. The **heat** inside the oven baked the potatoes.
2. If you **heat** something, you make it warm or hot. Let's **heat** up some soup for lunch. [**heating, heated**]

heavy (hev-ee)

Something that is **heavy** is hard to lift or carry because it weighs a lot. I need two hands to pick up this **heavy** watermelon. When we moved, it took two men to lift the **heavy** furniture. [**heavier, heaviest**]

heavy

heel (heel)

1. Your **heel** is the back part of your foot. Patrick thinks it is much easier to stand on his toes than on his **heels**.
2. A **heel** is also part of a shoe or a sock. The **heel** of my sock has a hole in it. [**heels**]

height (hite)

Height is how tall someone or something is. Jovine's **height** is 3 feet, 8 inches. Redwood trees grow to a **height** of 300 feet. [**heights**]

helicopter

helicopter (hel-uh-kahp-tuhr)
A **helicopter** is a machine that flies by its long, thin metal parts that turn around very fast and lift it off the ground. **Helicopters** can fly straight up and down or stay in one place in the air. **[helicopters]**

hello (hel-oh)
Hello is the first thing you say to people when you see them or talk to them on the phone. **[hellos]**

helmet (hel-muht)
A **helmet** is a hard hat worn to protect the head. Mike has a bicycle **helmet** and a football **helmet**. **[helmets]**

help (help)
1. When you **help** someone, you do something for that person. Katie **helps** Mrs. Waters shovel snow from her sidewalk in winter. We **helped** gather balls and bats after baseball practice. **[helping, helped]**
2. Help is what you get when someone does something for you or with you. Amanda needed **help** with her homework last night. We say **Help**! when we need something or are in trouble.

hen (hen)
A **hen** is a female chicken. Some other female birds are also called **hens**. **[hens]**

hero (hir-oh) and
heroine (her-uh-wuhn)
A **hero** is a person who has done something difficult or dangerous and has acted very bravely or in a good way. A **hero** helps and protects other people. A **hero** who is a girl or a woman is called a **heroine**. The mayor thanked the **heroes** and **heroines** who helped people after the earthquake. **[heroes, heroines]**

hide (hide)
When you **hide**, you cannot be seen. When you **hide** something, you put it where it cannot be seen. Joy's friends don't know where she is hiding. The dog **hid** under the bed during the storm. **[hiding, hid]**

hiding

high (hie)
Something that is **high** is far above the ground. My cat climbed **high** up in a tree. **[higher, highest]**

hike (hike)
1. A **hike** is a long walk. We took a **hike** in the mountains. **[hikes]**
2. To **hike** is to go on a hike. **[hiking, hiked]**

hill (hil)

A **hill** is a place where the land rises above the area around it. **Hills** are not as tall as mountains. [**hills**]

hippopotamus (hip-uh-**pot**-uh-muhs)

A **hippopotamus** is a wild animal from Africa. It has a large body with short legs and a huge head and mouth. [**hippopotamuses**]

hippopotamus

hit (hit)

If you **hit** something, you touch it hard. Jeannie **hit** the ball over the net to Tanya during their tennis game. Robert was punished for **hitting** his sister. [**hitting, hit**]

hive (hive)

A **hive** is the home that bees build to live in and make their honey. [**hives**]

hobby (hahb-ee)

A **hobby** is something that you do in your free time because you enjoy it. My dad works as a carpenter, but his **hobby** is fishing. My **hobby** is collecting shells. [**hobbies**]

ice **hockey**

hockey (hahk-ee)

Hockey is a game played by two teams using long sticks curved at one end. In ice **hockey** players on ice skates hit a disk. Field **hockey** is played on grass with a ball.

hold (hohld)

1. If you **hold** something or someone, you keep it close to you or in your hand or arms. Will you **hold** the baby for a moment? Bonny **held** up her painting for everyone to see. **2.** How much something can **hold** is the amount of room inside it. The van can **hold** up to eight people. [**holding, held**]

hole (hohl)

A **hole** is a place where there is an empty space. The rabbit dug a **hole** under the fence. There's a **hole** in this bag. [**holes**]

holiday (hahl-uh-day)

A **holiday** is a day or a time of year when we remember something special that happened in the past. July 4th, Thanksgiving, and Christmas are **holidays**. [**holidays**]

hollow (hahl-oh)

Something that is **hollow** has an empty space inside it. There's a long, **hollow** tube in the park that children can crawl through. **[hollower, hollowest]**

home (hohm)

Home is the place where a person or an animal lives. Jen's **home** is the house on the corner. The deer's **home** is the woods. **[homes]**

homework (hohm-wuhrk)

Homework is work that students are asked to do at home and bring back to school. Dad helped Maya with her **homework** last night.

honest (on-ist)

A person who is **honest** tells the truth and does not lie. Bruce broke Mr. Roberts' window and was **honest** and told him.

honey (huhn-ee)

Honey is a kind of thick, sweet food made by bees that looks like yellow syrup. Ann likes **honey** in her tea.

hook (huk)

A **hook** is a curved piece of metal or plastic that is used to catch or hold something. A fish **hook** has a sharp point at the end. The broom hangs on a **hook** by the stairs. **[hooks]**

hop (hahp)

When you **hop,** you jump on one leg. Sometimes animals **hop** on two legs. A rabbit has strong back legs used to **hop** quickly. **[hopping, hopped]**

hope (hohp)

To **hope** is to want very much for something to happen. I **hope** Dorita and Eric can come to my birthday party. **[hoping, hoped]**

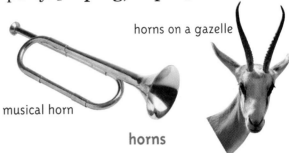

horns on a gazelle

musical horn

horns

horn (horn)

1. A **horn** is something that makes a loud noise when you blow into it or squeeze or press it. Some musical instruments are called **horns**. There are also toy **horns**, bicycle **horns**, and car **horns**.
2. A **horn** is also a hard and pointed part that grows on the heads of some animals like cattle. **[horns]**

horse (hors)

A **horse** is an animal with a large body and four thin legs. A **horse** has long hair on its neck, called a mane, and a long tail with hair. **[horses]**

galloping **horse**

hose (hohz)

A **hose** is a long rubber or plastic tube that carries water. Jameel used the garden **hose** to water plants. The **hose** on the fire truck was long and heavy. **[hoses]**

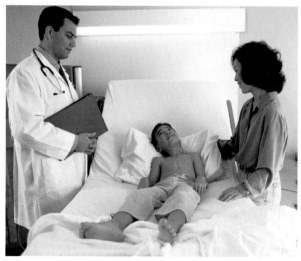

in the **hospital**

hospital (hahs-pit-l)

A **hospital** is a building where people who are sick or hurt go to be taken care of by doctors and nurses. When Chris was in the **hospital**, his mother and his doctor visited him often. **[hospitals]**

hot (haht)

Something that is **hot** has a very high temperature. Many things burn or melt when they get **hot**. People are taught to be careful around **hot** things. The oven stayed **hot** long after it had been turned off. When Tanya takes a bath, she likes the water to be warm, but not too **hot**. The soup was **hotter** than Ted thought it would be, so he blew on it. **[hotter, hottest]**

hotel (hoh-tel)

A **hotel** is a large building where people pay for a room to stay in when they are away from home. Most **hotels** also have restaurants in them. **[hotels]**

hour (our)

An **hour** is an amount of time equal to 60 minutes. There are 24 **hours** in every day. How many **hours** do you sleep at night? The movie was an **hour** and a half long. **[hours]**

house (hous)

A **house** is a building where people live. In some neighborhoods the **houses** are attached to each other, and in some neighborhoods each **house** has a yard and trees around it. An apartment **house** is a tall building with many places to live inside. **[houses]**

hug (huhg)

1. If you **hug** something, you put your arms tightly around it and hold it close. Janie **hugs** her teddy bear when she goes to sleep. **[hugging, hugged]**

a **hug**

2. When you put your arms tightly around someone you like a lot, you are giving that person a **hug**. **[hugs]**

a **huge** pumpkin

huge (hyooj)

Huge means very large. The alligator's mouth was **huge**. **Huge** cranes are used to build tall buildings. **[huger, hugest]**

human (hyoo-muhn)

A **human** is a person. **Human** is short for **human being**. Children and adults are **humans**, but animals are not. Scientists are learning about what happens to **humans**, animals, and plants when they travel in space. **[humans]**

hump (huhmp)

A **hump** is a large, round bump. Camels have one or two **humps** on their backs. **[humps]**

hundred (huhn-druhd)

One **hundred** is a large number that is written **100.** There are a **hundred** pennies in a dollar. The farmer picked **100** pumpkins to sell at the fair. **[hundreds]**

hung (huhng)

Hung comes from **hang**. The bat **hung** upside down from the tree.

hungry (huhng-gree)

Hungry means to want something to eat. We were **hungry** after the movie and went out for pizza. **[hungrier, hungriest]**

hunt (huhnt)

To **hunt** for something is to search for it carefully. Karin is **hunting** for her lost shoe. Some animals **hunt** for other animals for food. A person who **hunts** animals is called a **hunter**. **[hunting, hunted]**

hurricane (hur-uh-kayn)

A **hurricane** is a very big storm over the ocean. The wind and rain of the **hurricane** blew down houses and trees along the coast. **[hurricanes]**

hurry (huhr-ee)

When you **hurry**, you move quickly, because you are late or because you want to get somewhere very fast. If you don't **hurry**, we'll be late for the show. **[hurrying, hurried]**

hurt (huhrt)

If you **hurt** yourself or if a part of you **hurts**, you feel pain. José fell off the swing and **hurt** himself. My cat licked her paw because it **hurt**. **[hurting, hurt]**

husband (huhz-buhnd)

When a man and a woman marry, the man becomes the woman's **husband** and she becomes his wife. **[husbands]**

ice (ise)

Ice is water that is so cold that it has frozen. When water turns into **ice**, it changes from a liquid into a solid. Be careful not to slip on the **ice** on the sidewalk! Would you like some **ice** in your drink?

iceberg (ise-buhrg)

An **iceberg** is a huge block of ice that floats in very cold seas. Most of an **iceberg** is below the surface of the water. Only the top part of an **iceberg** is above the water. **[icebergs]**

iceberg

ice cream (ise kreem)

Ice cream is a frozen food made from milk or cream, sugar or honey, and sometimes eggs. **Ice cream** comes in many flavors. One of Janine's favorite sandwiches is an **ice-cream** sandwich. **[ice creams]**

on **ice skates**

ice skate (ise skayt)

An **ice skate** is a special boot for skating on ice. An **ice skate** has a long metal piece on the bottom that slides across the ice. Iesha tied her **ice skates** very tight around her ankles. A person who moves on ice wearing **ice skates** is called an **ice-skater**. **[ice skates]**

idea (ie-dee-uh)

An **idea** is something that you think of, like a plan or a picture in your mind. The children had a great **idea** for a class play. Jameel had no **idea** how Lindsay had done the card trick. **[ideas]**

igloo (ig-loo)

An **igloo** is a house built from hard blocks of snow or ice. The top of an **igloo** is round, and clear blocks of ice let in light. People enter and leave an **igloo** through a small tunnel. **[igloos]**

imagine (i-**maj**-uhn)

When you **imagine** something, you think of what something is like, or you have a picture of it in your mind. Can you **imagine** how it would feel to fly like an eagle or swim like a shark? If something is **imaginary**, it is only in your mind and is not real. Dylan likes to read stories about dragons even though he knows they are **imaginary**. **[imagining, imagined]**

important (im-**port**-nt)

Important means special for some reason. Something may be **important** because extra care is needed or because you feel something special about it. It is **important** to wear a seat belt when riding in a car. Sonja's cat is very **important** to her.

impossible (im-**pahs**-uh-buhl)

When something is **impossible**, it cannot happen. It is **impossible** for people to grow wings and fly.

inch (inch)

An **inch** is an amount used to measure the length of something. There are twelve **inches** in one foot. Ethan's arm is fifteen **inches** long. **[inches]**

information (in-fuhr-**may**-shuhn)

Information is one fact or many facts that are known about something. At the library, Tiesha found **information** about animals that live in the rain forest. **[information]**

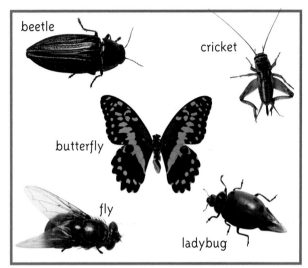

beetle

cricket

butterfly

fly

ladybug

insects

insect (in-sekt)

An **insect** is a kind of animal that is very small and has three pairs of legs. Some **insects** have wings. **Insects** also have a pair of antennae on the head, which are used to feel. Ants, bees, flies, mosquitoes, and butterflies are **insects**. **[insects]**

inside (in-side)

1. The **inside** of something is the part that is not on the surface. The **inside** of that shell is shiny.
2. Inside also means in a building. Our dog comes **inside** when it rains.

instrument (in-struh-muhnt)

1. An **instrument** is a kind of tool used to do a special job. A dentist uses metal **instruments** to check and clean your teeth. The pilot carefully watched the **instruments** in the airplane as he lowered the plane for a landing.
2. An **instrument** used to make music is called a **musical instrument**. **[instruments]**

interesting (int-uh-res-ting)
When something is **interesting**, you like it or want to learn more about it. At the zoo, the talk about penguins was so **interesting** that the children wanted to know more.

invent (in-vent)
To **invent** means to have a new idea and to make something that has not been made before. "If only I could **invent** a robot to put away my toys for me," thought Peter. Before cars were **invented**, people traveled on foot or on horses. A person who **invents** something is called an **inventor**. [inventing, invented]

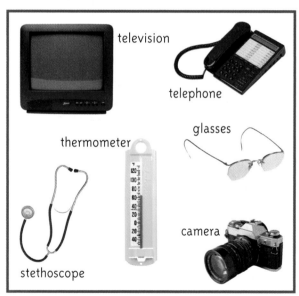

television
telephone
glasses
thermometer
camera
stethoscope

inventions

invention (in-ven-chuhn)
An **invention** is something that has not been made before. Before the **invention** of television, people got information by reading or listening to the radio. After the **invention** of rockets, astronauts went to the moon. [inventions]

invisible (in-viz-uh-buhl)
When something is **invisible**, no one can see it. The wind is **invisible**, but we can feel it when it blows.

invitation (in-vuh-tay-shuhn)
An **invitation** is what you give, send, or say to ask someone to do something with you. Sara used her computer to make **invitations** to her party. [invitations]

invite (in-vite)
Invite means to ask someone to do something with you. Danny decided to **invite** his grandparents to the next soccer game his team plays. [inviting, invited]

iron (ie-uhrn)
1. **Iron** is a metal that is dark, hard, and strong. **Iron** is dug up from underground. Some heavy cooking pots, stoves, pipes, and fences are made of **iron**.
2. An **iron** is a tool used to press wrinkles out of cloth or clothes by using heat and sometimes steam. The bottom of an **iron** is flat and shaped like a triangle. [irons]

island (ie-luhnd)
An **island** is a piece of land that has water all around it. We can use the bridge or take a ferry to get to the **island**. [islands]

itch (ich)
When you **itch**, your skin feels like it needs to be scratched. When his mosquito bites **itch**, Benjamin tries hard not to scratch them. [itching, itched]

hood

snap

sleeve

jacket

jacket (jak-it)

A **jacket** is a coat that is short. Brittany has a heavy **jacket** she wears when it's cold and a lighter one for warmer weather. [**jackets**]

jail (jayl)

Jail is a building where people who do not obey laws may be locked up and punished. The car thief was caught by the police and sent to **jail** for stealing. [**jails**]

jam (jam)

Jam is a sweet, sticky food made by cooking fruit with sugar until it gets thick. **Jam** often has small pieces of fruit in it. [**jams**]

jar (jahr)

A **jar** is a short, wide bottle. Most **jars** are made of glass and have covers that can be put on and taken off. When Carl forgot to cover the **jar** of paste, the paste dried up. [**jars**]

jeans (jeenz)

Jeans are pants made from very strong cotton cloth. Kirsten's favorite pair of **jeans** are the blue ones with patches all over them. [**jeans**]

jelly (jel-ee)

Jelly is a sweet, sticky food made from fruit juice and sugar heated together until it is thick and smooth. Tanya smiled when she opened her lunch bag and found a cream-cheese-and-**jelly** sandwich. [**jellies**]

jet (jet)

A **jet** is a kind of airplane that can travel very fast. An engine of a **jet** pushes the airplane forward by sending hot gases backward. [**jets**]

jewelry (joo-uhl-ree)

People wear **jewelry** to decorate their bodies and clothes. Bracelets, necklaces, rings, and earrings are different kinds of **jewelry**. **Jewelry** can be made of wood, metal, stones, glass, and many other things. [**jewelry**]

jars

job (jahb)

1. Having a **job** means doing work and getting paid for it. My aunt has a **job** as a police officer. **2.** Another kind of **job** is work that must be done for no money. Anthony's **job** today is to wash the car. **[jobs]**

today's **job**

jog (jahg)

When people **jog**, they run gently. **Jogging** is slower than running at full speed, but faster than walking. A person who **jogs** is called a **jogger**. **[jogging, jogged]**

join (join)

1. To **join** means to put things together and attach them to each other. When Megan's necklace broke, she **joined** the two ends with a knot. **2.** To **join** also means to become part of something. Gregg wants to **join** a singing group at school. **[joining, joined]**

joke (johk)

A **joke** is a short story that people find funny. Marie's uncle is very good at telling **jokes**. **[jokes]**

juggle (juhg-uhl)

To **juggle** means to keep two or more things moving in the air by throwing them and catching them. A person who **juggles** is called a **juggler**. **[juggling, juggled]**

juice (joos)

Juice is liquid that is pressed out of vegetables and fruits. We squeezed oranges to make fresh **juice**. A machine that gets liquids out of foods is called a **juicer**. **[juices]**

jump (juhmp)

When you **jump**, you stand up and push both feet off the ground. Risa **jumped** over the puddle so that she wouldn't get her new shoes wet. **[jumping, jumped]**

jumping rope

jungle (juhng-guhl)

A **jungle** is a warm, wet place filled with wild trees and plants that grow very close together. The **jungle** is home to insects, monkeys, snakes, and other animals that like hot, rainy weather. **[jungles]**

junk (juhngk)

Junk is something that is too worn out or broken to be used. Daryl threw out **junk** from his closet.

Kk

kangaroo (kang-guh-roo)

A **kangaroo** is a large animal with two very strong back legs for hopping. The female **kangaroo** has a kind of furry pocket, called a pouch, on top of her stomach to hold and carry her young. **[kangaroos]**

kangaroos

keep (keep)

1. To **keep** means to have something for yourself or to save something for later. Janelle **keeps** her toy panda and dolls on her bed. Extra batteries for the flashlight are **kept** in the kitchen.
2. Keep also means to continue in the same way or without stopping. The children tried to **keep** in a straight line. The milk will **keep** longer in the refrigerator.
3. To **keep** also means to stop from going somewhere or doing something. The fence **keeps** the dog in the yard. **[keeping, kept]**

key (kee)

1. A **key** is a piece of metal with bumps on one edge used for opening or closing a lock. Kara keeps the **key** to her diary in a special place.
2. Another kind of **key** is a bar or button that you press to make something work. Instruments like a clarinet and piano have **keys** to press to make music. **[keys]**

keyboard (kee-bord)

A **keyboard** has many keys lined up in one or more rows. There are different kinds of **keyboards**. A piano has a long **keyboard** with black and white keys. A computer **keyboard** often has five or six rows of keys with letters and numbers on them. **[keyboards]**

piano **keyboard**

kick (kik)

When you **kick**, you move your foot up to try to hit something. Jocelyn **kicked** the beach ball high in the air. **[kicking, kicked]**

kick

kid (kid)

1. Kid is the name for a baby goat. The **kid** stayed close to its mother.
2. Kid is also a name for a young child. The grown-ups talked in the living room, while the **kids** played games outdoors. **[kids]**

kid

kill (kil)

To **kill** means to end someone or something's life. When something is **killed**, it dies. Brian tried not to step on any ants because he did not want to **kill** them. **[killing, killed]**

kind (kinde)

1. Being **kind** means treating people in a nice way. A **kind** person is friendly and gentle and helps other people. Tyler was new in town and felt good when people were **kind** to him. **[kinder, kindest]**
2. Kind also means a group of things that are like each other in some way. Roses and tulips are two **kinds** of flowers. **[kinds]**

kindergarten (kin-duhr-gahrt-n)

Kindergarten is the grade in school before first grade. Chelsea's five-year-old brother started **kindergarten** this year. **[kindergartens]**

king (king)

A **king** is a man who rules a country or a kindgom. A **king** rules because he is part of the family that rules the country. The son of a **king** is called a prince. The daughter of a **king** is called a princess. **[kings]**

kingdom (king-duhm)

A **kingdom** is the land or country ruled by a king or queen. Meghan's book has pictures of life in a **kingdom** where the king and queen live in a castle. **[kingdoms]**

kiss (kis)

1. To **kiss** means to touch someone or something with your lips. Mikele and Leah **kiss** their grandfather on each cheek to say hello. **[kissing, kissed]**
2. A **kiss** is a touch made with your lips. Before Chris goes to sleep, her mom reads her a story and gives her a **kiss**. **[kisses]**

kiss

kit (kit)

A **kit** is a set of things that go together to help people do jobs or projects. Ariel's garden **kit** came with seeds, plant food, a pot, and a small shovel for digging. James built a small boat with a **kit** he received as a present. **[kits]**

kitchen (kich-uhn)

A **kitchen** is a room where people store and cook food. Many **kitchens** have a sink, a stove, and a refrigerator. In Lisa's house, the **kitchen** is big enough for a table where her family eats meals. **[kitchens]**

flying **kites**

kite (kite)

A **kite** is a toy that flies through the air on the wind while a person holds onto it with a long string. A **kite** is made of light sticks of wood wrapped in paper, plastic, or cloth. [**kites**]

kitten (kit-n)

Kitten is the name for a baby cat. The mother cat licked her **kittens** clean. [**kittens**]

kittens

knee (nee)

The **knee** is the part of the body that bends in the center of the leg. Your **knee** moves when you walk, sit, and kneel. Nana weeds the garden on her **knees**. [**knees**]

kneel (neel)

To **kneel** means to bend one or both knees and rest on your legs. Aaron **kneels** in the grass when he looks for worms. [**kneeling, kneeled**]

knife (nife)

A **knife** is a tool with a sharp edge called a blade. The chef used one **knife** to cut bread and another **knife** to cut meat. [**knives**]

knight (nite)

A **knight** was a soldier who worked for a king or a queen a long time ago. The job of a **knight** was to fight to keep the king and queen and their lands safe. **Knights** wore suits of armor made of metal to protect them when they fought with enemies. [**knights**]

knock (nahk)

To **knock** means to hit. When you **knock** on a door, you hit it enough to make a noise. If you **knock** something over, it falls over when you hit it. The mail carrier **knocks** on the door to deliver a package. As Holly ran by the table, her arm **knocked** over the vase and it broke. [**knocking, knocked**]

knot (naht)

A **knot** is made of ends of string, rope, thread, or ribbon tied together. When Tamika and Mitch went sailing, they learned how different kinds of **knots** are made. [**knots**]

knot

know (noh)

To **know** means to learn about and remember someone or something. Erin **knows** how to count to one hundred by fives. [**knowing, knew**]

label (lay-buhl)

A **label** is a piece of cloth, paper, or plastic that gives information about the thing it is attached to. **Labels** tell what something is made of, what it costs, or other things. The **label** on Jane's sweater says it can be washed in hot water. The **label** on the cough medicine tells how much medicine to take at one time. **[labels]**

ladder (lad-uhr)

A **ladder** is a set of wood or metal steps that can be carried around. Jack climbed up a tall **ladder** to fix the roof. We use a small **ladder** in the kitchen to reach the top shelf. **[ladders]**

ladder

lake (layk)

A **lake** is water with land all around it. **Lakes** are bigger than ponds. Most **lakes** have fresh water in them, but some **lakes** have salt water. Juan rode in a canoe on a **lake** last weekend. **[lakes]**

lamb (lam)

A **lamb** is a young sheep. At the farm Karen saw a **lamb** that was only two days old. The **lamb**'s wool was very soft. **[lambs]**

lamb

lamp (lamp)

A **lamp** gives off light and is used to light up places that are dark. Most **lamps** use electricity, but some burn oil or gas. If you need more light, you can turn on that **lamp** on the table. **[lamps]**

land (land)

1. Land is all the parts of the earth that are not covered with water. Islands and continents are **land**. In the middle of the ocean, the passengers on the ship could not see any **land**. **[lands]**

2. To **land** means to come to land from the air or from water. We watched the butterfly **land** on a flower. The pilot is going to **land** the seaplane in the harbor, right next to a large ship that has just **landed**. **[landing, landed]**

language (lang-gwij)

Language is made up of the words we use to speak, write, and read. A **language** is also the words used by one group of people. This dictionary is written in the English **language**. Alfredo's first **language** is Spanish. Ran speaks two **languages**, Japanese and English. **[languages]**

lap (lap)

When you are sitting down, the top part of your legs is called your **lap**. At the picnic we ate lunch on our **laps**. **[laps]**

large (lahrj)

Large is another word for big. **Large** things cover a lot of the ground or take up a lot of space. Alexandra's watermelon is very **large**. That truck is **larger** than our car. **[larger, largest]**

large watermelon

last (last)

1. The thing that is **last** comes after everything else. Z is the **last** letter in the alphabet. Bobbi ate the **last** banana in the bowl, so there are no more left.
2. Last also means the one before now. It was too cloudy **last** night to see any stars. We lost our **last** game, but we hope to win today.
3. To **last** is to go on, or to be the same for some time. The rain **lasted** all night. **[lasting, lasted]**

late (layt)

1. Late means after the time agreed upon, or after the time you should be there. Uncle Ted's train was **late**, so we had to wait.
2. Late also means near the end of a time. It was **late** in the afternoon, and the sun started to go down. The sun goes down **later** in the summer than in the winter. **[later, latest]**

laugh (laf)

To **laugh** is to make special sounds because you think something is funny. When we went to the circus, the bear's funny tricks made us **laugh**. **[laughing, laughed]**

laundry (lawn-dree)

Laundry is dirty clothes and other things that need to be washed. **Laundry** is also these things when they are being washed or have been washed. Michael put the **laundry** and soap into the washing machine, and Linda folded the **laundry** after it was dry.

law (law)

A **law** is a rule made by a country or state or city that everyone has to obey. There are many different kinds of **laws**. Traffic **laws** say that drivers must stop at a red light and a stop sign. **[laws]**

lay¹ (lay)

To **lay** means to put something down somewhere. Sally tried to **lay** the baby down carefully so he wouldn't wake up. **[laying, laid]**

lay² (lay)

Lay comes from **lie**. After the alarm went off, Dan **lay** in bed for five more minutes.

layer (lay-uhr)

A **layer** is something thin or flat that covers or lies on something else. We baked a cake with three **layers** for Nana's birthday. Vincent added a fresh **layer** of paint to the front door. **[layers]**

layer cake

lazy (lay-zee)

If you feel **lazy,** you do not want to work or do anything else. **[lazier, laziest]**

lead (leed)

1. To **lead** means to show where to go by going first. Peggy used a rope to **lead** the goat into the barn.
2. To **lead** also means to show a direction to a group. The president **leads** the country. A person who **leads** is called a **leader**. The **leader** of a state is the governor. **[leading, led]**

leaf (leef)

A **leaf** is a part of a plant or tree. Most **leaves** are green and flat. In the autumn, some **leaves** become brown, red, or yellow and fall to the ground. **[leaves]**

lean (leen)

To **lean** means to bend toward something. Polly was tired from hiking and had to **lean** against a tree to rest for a few minutes. **[leaning, leaned]**

learn (luhrn)

To **learn** something is to get to know it or to know how to do it. Today, we are going to **learn** about rhymes and

learning to float

how to write poems with them. Allen **learned** to read last year. Tricia is **learning** how to float and swim. **[learning, learned]**

leash (leesh)

A **leash** is a rope or long belt attached to an animal's collar, used to lead or control the animal. Our dog brings us its **leash** when it wants to go out. **[leashes]**

holding a **leash**

leather (leth-uhr)

Leather is made from the skin of cattle, sheep, pigs, and other animals. We use **leather** for shoes, belts, bags, clothes, and other things. Some balls, like baseballs, are made of **leather**. Jeremy has a new jacket made of **leather**. **[leathers]**

leave (leev)

1. To **leave** means to go away from somewhere. Nancy **leaves** for her art class at three o'clock. Eric **left** for soccer practice 15 minutes ago.
2. To **leave** something is to go away and not take it with you. When Joanie came to our house and we weren't home, she decided to **leave** us a note. I **left** my book at school yesterday. **[leaving, left]**

left (left)

The **left** side of something is the opposite of the right side. When we read, we start at the **left** and go to the right. Hakeem pressed the **left** arrow on the computer keyboard to go back to the beginning of the line. When we read, we read from **left** to right.

leg (leg)
1. A **leg** is the part of the body we use for standing, walking, and running. People have two **legs**, but many animals have four **legs**. Snakes and fish have no **legs**.
2. A **leg** is also a part that holds something up. Tables and chairs have **legs**. **[legs]**

lemon (lem-uhn)
A **lemon** is a small, round or oval, yellow fruit with a thick skin and a sour taste. **Lemons** grow on trees. **[lemons]**

lemon

lend (lend)
To **lend** means to give something to someone who plans to give it back. I'll **lend** you my pencil if you'll return it when you are finished with it. Mack **lent** Chester his jacket for the game. **[lending, lent]**

length (lengkth) or (lenth)
The **length** of something is how long it is. Barbara's hair is 10 inches in **length** and reaches the middle of her back. The **length** of our summer vacation from school is two months. **[lengths]**

less (less)
Less means an amount that is not as much as another amount. This glass holds **less** water than that bucket. Five dollars is **less** than ten dollars.

lesson (less-uhn)
A **lesson** is something you learn or an exercise to help you learn. Kim takes clarinet **lessons**. **[lessons]**

letter (let-uhr)
1. A **letter** is one of the parts of the alphabet. There are 26 **letters** in our alphabet. A is the first **letter** in many alphabets.
2. A **letter** is also a message that is written and sent from one person to another. Emily took her **letters** to the post office to mail. **[letters]**

lettuce (let-uhs)
Lettuce is a vegetable with large leaves that are usually green. **Lettuce** is often eaten in salads.

library (lie-brer-ee)
A **library** is a place to find different kinds of information and things to read. Many **libraries** have books, magazines, newspapers, tapes, and computers to be used there. You can also borrow books and tapes from a library. A person who is trained to work in a **library** is called a **librarian**. **[libraries]**

at the **library**

lick (lik)
You **lick** something when you move your tongue over it. Our cat **licks** herself clean and then takes a nap. **[licking, licked]**

lie¹ (lie)

When you **lie** somewhere, your body is flat. When you **lie**, you are not sitting, kneeling, or standing. You can **lie** on your back or your stomach. Herb likes to **lie** on the beach and listen to the ocean. **[lying, lay, lain]**

lie² (lie)

1. To **lie** means to say something that you know is not true. We were taught not to **lie**. **[lying, lied]**
2. A **lie** is something you say that is not true. Tenny was punished when her dad discovered she had told a **lie**. **[lies]**

life (life)

1. To have **life** is to be living or to be alive. **Life** is what people, animals, and plants have when they can breathe and grow. Rocks and machines do not have **life**.
2. A **life** is the time something or someone is alive. Maya is happy that her great-grandfather is one hundred years old and has lived a long **life**. Roy's plant had a short **life** because he forgot to water it. **[lives]**

lift (lift)

To **lift** something means to pick it up and raise it. Yolanda likes to **lift** Lyle into the air. Workers at the garage use a machine to **lift** the cars when they are putting on new tires. **[lifting, lifted]**

lift

light¹ (lite)

1. **Light** is energy from the sun and stars, and from lamps and fires. **Light** makes it possible to see.
2. A **light** is something that gives off light, like a lamp or a flashlight. Terry held a **light** so that we could see into the cave. **[lights]**
3. To **light** something is to start it burning. Bill's father used a match to **light** a fire in the fireplace. **[lighting, lighted or lit]**

light² (lite)

Light also means not heavy. A sheet of paper is **light**. This feather is much **lighter** than that stone. **[lighter, lightest]**

lighthouse

lighthouse (lite-hous)

A **lighthouse** is a building near or in the sea with a bright light that helps ships stay away from rocks and other dangerous things. **Lighthouses** often have horns that ships can hear when there is fog. **[lighthouses]**

lightning (lite-ning)

Lightning is a thin, bright light you see in the sky during some storms. **Lightning** is electricity passing suddenly between clouds, and sometimes between clouds and the ground. After there is **lightning**, thunder can often be heard.

lightning

like¹ (like)

If one thing is **like** another, it is the same or almost the same. A basketball is **like** a baseball in shape, but not in size. Paula's dress is blue, **like** Darrell's shirt.

like² (like)

To **like** something is to be pleased by it or to feel good because of it. Edy **likes** kittens a lot. At the zoo, Zachary **liked** the giraffes best. **[liking, liked]**

line (line)

1. A **line** is a long, thin mark. Steve made straight **lines** on his paper with a pencil and a ruler. Without a ruler Toby's **lines** might be crooked. **2.** Another kind of **line** is a row of people or things. Nancy saw a **line** of ants going into a hole at the bottom of the wall. **[lines]**

lions

lion (lie-uhn)

A **lion** is a large wild animal that is in the cat family. The fur of **lions** is a yellow-brown color. A male **lion** has a large circle of fur around its neck. The female **lion** hunts for most of the food. **[lions]**

lip (lip)

Your **lips** are the edges of your mouth. **Lips** are soft and pink on the inside. Louis put his **lips** together and whistled through them. **[lips]**

liquid (lik-wuhd)

A **liquid** is something wet that you can pour. Water, milk, and juice are **liquids**. **Liquids** change to solid when they freeze. **[liquids]**

list (list)

A **list** is a group of things, like names or words, that you write down, usually one under the other. Eduardo made a **list** of things to take to the picnic. **[lists]**

listen (lis-uhn)

When we **listen**, we want to hear something and try to hear it. Katie likes to **listen** to music and dance to it. **[listening, listened]**

little (lit-l)

1. Little means not taking up much room. Something that is **little** is small in size. Ants and beetles and mice are **little** animals. The opposite of **little** is big.
2. Little also means not very much. There is only a **little** milk left. **[littler, littlest]**

live (liv)

1. To **live** is to be alive. How can these plants **live** in a place so dark? Sandy's dog has **lived** almost 12 years.
2. To **live** also means to have a home somewhere. Mauricio **lives** in Arizona. **[living, lived]**

loaf (lohf)

1. A **loaf** is bread that is baked in one piece. Most **loaves** of bread are longer than they are wide. Sam took two slices from the **loaf** of bread to make a sandwich.
2. A **loaf** is also other food, like cake or meat, that is shaped like a rectangular **loaf** of bread. **[loaves]**

loaf

lobster (lahb-stuhr)

A **lobster** is an animal that lives in the sea. **Lobsters** crawl along the sea bottom on five pairs of legs. **Lobsters** have hard shells and two large claws that turn red when they are cooked. **[lobsters]**

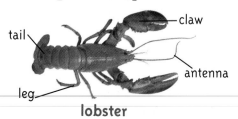

tail — claw — antenna — leg

lobster

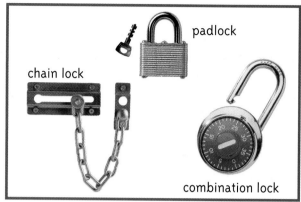

chain lock — padlock — combination lock

different kinds of **locks**

lock (lahk)

1. A **lock** is something used to keep things closed. Many doors, windows, and gates have **locks**. Some **locks** open and close with keys. **[locks]**
2. To **lock** means to close something with a lock. Joan pushed the button down to **lock** the car door. **[locking, locked]**

log (lawg) or (lahg)

A **log** is a long, round piece of wood cut from a tree. Kenny and Ruth rolled the big **log** across the yard. Uncle Hank put another **log** on the fire to keep it burning. **[logs]**

lonely (lohn-lee)

When you feel **lonely**, you are sad or unhappy about being by yourself. Marisa felt **lonely** when her friends Marilyn and Anne went away for the summer. **[lonelier, loneliest]**

long (lawng)

Long means that one end of something is not near the other end. **Long** is the opposite of short. The monkey was able to swing from its **long** tail. The rain lasted a **long** time. **[longer, longest]**

look (luk)

1. To **look** means to move your eyes to see or find something. **Look** at that big crocodile! Drew used a flashlight to **look** for the ball that rolled under the bed.

2. Look also means the way something appears to someone. Your car **looks** like the one we have. With that hat on his head, Paul **looks** like a firefighter. [**looking, looked**]

loose (loos)

1. Loose means attached but not in the way it should be. The wheel on the toy became **loose** and then fell off.

2. Loose also means not fitting tightly. Jay's old jeans are so **loose** that he needs a belt to hold them up. **Loose** clothes feel good on a hot day. [**looser, loosest**]

lose (looz)

1. To **lose** means not to have any more. The tree outside Ralph's window will **lose** its leaves if the storm is bad. Marta **lost** a baby tooth today.

2. To **lose** also means not to win. Ted and Joe were unhappy when their team was **losing**. They **lost** the first game, but then won the next two. [**losing, lost**]

lost (lawst)

1. Something is **lost** if you look for it and can't find it. The signs on the trees asked people to call a number if they found a **lost** cat named Fun.

2. If you don't know where you are, you are **lost**. When Rhonda got **lost** at the fair, a police officer helped her find her mom and dad.

lot (laht)

A **lot** means many. There are a **lot** of stars in the sky. We also say **lots** to mean many. Diane has **lots** of crayons. [**lots**]

a **lot** of crayons

loud (loud)

Loud means making a lot of noise. The television was so **loud** that we didn't hear the telephone ringing. [**louder, loudest**]

love (luhv)

To **love** is to like something or someone very much. When you care about someone a lot and feel very close to that person, you **love** that person. Mina **loves** Grandma Maria and likes to visit her on Sundays. Tony **loves** to skateboard, and Reid **loves** doing puzzles. [**loving, loved**]

low (loh)

Something that is **low** is near the ground or the floor. **Low** is the opposite of high. Tina and Tommy keep their toys on a **low** shelf so that they can reach them. [**lower, lowest**]

lunch (luhnch)

Lunch is a meal that is eaten in the middle of the day, between breakfast and dinner. Some children eat **lunch** at school at 12 o'clock. Roy is having a sandwich, an apple, and a drink for **lunch**. [**lunches**]

lunch

machine (muh-sheen)

A **machine** is something that is made to do work or to help make other things. Tractors, bulldozers, and computers are **machines** that do different kinds of work. [**machines**]

mad (mad)

Mad is another word for angry. Mrs. Block got **mad** at the twins when they picked the tulips in her yard. When Tommy hit his friend Ben, Ben got **mad** and yelled at Tommy. [**madder, maddest**]

magazine (mag-uh-zeen)

A **magazine** is like a big book with paper covers. **Magazines** have news, stories, and pictures. Most **magazines** are sold or mailed out every week or every month. Barbara likes to read the **magazine** with pictures and stories by other children. [**magazines**]

magic (maj-ik)

Magic is power to make impossible things look as if they are really happening. A person who does **magic** is called a **magician**. [**magicians**]

magnet (mag-nuht)

A **magnet** is a piece of metal or other material that pulls things made of iron and steel toward it. We used **magnets** to stick pictures on the refrigerator door. [**magnets**]

magnifying glass (mag-nuh-fie-ing glass)

A **magnifying glass** is a piece of special glass that makes things look bigger when you look through it. We can see the parts of the flower better with a **magnifying glass**. [**magnifying glasses**]

magnifying glass

mail (mayl)

1. **Mail** means the letters, cards, magazines, packages, and other things that are delivered to us by someone who works for the post office. The box where you put **mail** to be sent, or where your **mail** is left, is called a **mailbox**. Letters and notes sent and received on a computer are called **e-mail**.
2. To **mail** means to put an address and a stamp on a letter, card, or other kind of mail and put it in a mailbox or take it to the post office. Sam **mailed** a letter to his friend. [**mailing, mailed**]

mail in a **mailbox**

making jewelry

make (mayk)

1. When you **make** something, you put it together, create it, or change it into something else. Let's use these vegetables to **make** soup. Jaime **made** a hat by folding a piece of paper.
2. Make also means to cause things to happen. During the earthquake, the ground moved and **made** dishes and books fall off the table. **[making, made]**

male (mayl)

People and animals are either **male** or female. Boys and men are **male**. Fathers, grandfathers, uncles, and brothers are **male**. **Male** grown-ups can grow beards. Some **male** animals, like goats and cattle, grow horns, and some **male** birds have feathers that are bright in color.

mammal (mam-uhl)

A **mammal** is an animal that gets milk from its mother when it is young. Most **mammals** have hair on their bodies. Bears, cats, dogs, giraffes, kangaroos, monkeys, seals, whales, zebras, and people are **mammals**. **[mammals]**

man (man)

A **man** is a male person who has grown up. Boys grow up to become **men**. **[men]**

manners (man-uhrz)

Manners mean the way someone acts with other people. When you are polite and friendly, you have good **manners**. A person who talks at a concert while the musicians are playing has bad **manners**.

many (men-ee)

1. Many means a large number or a lot. There were **many** people at the circus. We saw **many** geese flying over us. There are **many** books at the library.
2. When you ask a question with the word **many**, the answer is a number. How **many** days are there in a week? How **many** people are there in your family?

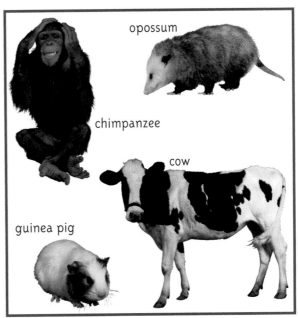
opossum
chimpanzee
cow
guinea pig
some **mammals**

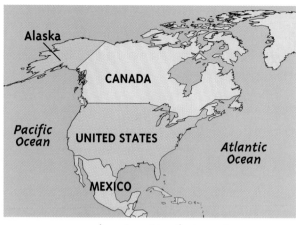

map showing North America

map (map)

A **map** is a picture that shows where places or things are. There are **maps** that show continents, countries, oceans, rivers, and mountains. Some **maps** show cities and streets. A book of **maps** is called an **atlas**. A round ball with a **map** on it is called a **globe**. [**maps**]

maple (may-puhl)

A **maple** is a kind of tree. Sugar and syrup are made from some **maples**, and **maple** wood is used in making furniture. [**maples**]

marble (mahr-buhl)

1. Marble is a kind of hard stone used to make some buildings and statues. There is a big **marble** statue of a horse in the park on Center Street.
2. A **marble** is also a small ball of glass used to play games. [**marbles**]

march (mahrch)

To **march** is to walk together with other people all stepping the same way. At the parade the school band will **march** and play the school song. [**marching, marched**]

mark (mahrk)

1. A **mark** is a line or a spot on something. The **marks** on the pool show how deep the water is.
2. A **mark** is also a letter or number that is given to show how good your work in school is. Janelle received a good **mark** on her science project. [**marks**]
3. To **mark** something is to put a mark on it. Mr. Limon **marks** the ground to show how far each person has jumped. The teacher is **marking** our spelling tests. [**marking, marked**]

marry (mar-ee)

When people **marry**, they become a new family as husband and wife. [**marrying, married**]

marshmallow (mahrsh-mal-loh)

A **marshmallow** is a piece of soft white candy made from sugar, corn syrup, and other things. At the campground after supper, we cooked **marshmallows** on long sticks over the fire. [**marshmallows**]

mask (mask)

A **mask** is something a person wears to cover all or part of the face. I'm going to wear a rabbit

surgeon's mask   catcher's mask

mask to the costume party. Some people wear special kinds of **masks** over their mouth and nose to protect them while they work. [**masks**]

mat (mat)

A **mat** is something flat that covers a part of the floor. We put a rubber **mat** in the bathtub so that no one would slip. **[mats]**

match (mach)

1. To **match** means to look the same. Things that **match** are made from the same cloth or wood or have the same design or color. In Lili's room, the curtains **match** her quilt. **[matching, matched]**

2. A **match** is also a small stick with something on it used to make fire. You can use this **match** to light the candles. **[matches]**

picture sewn from pieces of cloth **material**

material (muh-tir-ee-uhl)

Material is what is used to make something. Cloth is **material** used to make clothes and other things. Boards and bricks are **materials** used in buildings. **[materials]**

meal (meel)

A **meal** is the food we eat at one time. We eat three **meals** a day, called breakfast, lunch, and dinner. **[meals]**

mean (meen)

1. If you know what something **means**, you understand what it is saying. If I say the room is messy, I **mean** that things are all around and not where they belong. Do you know what the word *tickle* **means**?

2. If you **mean** to do something, you want to do it or plan to do it. I did **mean** to call you yesterday, but I forgot. **[meaning, meant]**

3. A person who acts **mean** is not being kind or friendly, and hurts other people. When Jack teases his little sister and makes her cry, he is being **mean**. **[meaner, meanest]**

measure (mezh-uhr)

To **measure** is to find out what size something is. When Mr. Cooper **measured** me, I was four feet, three inches tall. Let's **measure** the rug to see if it will fit. **[measuring, measured]**

measure

meat (meet)

Meat is the part of an animal that is used for food. Chicken, beef, and lamb are different kinds of **meat**. **[meats]**

medicine (med-uh-suhn)

Medicine is something people take when they are sick to help them feel better and get well. **Medicine** is often a pill, a liquid, or a powder. **[medicines]**

meet (meet)

1. To **meet** means to come together in the same place at the same time. I'll **meet** you at the library at 10 o'clock.
2. To **meet** also means to talk to someone for the first time. I'm glad to **meet** you. **[meeting, met]**

melt (melt)

To **melt** means to go from being solid to being liquid. Heat makes things **melt**. When ice **melts**, it becomes water. When the sun came out, the snow on the roof **melted**. **[melting, melted]**

memory (mem-uh-ree)

Memory means the power to remember things. Marta has a good **memory** for addresses and telephone numbers. **[memories]**

menu (men-yoo)

A **menu** is a list of the different kinds of food you can order at a restaurant and what each one costs. Sara ordered from the children's **menu** at the restaurant. **[menus]**

menu

mess (mes)

When a place is a **mess**, it is not neat and many things are not where they should be. When a place is a **mess**, we say it is **messy**. Brian's mom thinks his room is a **mess**. Brian thinks his sister's room is also **messy**.

metal pot and cornet

metal (met-l)

Metal is a hard material that comes from the ground. **Metal** is used for many things, like pots, coins, parts of cars, and jewelry. Iron, gold, and silver are **metals**. **[metals]**

microphone (mie-kruh-fohn)

A **microphone** is an instrument that uses electricity to record sound or to make sounds louder. A short word for **microphone** is **mike**. **[microphones]**

microscope (mie-kruh-skohp)

A **microscope** is an instrument that makes tiny things look large. Looking into a **microscope** is like looking through a magnifying glass. Through a **microscope**, a person can see things that the human eye cannot see by itself. **[microscopes]**

microscope

microwave oven (mie-kroh-wave uhv-uhn)

A **microwave oven** is an oven that cooks food very fast by changing microwave energy into heat. It takes us an hour to bake two potatoes in the large oven and only 10 minutes in the **microwave oven**.
[microwave ovens]

middle (mid-l)

The **middle** of something means its center. The **middle** is the same distance from all the edges or ends. To make a card, Henry folded his paper down the **middle**. [**middles**]

midnight (mid-nite)

Midnight is 12 o'clock at night. The time after **midnight** is the early morning. The day and the date change at **midnight**. [**midnights**]

milk (milk)

Milk is a white liquid that comes from cows and other mammals. Mothers make **milk** in their bodies to feed their babies. Cheese, yogurt, and butter are made from cows' **milk**.

mind (minde)

A person's **mind** is what thinks, understands, remembers, learns, feels, imagines, and dreams. When you read, draw, use a computer, play, and do other things, you are using your **mind**. [**minds**]

mine (mine)

1. Something that is **mine** belongs to me. That purple crayon is **mine**. The blue one is yours, not **mine**.
2. A **mine** is also a large area where people have dug out the ground. Gold, silver, and diamonds come from **mines**. [**mines**]

minus (mie-nuhs)

Minus means to take something away. We use **minus** when we are subtracting numbers. A **minus** sign is written −. Six **minus** two equals four is often written 6 − 2 = 4.

minute (min-uht)

A **minute** is a short amount of time equal to 60 seconds. There are 60 **minutes** in one hour. It took 10 **minutes** to cook the fish for dinner. [**minutes**]

mirror (mir-uhr)

A **mirror** is a special kind of glass that you can look at and see yourself. Candi put on her new dress and smiled when she looked at herself in the **mirror**. The dentist used a small **mirror** to look at Pedro's back teeth. [**mirrors**]

missing teeth

miss (mis)

1. To **miss** something is not to do or get something you are planning or trying to do. Mindy sometimes **misses** the ball when Sarah throws it.
2. To **miss** is also to see or feel that something is absent. This book is **missing** a page. Sal is **missing** two teeth in the front.
3. When you **miss** people, pets, or other things, you are sad that they are not with you. Roberto enjoyed the trip, but **missed** his dog Herman. [**missing, missed**]

mistake (muh-stayk)

A **mistake** is something that is not right. It is something that is wrong. If you add 2 + 1 and get 4, you have made a **mistake**. [**mistakes**]

mittens

mitten (mit-n)

A **mitten** is something to wear on your hand when the weather is cold. A **mitten** is like a glove with one place for the thumb and one place for the rest of the fingers. [**mittens**]

mix (miks)

To **mix** is to put things together to make something new. The cook will **mix** flour, milk, eggs, sugar, and melted chocolate for the cake she is baking. [**mixing, mixed**]

model (mahd-l)

A **model** is a small copy of something large. In the bank there is a **model** of the new bank to be built next year. Uncle Kele has a collection of **model** cars. [**models**]

mom (mahm) and mommy (mahm-ee)

Mom and **mommy** are names for a mother. Our **moms**, dads, and friends were invited to school to watch us in a play. [**moms, mommies**]

money (muhn-ee)

Money is what we use to pay for things we buy. Quarters, dimes, nickels, pennies, and dollar bills are American **money**. Many people save **money** in banks. Nikki saves **money** in a jar for things she wants to buy. [**moneys**]

monkey (muhng-kee)

A **monkey** is a furry animal with long arms and legs, and usually a long tail. Most **monkeys** live in trees, but some live on the ground. **Monkeys** can hold things with their hands and feet and sometimes hang from trees by their tails. [**monkeys**]

vervet monkey   capuchin monkey

monkeys

monster (mahn-stuhr)

A **monster** is a large imaginary animal or person that usually seems scary. There are stories, games, and movies with **monsters** in them. Some **monsters** are mean, and some are friendly. [**monsters**]

month (muhnth)

A **month** is one of the 12 parts a year is divided into. All **months** except February have 30 or 31 days. The names of the **months** are January, February, March, April, May, June, July, August, September, October, November, and December. [**months**]

moon (moon)

A **moon** is something that travels around a planet. The planet we live on, called Earth, has one **moon**. Our

moon over mountains

moon goes around Earth in four weeks. Sometimes our **moon** looks like a whole circle in the sky, and sometimes we can see only a small curved part. [**moons**]

more (mor)

More means a larger amount or a larger number. Six is **more** than five. A bathtub holds **more** water than a bucket. Do you know that an ant has **more** legs than an elephant?

morning (mor-ning)

The **morning** is the earliest part of the day. It is the time between midnight and noon. The sun rises in the **morning**. At the farm, the sound of a rooster wakes Falisha each **morning**. [**mornings**]

mosquito (muh-skeet-oh)

A **mosquito** is a kind of insect. The bite of a **mosquito** itches. Where Lou lives, there are many **mosquitoes** during the warm, wet summer months. [**mosquitoes**]

most (mohst)

Most means the largest amount or number. The person who gets the **most** points wins the game.

mother (muhTH-uhr)

A **mother** is a woman who has a child or children. Your **mother** is your female parent. Both Meghan and her **mother** have brown eyes and red hair. [**mothers**]

motor (moht-uhr)

A **motor** is a special kind of machine that makes other machines work. Cars, boats, motorcycles, and refrigerators use **motors** to make them work. Most **motors** get their power from gas or electricity. [**motors**]

motorcycle (moht-uhr-sie-kuhl)

A **motorcycle** is like a big, heavy bicycle that has an engine that runs on gas. Some **motorcycles** are used by the police and some are used in races. [**motorcycles**]

mountain (moun-tuhn)

A **mountain** is a very high hill. Some **mountains** have snow on top even in summer. [**mountains**]

mouse   computer **mouse**

mouse (mous)

1. A **mouse** is a small animal with a long tail, sharp teeth, and gray or brown fur. Some **mice** live in houses and some live outside in fields. [**mice**]
2. Another kind of **mouse** is used to move things around on a computer screen.

mouth (mouth)

Your **mouth** is part of your face. Your tongue and teeth are in your **mouth**. You open and close your **mouth** to talk and eat. You sometimes breathe through your **mouth**. The dentist asked Ana to open her **mouth** wide. **[mouths]**

move (moov)

1. To **move** means to go from one place to another. When the sun got too hot, Hal and Ryan decided to **move** under the tree to continue their game.
2. To **move** is also to go somewhere new to live. Irisa and her mother are planning to **move** to Ohio to live with her grandmother.
3. To **move** is also to take something from one place to another. Let's **move** these plants to another window where they will get more sun. **[moving, moved]**

movie (moo-vee)

When you watch a **movie**, you are looking at a group of pictures that move to tell a story. Last month we went to a theater and saw a **movie** about animals that talk and sing. Yesterday, my friends and I saw the same **movie** on television. **[movies]**

mud (muhd)

Mud is wet dirt. The **mud** stuck to our shoes and made dirty footprints on the kitchen floor. When something is covered with **mud**, we say it is **muddy**. What **muddy** feet that duck has. **[muddier, muddiest]**

multiply (muhl-tuh-plie)

When we **multiply** a number by 2 or more, we add the number to itself over and over again. If we **multiply** by one, the number stays the same. When we **multiply**, we use the word *times* or the sign x. To **multiply** 2 times 4 (2 x 4), add the number 2 four times (2 + 2 + 2 + 2) or add the number 4 two times to equal 8. Calculators and computers can **multiply** numbers very fast. **[multiplying, multiplied]**

muscle (muhs-uhl)

A **muscle** is a part of the body that stretches and makes other parts of the body move. People use **muscles** whenever they walk, run, dance, eat, talk, or carry things. **Muscles** get stronger when they are exercised. **[muscles]**

museum (myoo-zee-uhm)

A **museum** is a place that collects beautiful or interesting things for people to look at. **Museums** are places to learn about art, animals, science, computers, and history. **[museums]**

rhinoceros in the **mud**

mushrooms

mushroom (muhsh-room)

A **mushroom** grows like a plant, but has no leaves or flowers. Many **mushrooms** look like little umbrellas. **Mushrooms** grow in dark places where the ground is damp. Some **mushrooms** can be eaten, but some are dangerous. In his science class, Michael learned not to pick wild **mushrooms**. [**mushrooms**]

music (myoo-zik)

The sounds that people make when they sing or play musical instruments are called **music**. Some people like to make **music**, some like to listen to **music**, and some like to dance to it. A person who makes **music** is called a **musician**. The **musicians** arrived at the park with their guitars and drums and played a concert all Saturday afternoon.

musical instrument
(myoo-zi-kuhl in-struh-muhnt)

A **musical instrument** is something you play to make music. Trumpets, pianos, flutes, violins, clarinets, and harmonicas are kinds of **musical instruments**. [**musical instruments**]

mustache (muh-stash)

A **mustache** is the hair that grows on the face above the mouth and below the nose. Sean's dad has a black **mustache** and beard. [**mustaches**]

mystery (mis-tuh-ree)

1. A **mystery** is something that is hard or impossible to understand or explain. Where Jason's dog went when it ran away is still a **mystery** to all of us.
2. A **mystery** is also a story or show about people who disappear or are killed. Christopher likes to read and write **mystery** stories. [**mysteries**]

flute ▼

harmonica ▼

clarinet ▼

violin ▼

piano ▼

playing **musical instruments**

Nn

nail (nayl)

1. A **nail** is a thin piece of metal that is used to hold pieces of wood and other things together. The top of a **nail** is flat and the bottom comes to a point. Julienne held her hands over her ears while her mom hammered a **nail** into the wall.
2. A **nail** is also the thin, hard part that covers the end of a finger or toe. **[nails]**

name (naym)

A **name** is the word that a person or thing is called. Tiger, giraffe, and monkey are **names** of animals. Tulip and rose are **names** of flowers. People, places, and most other things have **names**, too. Rhode Island is the **name** of the smallest state in the United States. **[names]**

nap (nap)

When you take a **nap**, you go to sleep for a short time. Rod took a **nap** in the car on the way home from the beach. **[naps]**

narrow (nar-oh)

When something is **narrow**, there is only a small amount of space between its sides. The opposite of **narrow** is wide. The bridge is so **narrow** that only one car can cross it at a time.
[narrower, narrowest]

nature (nay-chuhr)

All of the things in the world that are not made by people are part of **nature**. Oceans, rivers, forests, plants, animals, and people are all part of **nature**. The air, weather, moon, and stars are part of **nature**, too. When people recycle things and work to keep the air and water clean, they help protect **nature**.

near (nir)

Near means being close to something or someone. When something is **near**, it is not far away. Mara lives so **near** her school that she and her friends can walk there. **[nearer, nearest]**

neat (neet)

Neat means that things are in the places where they belong. The teacher told the children to hang their hats, coats, and backpacks on hooks so that the coat area would stay **neat**. **[neater, neatest]**

narrow   wide

neck (nek)

The **neck** is the part of a person's or animal's body that attaches the head to the rest of the body. A heron is a bird with a long **neck**. [**necks**]

long **neck**

necklace (nek-luhs)

A **necklace** is a kind of jewelry that is worn around the neck. Karla wore a **necklace** made of two beads on a leather string. [**necklaces**]

need (need)

When you **need** something, you cannot do without it. Everyone **needs** food, water, and a place to live. Erica **needs** her medicine every day. [**needing, needed**]

needle (need-l)

1. A **needle** is a thin piece of metal used for sewing. One end of a **needle** has a hole for thread to go through, and the other end comes to a point. Terry took out a **needle** and thread to sew a patch on his jeans.
2. The leaves of some kinds of trees are called **needles** because they are thin, pointed, and sharp. The forest was covered with pine **needles** and smelled good. [**needles**]

neighbor (nay-buhr)

Your **neighbor** is a person who lives close to where you live. Tamara took cookies to the new **neighbors** across the street. [**neighbors**]

neighborhood (nay-buhr-hud)

An area of homes where neighbors live is called a **neighborhood**. Most of the children in Jackie's **neighborhood** go to the same school. There are lots of houses but not many stores in Monica's **neighborhood**. There are many stores in Boris's **neighborhood**. [**neighborhoods**]

nest (nest)

A **nest** is a home made by birds to lay eggs and protect the new baby birds. Birds use dry grass, mud, and sticks to build their **nests**. **Nests** are also made by reptiles, insects, some fish, and mammals like mice and squirrels. [**nests**]

▲ wasp's nest

osprey's nest ▼

nests

net (net)

A **net** is made of pieces of string or rope tied together to leave spaces between them. **Nets** are used in games like basketball, tennis, and hockey. **Nets** are also used to catch fish and other animals. Liz used a **net** to catch a butterfly. **[nets]**

basketball **net**

never (nev-uhr)

Never means at no time or not ever. Jasmine has **never** flown in an airplane, but wants to someday. Tyler hopes he **never** loses the watch his grandfather gave him.

new (noo) or (nyoo)

1. New means not old, used, or worn. Corey is saving money to buy a **new** pair of skates.
2. New also means not known, seen, or discovered before. Scientists continue to discover **new** facts about the planets.
3. New also means just starting. We have two **new** students in our class. Todd is looking forward to the **new** soccer season. **[newer, newest]**

news (nooz)

The **news** tells you about things that have just happened. People can read the **news** in newspapers or magazines. Some people watch the **news** on television or listen to it on the radio. Amber used a computer to find **news** about children's projects in other countries.

newspaper (nooz-pay-puhr)

A **newspaper** is made of big sheets of paper and has the news printed on it. **[newspapers]**

next (nekst)

When something is **next**, it comes right after something else. Tara was thirsty and glad that she was **next** in line for a drink of water.

nice (nise)

1. Being **nice** means being polite or kind to people. When Shayna forgot her lunch, her friends were **nice** and shared their food with her.
2. When we say that something is **nice**, we mean that we like it. Angel told Bernie that his new skates were very **nice**. **[nicer, nicest]**

nickel (nik-uhl)

A **nickel** is a coin that is silver and gray in color and is the same amount of money as five pennies. Two **nickels** equal ten pennies or one dime. Ray needed one more **nickel** to buy a birthday card for his friend. **[nickels]**

nickel

night (nite)

Night is the time that starts when the sun goes down and ends when the sun rises. Raccoons and owls search for food at **night**. **[nights]**

nightmare (nite-mair)

A **nightmare** is a very scary dream. Nils does not watch scary shows on television because they seem to give him **nightmares**. **[nightmares]**

nine (nine)

Nine is the number that comes after eight and before ten. The number **nine** is written **9**. Beatrice's birthday cake had **nine** candles on it. [**nines**]

no (noh)

1. No is the opposite of yes. People say **no** when they do not agree with something or when they do not want to do something. When Tamika asked her mother if she could go to the park, her mother said, "**No**, we are going to eat dinner soon."
2. No also means not any. There was **no** turkey left from dinner last night, so Jed made a cheese sandwich. [**noes**]

nobody (noh-bahd-ee)

Nobody means not a single person. **Nobody** in Chris's class is allowed to cross the street without an adult.

nod (nahd)

When you **nod**, you move your head up and down. When people **nod**, they are often showing that they agree with something or are saying yes. When asked if he would like a glass of milk, Gerald **nodded**. [**nodding, nodded**]

noise (noiz)

Noise is a kind of sound. When people use the word **noise**, they often mean loud sounds or a strange sound they don't like. When Mandy's dad wanted to sleep late, he asked her not to make **noise** when she woke up. [**noises**]

noodle (nood-l)

A **noodle** is a kind of pasta that is usually wide and flat like pieces of wide ribbon. Gretchen likes to eat **noodles** with

noodle soup

tomato sauce or melted butter on top. [**noodles**]

noon (noon)

Noon is 12 o'clock in the middle of the day. Mara ate such a late breakfast that she was not hungry for lunch at **noon**. [**noons**]

north (north)

North is a direction on a compass opposite south. The needle on a compass always points to the **north**. When you face the direction of the setting sun, **north** is the direction to your right. On most maps **north** is at the top. The state of North Dakota is **north** of South Dakota and lies above it.

nose (nohz)

The part of the body used to smell and breathe is called the **nose**. Your **nose** is in the center of your face. Leslie held the piece of fresh bread up to her

nose to **nose**

nose and smelled it before she took a big bite. [**noses**]

note (noht)

1. A **note** is a way of saying something by writing it down. **Notes** are short and can be just one sentence

musical **notes**

long. When Dora was sick, her friends at school sent her cards and get-well **notes**.
2. Another kind of **note** is a musical sound. This kind of **note** can be sung or played on a musical instrument. [**notes**]

nothing (nuhth-ing)

Nothing means not anything. Tiffany reached into the cookie jar, but all the cookies were gone, and there was **nothing** left.

now (nou)

Now means at this very time or moment. Greg asked if he could do his homework after supper, but his mother told him to do it **now**. What are you doing **now**?

number (nuhm-buhr)

A **number** is what we use when we count. We use **numbers** to show how many things there are. The **numbers** five, twelve, and one hundred are written 5, 12, and 100. The **numbers** on a ruler show how many inches there are in one foot. We use **numbers** when we add, subtract, multiply, and divide. Mariah wrote **numbers** on the chalkboard to show how many points each team had. [**numbers**]

nurse (nurs)

A **nurse** is someone who works with doctors to help take care of people when they are sick or hurt. Many **nurses** work in hospitals, doctors' offices, schools, and people's homes. [**nurses**]

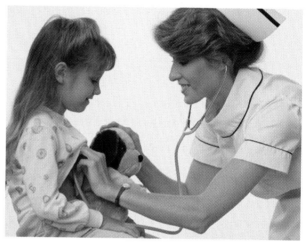
nurse listening to a child's heart

nut (nuht)

A **nut** is the fruit or seed of a tree. Most **nuts** have hard shells on the outside. Inside the shells there are softer parts that can be eaten. Walnuts and almonds are kinds of **nuts**. Salik took a bag of **nuts** and raisins on his hike. [**nuts**]

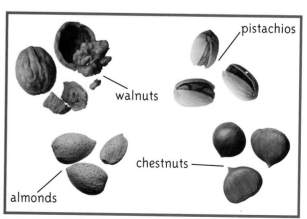
pistachios
walnuts
chestnuts
almonds
nuts

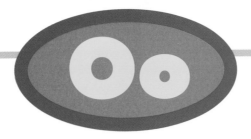

oak (ohk)

An **oak** is a kind of tree with hard, strong wood and seeds called acorns. That table is made of **oak**. **[oaks]**

obey (oh-**bay**)

To **obey** is to do what someone tells you to do, to follow rules, or to do what a law says to do. Drivers must **obey** the law and make room for fire engines on their way to a fire. **[obeying, obeyed]**

the **oceans**

ocean (oh-shuhn)

An **ocean** is one of the very large areas of salt water that cover most of the earth. There are four **oceans**, the Atlantic **Ocean**, the Pacific **Ocean**, the Indian **Ocean**, and the Arctic **Ocean**. We took a boat ride to watch whales in the **ocean**. **[oceans]**

o'clock (uh-klahk)

O'clock is a word we use when we are saying what time it is. Twelve **o'clock** in the middle of the day is the same as noon. Michelle's school day ends at three **o'clock**.

octopus (ahk-tuh-puhs)

An **octopus** is an animal that lives in the sea. An **octopus** has eight long arms called tentacles that it uses to move from place to place and to get food. **[octopuses]**

off (awf)

1. Off means away from something. Please take this bug **off** my shoulder! Arnie took the plates **off** the table and put them in the sink. **Off** is the opposite of on.
2. Off also means not on or not working. Melody tries to remember to turn the lights **off** when she leaves a room. Dad turned the saw **off** after he cut the piece of wood.

office (ahf-is) or (awf-is)

An **office** is a room or building where people work. We parked in front of the doctor's **office**. Worker's gathered at the **office** to look at the new computer. **[offices]**

at the **office**

often (**aw**-fuhn) or (**awf**-tuhn)

Often means many times. If Janine practices **often**, she may become good at juggling.

oil (oil)

Oil is a thick liquid. It can float on water, and slips and slides if you touch it. The **oil** that people burn to make heat or to run machines comes from the ground. **Oils** often used in cooking come from plants or animals. **[oils]**

old (ohld)

1. Old means that someone or something has lived for a long time. **Old** is the opposite of young. A person who is **old** has been alive for many years.
2. Old also means that something has been there for a long time or has been used a lot. **Old** is the opposite of new. Sally bought a new jacket almost the same color as her **old** one.
3. We also use the word **old** when we talk about the age of someone or something. Marius is ten years **old**. **[older, oldest]**

on (ahn)

1. On means touching something or somebody. Harry has a hat **on** his head.
2. On also means working or running. The light was **on** all night.
3. We also use **on** when we talk about a time when something happens. I go to school **on** Monday.

birds **on** a birdfeeder

one (wuhn)

1. One is a number. **One** means a single thing. The number **one** is written **1**. When you have **1** apple and **1** orange, you have 2 pieces of fruit.
2. We also say **one** when we are talking about someone or something. Sandi is **one** of Terri's best friends. I have three pairs of shoes, but no brown **ones**. **[ones]**

onion (**uhn**-yuhn)

An **onion** is a vegetable with a strong smell and taste. It is the bulb of a plant, and it grows under the ground. Most **onions** are round. Sometimes **onions** are eaten raw, and sometimes they are cooked. **[onions]**

onions

only (**ohn**-lee)

1. Only means that there is one and no more. When Karla lost her **only** pair of gloves, she had to borrow a pair from her sister. Al is the **only** boy I know in the second grade.
2. We also use **only** to mean not more than some number. There were **only** five people at the party, not six. I have **only** fifty cents in my pocket.

open (**oh**-puhn)

1. Open means not closed, shut, or covered. A big mosquito flew into the room through an **open** window. The paste dried up in the **open** jar.
2. To **open** means to change something from being closed, shut, or covered to being open. Rob is going to **open** a can of rice and beans for lunch. **[opening, opened]**

opposite (ahp-uh-zuht)

1. Opposite means across from. Your left hand is **opposite** your right. When Dad and my brother Todd play chess, they sit **opposite** each other.

sitting **opposite**

2. Opposite also means different in every way. Wide is the **opposite** of narrow. **[opposites]**

orange (ahr-uhnj)

1. An **orange** is a sweet fruit that is round and has a thick skin. **Oranges** come from trees that grow in warm places. **[oranges]**

2. Orange is also a color. Pumpkins, carrots, and oranges are **orange**. You can make the color **orange** by mixing red and yellow.

orbit (or-buht)

1. To **orbit** is to move around something in space following a path. Earth is one of the nine planets that **orbit** the sun. **[orbiting, orbited]**

2. An **orbit** is the path that something in space follows as it goes around something else. Earth's **orbit** is oval in shape. **[orbits]**

orchestra (or-kuh-struh)

An **orchestra** is made up of a large group of musicians who play musical instruments together. Some of the instruments in an **orchestra** are the violin, cello, clarinet, flute, horn, and drums. **[orchestras]**

order (ord-uhr)

1. Order means everything is in the right place. Billy can say all 26 letters of the alphabet in **order**. We put our guest room in **order**.

2. To **order** is to tell someone to do something. When Mr. Martin smelled smoke, he **ordered** everyone to leave the building and called the firefighters.

3. To **order** also means to ask for something you will pay for. In a restaurant, Greg often **orders** a hamburger. **[ordering, ordered]**

ostrich

ostrich (ahs-trich)

An **ostrich** is the largest bird in the world. An **ostrich** has a long neck and long legs. It cannot fly, but it runs very fast. **Ostriches** are found in Africa. **[ostriches]**

ounce (ouns)

An **ounce** is an amount used in measuring. There are 8 **ounces** in a cup. There are 16 **ounces** in a pound. **[ounces]**

outdoors (out-dorz)

Outdoors means not inside a building. When it stops raining, we can play **outdoors**.

outer space (out-uhr **spayss**)

Outer space is all the space above Earth, but far away from it. Astronauts wear special suits to protect them in **outer space**.

outgrow (out-**groh**)

To **outgrow** is to become too big or too tall for something. When Sally **outgrows** her clothes, she gives them to her younger sister Mary. Pete has **outgrown** easy puzzles and now likes the harder ones. **[outgrowing, outgrew, outgrown]**

outside (out-side)

1. The **outside** of something is its surface, or the part that we can see. The **outside** of a banana is yellow. We painted the **outside** of the barn bright red.
2. Outside also means not inside a building. Another word for **outside** is **outdoors**.

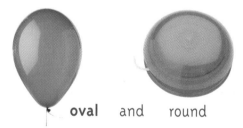

oval   and   round

oval (oh-vuhl)

An **oval** is a shape like an egg. Our table is shaped like a circle, but when we add an extra piece in the middle it becomes an **oval** in shape. **[ovals]**

oven (uhv-uhn)

An **oven** is a place where food is baked or roasted. Most stoves have **ovens** inside. **[ovens]**

over (oh-vuhr)

1. Something that is **over** is above something else. Herb hit the ball **over** the fence. Bonnie has a circus poster **over** her bed.
2. Over also means covering so that something touches something else. There was snow all **over** the city.
3. Over also means more than. Are you **over** seven years old?
4. Something that is finished is **over.** When the game was **over**, we went home.
5. Over can also mean again. Please play that CD **over**, so I can learn the words.

owe (oh)

If you **owe** something, you need to give it back or give something in return. Jeremy **owes** Sal the dollar he borrowed. **[owing, owed]**

owl (oul)

An **owl** is a bird with a large, round head and large eyes on the front of its head. Most **owls** hunt for food at night. **[owls]**

snowy **owl**

own (ohn)

1. To **own** something means that it belongs to you. It is yours to keep. Mickey **owns** a baseball glove, but he had to borrow a bat to play ball. Patti is happy to **own** her first watch. **[owning, owned]**
2. We also say **own** when we talk about something that belongs to us. Each of us has our **own** toothbrush. Emily has her **own** bicycle.

packing the car

pack (pak)

To **pack** means to put things in a box, suitcase, car, or other container to take with you or send somewhere. Erica put a sweater, blouse, and skirt on her bed to **pack** in her suitcase. [**packing, packed**]

package (pak-ij)

A **package** is a box or other container that is packed or wrapped. Did you get the **package** we sent? Let's wrap these **packages** with paper and ribbon. [**packages**]

pad (pad)

A **pad** is something thick and often flat. A **pad** of paper has many pieces of paper that are glued together at one end. [**pads**]

page (payj)

A **page** is one of the pieces of paper in a book, magazine, or newspaper. The book you are reading has 224 **pages**. [**pages**]

pail (payl)

A **pail** is a round container for water, sand, or other things. It has a handle and a flat bottom. Another word for **pail** is **bucket**. At the beach Greer plays with a plastic **pail** and shovel. [**pails**]

pain (payn)

When something hurts you, you feel **pain**. The doctor gave Al medicine for the **pain** in his ear. [**pains**]

paint (paynt)

1. Paint is a liquid with color in it that is used to cover things or to make pictures. We mix colored powder and water to make **paint** for art class. [**paints**]
2. To **paint** is to cover something with paint or to use paint to make pictures. Let's **paint** the house blue instead of white. Maggie is going to **paint** a picture of her cat. A person who paints is called a **painter**. [**painting, painted**]

painting

painting (paynt-ing)

A **painting** is a picture that is made using paint. At the museum the children saw **paintings** by many famous artists. [**paintings**]

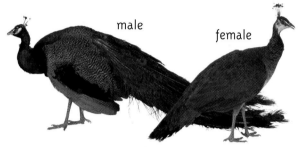

male   female

pair of peacocks

pair (pair)

1. A **pair** is two things that match or go together. Jim can't find one sock from his red **pair**.
2. A **pair** is also something that has two matching parts. Grandpa got a new **pair** of pants for his birthday. [**pairs**]

pajamas (puh-jahm-uhz)

Pajamas are clothes that are worn for sleeping. **Pajamas** have a loose shirt and pants.

palace (pal-uhs)

A **palace** is a large house that people like kings and queens and some presidents live in. **Palaces** have many rooms. [**palaces**]

pan (pan)

A **pan** is a metal or glass container used for cooking. A **pan** is usually flatter than a pot. A frying **pan** has a handle. A **pan** used for baking is often wide and low. We have two cake **pans**. [**pans**]

pancake (pan-kayk)

A **pancake** is a thin, flat, round cake that is cooked on both sides in a hot pan. Sometimes Luke's family has **pancakes** and syrup for breakfast. [**pancakes**]

panda (pan-duh)

A giant **panda** is a large animal that has black and white fur and looks like a bear. A smaller **panda** has reddish-brown fur, a long tail, and looks like a raccoon. **Pandas** are mammals that are in the raccoon family. Giant **pandas** live in China and eat a tall, thin plant called bamboo. [**pandas**]

giant **panda**

pants (pants)

Pants are clothes that cover the body from the waist down the legs. A pair of **pants** has two openings that a person puts his or her legs into.

paper (pay-puhr)

1. Paper is a thin piece of material made from tiny pieces of wood and used for writing, drawing, and painting. Packages and presents are wrapped in **paper**. Books, magazines, and newspapers are printed on **paper**.
2. The word **paper** is also short for **newspaper**. [**papers**]

parachute (par-uh-shoot)

A **parachute** is used for jumping from an airplane or other very high place and floating slowly down to the ground. **Parachutes** are made of cloth and thin ropes. [**parachutes**]

parachute

parade (puh-**rayd**)

A **parade** is a group of people walking or marching together down the street. In some **parades** there are cars that have been decorated, large balloons, and marching bands. [**parades**]

parent (par-uhnt)

A **parent** is a mother or father. A man or woman who has a child is a **parent**. [**parents**]

park (pahrk)

1. A **park** is a place where people go to walk or rest or play games and have fun outside. Most **parks** have grass and trees. Some **parks** have playgrounds. [**parks**]
2. To **park** means to stop driving a car and to leave it somewhere for a time. We were able to **park** in front of the store. [**parking, parked**]

parrot (par-uht)

A **parrot** is a bird with a large, curved beak and feathers of bright colors. **Parrots** live in rain forests. [**parrots**]

parrot

part (pahrt)

A **part** of something is some of it or a piece of it, but not all of it. A year is divided into 12 **parts** called months. A page is **part** of a book. [**parts**]

party (pahrt-ee)

A **party** is a group of people who come together to have a good time. Aleshia is opening presents at her birthday **party**. [**parties**]

birthday **party**

pass (pas)

1. To **pass** means to go by without stopping. This bus **passes** the train station on its way to the airport.
2. To **pass** also means to hand something to someone. Will you please **pass** the pepper?
3. To **pass** also means to do well in something you study or do at school. Dale studied for the test and **passed** it. [**passing, passed**]

passenger (pas-uhn-juhr)

A **passenger** is a person riding on a train, bus, plane, or ship. Everyone who is riding, except the driver, is called a **passenger**. [**passengers**]

past (past)

1. Past means any time before what is happening now. Yesterday, last week, last year, and five years ago are all part of the **past**.
2. Past also means going by a place without stopping. Ned ran **past** us on his way to school.

pasta (pahs-tuh)

Pasta is a food made of flour that come in many shapes. Dry **pasta** is boiled in water before it is eaten. Noodles and spaghetti are two kinds of **pasta**. [pastas]

raw and cooked **pasta**

paste (payst)

1. Paste is a soft, thick mixture that is a little wet when you put it on and makes things stick together as it dries. [pastes]
2. To **paste** means to put paste on something so that it will stick to something else. Rachel is going to **paste** a picture of a flower on her card. [pasting, pasted]

path (path)

A **path** is a narrow area along the ground where you can walk or pass through something like the woods or a park. Another word for **path** is **trail**. Mel walks on a **path** through a field when he goes to the lake to fish. [paths]

patient (pay-shuhnt)

1. A **patient** is someone a doctor or nurse is caring for. Crystal was a **patient** in the hospital last year when she was very sick. [patients]
2. A person who is **patient** is able to wait without getting upset or angry. Please be **patient** while I explain the rules of the game.

paw (paw)

The foot of some animals with four legs, like cats, dogs, and bears, is called a **paw**. [paws]

pay (pay)

To **pay** for something is to give money for it. When you buy something, you **pay** for it. Do you have enough money to **pay** for a slice of pizza for me too? [paying, paid]

pea (pee)

A **pea** is a small, round vegetable. **Peas** grow in pods, and most are green. [peas]

peace (pees)

Peace is a time when there is no fighting or war. After the war, soldiers from different countries worked together to help keep **peace**.

walking on a **path**

peach (peech)

A **peach** is a round fruit with yellow and red skin. **Peaches** grow on trees and have large seeds inside. Are those **peaches** ripe enough to eat? [**peaches**]

peanut (pee-nuht)

A **peanut** is a food that grows in shells under the ground. **Peanuts** are the seeds of a plant. **Peanuts** can be eaten raw or cooked after the outside shells are removed. [**peanuts**]

peanuts

peanut butter (pee-nuht buht-uhr)

Peanut butter is a food made from peanuts. It is smooth like butter, and sometimes has small pieces of peanuts in it. Faye likes **peanut butter** sandwiches.

pear (pair)

A **pear** is a fruit that grows on trees. The bottom of a **pear** is bigger around than the top. The skin of a **pear** can be green, yellow, brown, or red, but the fruit inside is white. [**pears**]

pebble (peb-uhl)

A **pebble** is a very small stone. Most **pebbles** are round and smooth. This beach has **pebbles** instead of sand. [**pebbles**]

pedal (ped-l)

A **pedal** is a part of a machine that you push with your foot to make the machine work in some way. Pianos, bicycles, and motorcycles have **pedals**. [**pedals**]

peel (peel)

To **peel** something is to take the skin or outside layer off. We can eat the skin of apples and pears, but we **peel** bananas and oranges before eating them. [**peeling, peeled**]

pelican (pel-uh-kuhn)

A **pelican** is a bird that lives by the sea. It has a big body and a long neck. The skin under a **pelican's** beak can stretch like a balloon to hold fish. [**pelicans**]

pelican

pen (pen)

1. A **pen** is a writing tool that you hold in your hand. It is long and thin, has a point at one end, and is filled with a liquid called ink.
2. A **pen** is also a place with a fence around it, where animals like pigs or goats are kept. [**pens**]

pencil (pen-suhl)

A **pencil** is a writing tool filled with a very thin stick called lead. Some **pencils** are made of wood with an eraser at one end. [**pencils**]

penguin (pen-gwin)

A **penguin** is a bird that lives in very cold places. **Penguins** are black and white. **Penguins** don't fly, but they are very fast swimmers. [**penguins**]

penguins

penny (pen-ee)

A **penny** is a small metal coin that is reddish-brown in color. The **penny** is not the smallest in size, but it is the smallest in amount of American money. One hundred **pennies** make one dollar. Another word for **penny** is **cent**. [**pennies**]

penny

people (pee-puhl)

People are men, women, or children. There are many **people** in our town. Do you know many **people** where you live?

peppers

pepper (pep-uhr)

1. Pepper is something we put on food to make it taste hot. **Pepper** is made from tiny dried berries and is usually a powder.
2. A **pepper** is also a kind of vegetable. **Peppers** are the fruit of a kind of plant. They are eaten raw or cooked. [**peppers**]

perfect (puhr-fikt)

When something is **perfect**, everything about it is right, and there are no problems or mistakes. Today is a **perfect** day for baseball. Earl and Sharlene's math tests are **perfect** because all of their answers are correct.

period (pir-ee-uhd)

1. A **period** is an amount or length of time. The **period** of time in one day is 24 hours.
2. A **period** is also a small dot that marks the end of most sentences. Sentences that are questions end with a question mark. [**periods**]

person (puhr-suhn)

A **person** is a man, woman, or child. When we talk about more than one **person**, we usually say **people** instead of **persons**. I know only one **person** with red hair. [**persons**]

pet (pet)

A **pet** is an animal that lives with you in your home and that you take care of. Many people have dogs or cats as **pets**. Jasper has a **pet** lizard that likes to eat insects and lettuce. [**pets**]

tulip petal   mum petal
daisy petal   rose petal

petals

petal (pet-l)

A **petal** is the part of a flower that is often bright in color and comes in many shapes. The **petals** of some flowers smell sweet. [**petals**]

phone (fohn)

Phone is short for **telephone**. May I please use your **phone**? [**phones**]

photograph (foht-uh-graf)
A **photograph** is a picture that someone takes with a camera. Jodi likes to take **photographs**. The word **photo** is short for **photograph**. [**photographs**]

piano (pee-an-oh)
A **piano** is a large musical instrument with black and white keys outside and metal wires inside. You press the keys with your fingers to make music. Aaron is learning to play the **piano**. [**pianos**]

pick (pik)
1. To **pick** means to choose something or to decide you want it. **Pick** a ball and let's play catch.
2. To **pick** also means to take something by pulling it with your hand. Earl likes the farm where you can **pick** your own strawberries. [**picking, picked**]

picnic (pik-nik)
A **picnic** is a meal that you eat outdoors. Our family likes **picnics** in the park. [**picnics**]

having a **picnic**

picture (pik-chuhr)
A **picture** shows something. People can make **pictures** by painting them or drawing them. Some **pictures** are photographs. There is a **picture** of Jana's grandparents on the wall. [**pictures**]

pie (pie)
A **pie** is a kind of food that is round and almost flat and is baked in an oven. The bottom and sides of a **pie** are called the crust. **Pies** can be filled with fruit, meat, or other foods. Some **pies** are eaten as dessert. [**pies**]

piece (pees)
A **piece** is one part of something that is larger or has more than one part. This puzzle has two hundred **pieces**. [**pieces**]

pig and piglets

pig (pig)
A **pig** is an animal with a fat body and short legs. It has big ears, a flat nose called a snout, and a short tail that curls. A baby **pig** is called a **piglet**. A grown **pig** is also called a **hog**. [**pigs**]

piles of CDs, disks, and books

pile (pile)

1. A **pile** is a large amount of something or a lot of things lying together, one on top of the other. Randell raked the leaves into a huge **pile**. Don't leave that **pile** of muddy clothes in the hall! **[piles]**

2. To **pile** means to put things one on top of the other. Brittany **piled** all her toys into one corner of her bedroom. **[piling, piled]**

pill (pil)

A **pill** is a small piece of medicine. Most **pills** are swallowed, but some can be chewed. When Spencer was sick, his mom gave him a **pill** to take with a glass of water. **[pills]**

pillow (pil-oh)

A **pillow** is something soft that you put your head on when you sleep. Some **pillows** are filled with soft, light rubber, and some are filled with feathers. **[pillows]**

pilot (pie-luht)

A **pilot** is the person who flies an airplane or helicopter or who helps ships make their way in and out of a harbor. **[pilots]**

pin (pin)

1. A **pin** is a thin piece of metal with a sharp point. **Pins** are used to hold things together. These **pins** will hold the pocket on your jacket until it can be sewn.

2. A **pin** is also a piece of jewelry with a pin attached to it. **[pins]**

pine (pine)

A **pine** is a kind of tree with thin, pointed leaves called needles. The small brown part of a **pine** tree that holds seeds is called a **pinecone**. The forest was filled with **pine** trees. **[pines]**

pineapple (pie-nap-uhl)

A **pineapple** is a large fruit that grows in hot places. It has yellow-brown skin with sharp points and has sharp, pointed green leaves on top. The fruit inside is yellow and sweet. **[pineapples]**

pink (pingk)

Pink is a color that is a mixture of red and white. Kristie gave **pink** flowers to her neighbor, Mrs. Sims.

pilots in an airplane

pint (pinte)

A **pint** is an amount of liquid equal to 2 cups or 16 ounces. A **pint** is half a quart. **[pints]**

pipe (pipe)

A **pipe** is a tube that carries things like water or gas. **Pipes** are used in buildings and underground. **Pipes** are often made of metal or plastic. **[pipes]**

pipes

pirate (pie-ruht)

A **pirate** is someone who robs ships. Pete likes to read stories about **pirates** and their adventures at sea. **[pirates]**

pizza (peet-suh)

Pizza is a large, flat pie baked with tomatoes and cheese, and sometimes other foods. **Pizza** has bread on the bottom and everything else on top. We ordered two **pizzas**, one with meat and one with peppers. **[pizzas]**

place (plays)

1. A **place** is where you are, or where something or somebody else is. A **place** is also where something happens. A lake is Robin's favorite **place** to swim. Save a **place** for me on the bus. This is the **place** where the game will be played on Saturday. **[places]**
2. To **place** something is to put it somewhere. I **placed** the glasses on the table. **[placing, placed]**

plain (playn)

Plain means simple without added or extra things. Mitch liked the **plain** green shirt without stripes. **[plainer, plainest]**

plan (plan)

1. To **plan** is to think about something and decide how to do it. Let's **plan** what we want to do when Grammy and Gramps come to visit. **[planning, planned]**
2. A **plan** is the way you think you will do something. Carmen's **plan** to make money for her class trip was to have a cake sale. **[plans]**

plane (playn)

Plane is short for **airplane**. Our **plane** leaves at six o'clock. **[planes]**

planet (plan-it)

A **planet** is very large and travels around the sun. Earth, where we live, is a **planet**. The nine **planets** that travel around the sun are Mercury, Venus, Earth, Mars, Jupiter, Saturn, Neptune, Uranus, and Pluto. **[planets]**

Jupiter

the **planet** Jupiter and two of its moons

plant (plant)

1. The two kinds of living things on Earth are **plants** and animals. **Plants** do not move around as animals do. **Plants** make their own food from the light of the sun and from water. Most **plants** have stems and leaves. Many **plants** have flowers and seeds. **[plants]**
2. To **plant** means to put something in the ground so that it will grow. You can **plant** tulip bulbs in the fall to bloom in spring. **[planting, planted]**

plastic (plas-tik)

Plastic is a material that is strong and light and does not break easily. Many containers and toys are made from **plastic**. **[plastics]**

plate (playt)

A **plate** is a dish that is round and flat and holds food. People eat from **plates**. **[plates]**

play (play)

1. To **play** is to do things just for fun and to enjoy yourself. Allie likes to **play** outdoors.
2. To **play** also means to act a part or to make music on a

playing the tuba

musical instrument. Matt likes to **play** the tuba. **[playing, played]**
3. A **play** is a kind of story with people acting in different parts. We went to the theater to see a **play**. **[plays]**

playground (play-ground)

A **playground** is a place where you can play outside. The school has two **playgrounds**, one for basketball and another with swings and slides. **[playgrounds]**

please (pleez)

1. Please is a word you use to be polite when you ask for something. *Shh*, **please** be quiet. May I **please** have a glass of water?
2. To **please** someone is to make that person happy. Erin and Alex hope their present will **please** their mother. **[pleasing, pleased]**

plow (plou)

A **plow** is a tool a farmer uses to cut through the ground so the soil is ready for plants or seeds. A **plow** is made of metal and is usually pulled by a tractor. **[plows]**

plumber (pluhm-uhr)

A **plumber** is a person who works on pipes that carry water. When water was dripping from the bathroom ceiling, we called a **plumber**. **[plumbers]**

plus (pluhs)

Plus means to add something. We use **plus** when we are adding numbers. A **plus** sign is written **+** "Four **plus** two equals six" is often written $4 + 2 = 6$.

pocket (pahk-uht)

A **pocket** is a small bag that is sewn into your clothes to hold things. Pants, shirts, and jackets often have **pockets**. **[pockets]**

peas in a **pod**

pod (pahd)
A **pod** is a part of some plants that holds seeds. [**pods**]

poem (poh-uhm)
A **poem** is a special way of using words. **Poems** sound different from the way we usually talk. Sometimes words in **poems** rhyme.

In the river Lee saw a crocodile
With big bright eyes and a winning smile.
Thinking she had found a friend,
Toward it she began to bend.
Then Lee spotted its pointed teeth
And backed away with great relief,
For suddenly she had the hunch
That the crocodile wanted her for lunch!

A person who writes **poems** is called a **poet**. [**poems**]

point (point)
1. A **point** is a sharp or thin end. Pencils, pins, and arrows have **points**. [**points**]
2. To **point** is to show something by using your finger. The teacher asked Bart to **point** to a place on the map. [**pointing, pointed**]

pole (pohl)
A **pole** is a long, round piece of wood, metal, or plastic. **Poles** are used for fishing and to hold flags and other things. [**poles**]

police (puh-lees)
The **police** are people who work to protect other people and the things they own. The **police** try to catch people who have broken laws. A man or woman who is one of the **police** is called a **police officer**.

polite (puh-lite)
To be **polite** means to have good manners and to treat people in a nice way. Saying *please* and *thank you* is a good way to be **polite**. [**politer, politest**]

pollution (puh-loo-shuhn)
Pollution happens when dirt gets in water, soil, air, and other things in nature and makes them no longer safe. **Pollution** is caused by things that people do. Some factories and cars create **pollution**.

pond (pahnd)
A **pond** is a place where there is water with land all around it. This **pond** freezes in winter. [**ponds**]

pointing at a map

Shetland **pony**

pony (poh-nee)

A **pony** is a kind of horse that is smaller than most horses. The children took **pony** rides at the fair. **[ponies]**

pool (pool)

A **pool** is something filled with water and used for swimming. Swimming **pools** often have a shallow end and a deep end for diving. **[pools]**

poor (pur)

To be **poor** is to have only a very small amount of money. When people are **poor**, they sometimes cannot buy things that they need or would like. **[poorer, poorest]**

popcorn (pahp-korn)

Popcorn is a kind of corn that opens up when it is cooked. Cooked **popcorn** is white.

possible (pahs-uh-buhl)

Something that is **possible** can happen or can be done. It is **possible** to climb this tree, but it's going to be hard.

postcard (pohst-kahrd)

A **postcard** is a small card you can send in the mail. **Postcards** often have a picture on one side and a place to write on the other side. Adia sent a **postcard** home from camp. **[postcards]**

poster (poh-stuhr)

A **poster** is a large piece of paper with pictures or words on it. Some **poster**s have art or information on them. Sydney hung **posters** from the zoo in his room. **[posters]**

post office (pohst-ahf-is)

A **post office** is a place where people go to buy stamps and send packages or other mail. People who work for the **post office** also collect and deliver mail. **[post offices]**

pot (paht)

A **pot** is a round container that is deeper than a pan. Many **pots** are used for cooking. Flower **pots** are used for holding plants. Miguel put rice and water in a large **pot**. **[pots]**

flower **pot**

potato (puh-tayt-oh)

A **potato** is a vegetable that grows under the ground. Most **potatoes** are brown on the outside and white on the inside. Some **potatoes** are orange or yellow inside. **[potatoes]**

potatoes

poultry (pohl-tree)

Poultry is a word for birds that we eat for meat or get eggs from. Chickens, ducks, turkeys, and geese are all **poultry**.

pound (pound)

A **pound** is an amount used in measuring weight. There are 16 ounces in 1 **pound**. Ostriches are the biggest living birds and sometimes weigh as much as 300 **pounds**. [**pounds**]

pour (por)

To **pour** means to make something flow down and out of a container. You can **pour** liquids or something like sand. Seth **poured** a tall glass of juice. [**pouring, poured**]

powder (poud-uhr)

A **powder** is made of very tiny pieces of something dry. Flour is made from grains that have been turned into a **powder**. Mom puts **powder** all over the baby's body after his bath. Some foods, like milk, are made into **powder** so they will last longer. [**powders**]

power (pou-uhr)

Having **power** means being able to do things or make things happen. Many machines run on electrical **power**. In America, people have the **power** to choose the president by voting. Being **powerful** means having a lot of **power**. It took a **powerful** machine to lift a container of automobiles on and off the ship. [**powers**]

practice (prak-tuhs)

To **practice** means to do something over and over so that you get better at doing it. The school orchestra **practices** every Thursday. Ralph **practiced** batting until he could hit the ball most of the time. [**practicing, practiced**]

prepare (pri-pair)

1. To **prepare** means to get ready for something. To **prepare** for the concert the children practiced their songs.
2. Prepare also means to make something by putting things together or by following a plan. Let's **prepare** a salad for dinner. [**preparing, prepared**]

presents

present (prez-uhnt)

1. A **present** is something you give to someone, often for a special reason. Another word for **present** is **gift**. Letty wrapped the **present** for her cousin Sean's birthday. [**presents**]
2. The **present** is the time that is happening now. At **present** you are reading a dictionary. If tomorrow is Saturday, Friday is the **present**.

president (prez-uhd-uhnt)
A **president** is the leader of a country or a group of people. [**presidents**]

press (pres)
To **press** means to push on something. When Kendra plays her clarinet, she **presses** the keys to make different sounds. [**pressing, pressed**]

pretend (pri-**tend**)
To **pretend** means to say or act as if something that is not true is true. We like to listen to music and **pretend** to be our favorite singers. [**pretending, pretended**]

pretty (prit-ee)
Pretty means nice to look at. Greta smiled when she saw how **pretty** she looked in the photograph. That is the **prettiest** garden I have ever seen! [**prettier, prettiest**]

price (prise)
The **price** of something is how much you have to pay for it. What is the **price** of those peppers? [**prices**]

vegetables and their **prices**

prince (prins)
A **prince** is a son of a king or queen. [**princes**]

princess (prin-suhs)
A **princess** is a daughter of a king or queen. [**princesses**]

principal (prin-suh-puhl)
A **principal** is the person who leads a school. The students and the teachers listened to the **principal** as she spoke about plans for the school year. [**principals**]

print (print)
1. To **print** means to write so that the letters do not touch each other. When you **print**, the letters have spaces between them, as they do in a book. When Elly draws a picture, she **prints** her name at the bottom of the page.
2. To **print** also means to put letters, pictures, or patterns on paper or cloth with a machine or something

printing on a shirt

else. A machine that **prints** or a person who **prints** is called a **printer**. [**printing, printed**]

prize (prize)
A **prize** is what a person wins for being the best at something or for doing something well. Eileen won first **prize** in the art contest for her clay sculpture of a squirrel. [**prizes**]

problem (prahb-luhm)

A **problem** is something you have to think about carefully and try to solve. Noah can add and subtract, and his older sister can solve multiplication **problems**. [problems]

program (proh-gruhm)

A **program** on television or on the radio is a show you watch or hear at a special time. Jana has two favorite **programs** — one is about animals and one is a cartoon. [programs]

project (prahj-ikt)

A **project** is something that you plan and then do. Brandon's **project** for the summer is to build a house with his dad for their dog. [projects]

promise (prom-uhss)

To **promise** means to say that you will do or not do something. We **promise** not to lie. Caitlin **promised** to play quietly while the baby napped. [promising, promised]

protect (pruh-tekt)

To **protect** means to keep something or someone safe from some danger. Emma wears a helmet to **protect** her head when she rides her bike. The fence **protected** us from the barking dogs. [protecting, protected]

protect

proud (proud)

To feel **proud** is to be happy about something you have done. A person can also feel **proud** of someone else. Bethany's parents are **proud** of her. [prouder, proudest]

public (puhb-lik)

Something that is **public** is for everyone. Terry goes to **public** school. Yesterday, I used the computer at the **public** library.

puddle (puhd-l)

A **puddle** is a small amount of water or other liquid. After the rain shower, there were **puddles** all over the playground. [puddles]

pull

pull (pul)

To **pull** means to tug at something to move it toward you. Doug likes to **pull** Mara on skates. [pulling, pulled]

pumpkin (puhmp-kin)

A **pumpkin** is a large, round, orange fruit with a hard skin. **Pumpkins** grow on the ground. Ben is going to cut a face in the **pumpkin** for Halloween. We eat **pumpkin** pie for dessert on Thanksgiving. [pumpkins]

punish (puhn-ish)

To **punish** means to do something to make a person feel bad about having done something wrong. Lauren was **punished** for hitting another soccer player and was not allowed to play for the rest of the game. **[punishing, punished]**

pupil (pyoo-puhl)

A **pupil** is a young person who is going to school. **Pupil** is another word for **student**. **[pupils]**

puppet (puhp-uht)

A **puppet** is a kind of doll that moves. Some **puppets** are moved by strings. A **hand puppet** fits over one hand and can be moved with the fingers. **[puppets]**

playing with a **puppy**

puppy (puhp-ee)

A **puppy** is a dog that has just been born or is still young. Phylicia likes to play with her new **puppy**. **[puppies]**

pure (pyur)

Something that is **pure** has nothing else mixed with it. This carton says it is filled with **pure** fruit juice. **[purer, purest]**

purple (puhr-puhl)

Purple is a color. If you mix red and blue, you get **purple**. Violets are **purple** flowers.

push (push)

To **push** means to press on something to move it away. Let's **push** the table against the wall. **[pushing, pushed]**

put (put)

To **put** means to move something or to set it down. Please **put** your coats in the closet, not on the chair. Dad always forgets where he **puts** his keys. **[putting, put]**

puzzle (puhz-uhl)

1. A **puzzle** is a kind of game. Some **puzzles** are guessing games. A **puzzle** that has small pieces that fit together is called a **jigsaw puzzle**.
2. A **puzzle** is also something you try to understand. How that magic trick is done is a **puzzle** to us. **[puzzles]**

doing a jigsaw **puzzle**

Qq

quart (kwort)

A **quart** is an amount of a liquid. Four cups or two pints equal one **quart**. Four **quarts** equal one gallon. [**quarts**]

quarter (kwort-uhr)

quarter

1. If you divide something into four parts that are the same size, each part is called a **quarter**. Arnold divided his paper into **quarters** and had room for four small pictures.
2. A **quarter** is also a coin equal to 25 pennies. A **quarter** is also equal to two dimes plus one nickel, or to five nickels. Four **quarters** make one dollar. [**quarters**]

queen (kween)

A **queen** is a woman who rules a country. A **queen** can also be the wife of a king who rules a country. A son of a **queen** is called a prince, and the daughter of a **queen** is called a princess. [**queens**]

question (kwes-chuhn)

A **question** is what you ask when you want to know something. Our teacher asked the **question**, "Who knows the name of the capital of the United States?" When a question is written, it has a **question mark** at the end of it. [**questions**]

quick (kwik)

Quick means that something happens fast or in a short time. The mouse was too **quick** for the cat to catch it. When something happens in a short time, it happens **quickly**. The storm passed **quickly** and the sun came out again. [**quicker, quickest**]

quiet (kwie-uht)

Quiet means a little sound or no sound. Everyone became **quiet** when Ellen started singing her song. [**quieter, quietest**]

quilt (kwilt)

A **quilt** is a cover or blanket of small pieces of cloth that have been sewn together. **Quilts** are made in many different designs. [**quilts**]

quilt

quiz (kwiz)

A **quiz** is a test to see how much someone knows about something. On the spelling **quiz**, Luis got 8 words right out of 10. [**quizzes**]

Rr

rabbit (rab-it)

A **rabbit** is an animal with soft, thick fur and long ears. **Rabbits** have short tails, and they hop using their strong back legs. [**rabbits**]

raccoon

raccoon (ra-koon)

A **raccoon** is an animal that looks like it is wearing a mask. Its furry tail has black rings. [**raccoons**]

race (rays)

1. A **race** is a contest that measures what or who is fastest. There is a sailboat **race** on the lake every summer. [**races**]

2. To **race** is to go very fast, or to be in a race. Ted and Miranda like to **race** to the end of the block to see who can get there first. [**racing, raced**]

radio (rayd-ee-oh)

A **radio** is an instrument that uses electricity to send sounds or to receive sounds that travel through the air from far away. Ariel listens to songs on the **radio**. [**radios**]

railroad (rayl-rohd)

When people or things travel by train from one place to another, they are using the **railroad**. **Railroad** trains travel on metal tracks called **rails**. [**railroads**]

rain (rayn)

1. Rain is drops of water that fall to the ground from clouds. Please close the windows so the **rain** doesn't come in. [**rains**]

2. To **rain** means to fall as drops of water from the clouds. When it **rains**, Sherry and her friends play inside. [**raining, rained**]

rainbow

rainbow (rayn-boh)

A **rainbow** is a band of different colors created when light from the sun passes through drops of water. **Rainbows** can stretch across the sky in a curve when the sun shines right after it has rained. After the rain, Zach saw two **rainbows**, one above the other. [**rainbows**]

rain forest (rayn for-uhst)

A **rain forest** is a forest in a warm place with a lot of rain. In a **rain forest**, trees stay green all year, and there are many different kinds of plants and animals. **[rain forests]**

raising hands

raise (rayz)

1. To **raise** something is to lift it up. We **raise** the flag in front of our school every morning. **Raise** your hand if you know the answer.
2. To **raise** also means to care for something and to help it grow. The farmer down the road **raises** pigs. Grandma **raised** my mom and her sisters. **[raising, raised]**

raisin (ray-zuhn)

A **raisin** is a sweet fruit that comes from a grape that has been dried. Jeffrey likes **raisins** in his cereal. **[raisins]**

rake (rayk)

1. A **rake** is a tool with a long handle and a row of separate parts called teeth. It is pulled across the ground to move or gather things. **[rakes]**
2. To **rake** is to pull a rake across the ground. Lila **rakes** the leaves into a pile. **[raking, raked]**

ramp (ramp)

A **ramp** is like a small hill. **Ramps** help people in wheelchairs, and workers moving heavy things, get in and out of places more easily. **[ramps]**

ran (ran)

Ran comes from **run**. Melanie **ran** from the car to the back door because it was raining.

ranch (ranch)

A **ranch** is a farm where cattle, horses, or sheep are raised or kept. **[ranches]**

raspberry (raz-ber-ee)

A **raspberry** is a small fruit with lots of tiny seeds. **Raspberries** are red or black. **[raspberries]**

rat (rat)

A **rat** is an animal with a long tail and sharp teeth. A **rat** looks like a large mouse. **[rats]**

raw (raw)

Raw means not cooked. Carrots are often eaten **raw**. Rice and potatoes are not eaten **raw**. **[rawer, rawest]**

raking leaves

reach (reech)

1. To **reach** means to move your hand or stretch your arm to touch something. Perry tried to **reach** for a book on the top shelf.
2. To **reach** also means to arrive at. Our bus should **reach** the city by noon. **[reaching, reached]**

read (reed)

When you **read** words, you look at them and understand what they mean. You can **read** words aloud or you can **read** them to yourself. Joan likes to **read** before she goes to sleep. **[reading, read (rhymes with red)]**

reading

ready (red-ee)

Ready means that something can be done without waiting any longer. Dinner is **ready**, so you can sit down at the table now. **[readier, readiest]**

real (ree-uhl)

1. **Real** means true and not made up or imaginary. That book tells the **real** story of astronauts who walked on the moon.
2. When something is part of nature, we also say it is **real**. People are **real** and ghosts are imaginary.

reaching for the ball

reason (ree-zuhn)

The **reason** for something is why it is or why it happened. The **reason** we couldn't see the moon was that clouds were covering it up. Tyrone is trying to find the **reason** that his computer isn't working. **[reasons]**

recipe (res-uh-pee)

A **recipe** is written directions that tell how to prepare or cook food. Do you have a **recipe** for oatmeal raisin cookies? **[recipes]**

record¹ (rek-uhrd)

1. If you set a **record**, you do something better than anyone else has ever done it. Thelma set a school **record** for running.
2. A **record** is also a large plastic disk with music recorded on it. **[records]**

record² (ri-kord)

1. To **record** means to write down facts and keep them for use at a later time. The owners of the store **record** everything they sell so they will know when they need more of something.
2. To **record** also means to use a machine to put music, words, or other sounds on a tape or disk. The singer hopes to be able to **record** her songs. **[recording, recorded]**

recorder (ri-kord-uhr)

A **recorder** is a flute made of plastic or wood, played by blowing into the top and covering holes with your fingers. **[recorders]**

rectangle   and   square

rectangle (rek-tang-guhl)

A **rectangle** is a shape with four sides. Two sides of a **rectangle** are long and two are short. Most towels and many rugs are shaped like **rectangles**. **[rectangles]**

recycle (ree-sie-kuhl)

To **recycle** means to collect something and send it to a special place so it can be used again.

recycling

Our town **recycles** bottles, cans, and papers. **[recycling, recycled]**

red (red)

Red is a color. Strawberries, cherries, tomatoes, and some flowers are **red**.

reflection (ri-flek-shuhn)

A **reflection** is something you see when you look at a shiny surface like a mirror or a quiet pool of water. There is a **reflection** of the castle in the water. **[reflections]**

refrigerator (ri-frij-uh-rayt-uhr)

A **refrigerator** is a machine that uses electricity to keep food cold and fresh. Most **refrigerators** have an area that keeps ice and some foods frozen. **[refrigerators]**

relax (ri-laks)

To **relax** means to stop doing work or other things you have to do and to rest and have fun. Rosa likes to **relax** by reading or watching TV. Jim **relaxes** by playing computer games. **[relaxing, relaxed]**

remember (ri-mem-buhr)

To **remember** is to have something in your mind and not forget it. Emily tried to see how many names of the states she could **remember**. **[remembering, remembered]**

repair (ri-pair)

To **repair** something is to make it work again, or to put it together if it is broken or torn. When you **repair** something, you fix it. **[repairing, repaired]**

reflection

some **reptiles**

reptile (rep-tile)

A **reptile** is an animal with dry skin, short legs, and a long, low body. Most **reptiles** live on land and lay eggs. Crocodiles, alligators, turtles, and snakes are **reptiles**. [**reptiles**]

rescue (res-kyoo)

To **rescue** means to save someone or something from danger. The swimmer was able to **rescue** the boy who fell out of the boat. [**rescuing, rescued**]

rest (rest)

1. To **rest** is to stop what you are doing because you are tired. When people **rest**, they stay quiet until they feel ready to do things again. [**resting, rested**]
2. A **rest** is the time when you are resting. We needed a **rest** after playing football for an hour. [**rests**]
3. The **rest** of something is the part that is left after some is taken away. Karen took out two crayons and left the **rest** in the box.

restaurant (res-tuh-rahnt)

A **restaurant** is a place where people go to eat and pay for their meals. Jake gets spaghetti when he eats at a **restaurant**. [**restaurants**]

rest room (rest room)

Rest room is a name for a bathroom in a public place. When we stopped to get gas, we also used the **rest rooms**. [**rest rooms**]

return (ri-tuhrn)

1. To **return** is to go back or come back from somewhere. We had to **return** to the grocery store because we forgot to buy bread.
2. To **return** something is to give it back or send it back to the person or place you got it from. I must **return** the videos I borrowed from the library. [**returning, returned**]

rhyme (rime)

Words or parts of words **rhyme** when they end in the same sound. The words *bean, green,* and *machine* **rhyme**. Do you know any words that **rhyme** with *blue?*
[**rhyming, rhymed**]

ribbon (rib-uhn)

A **ribbon** is a long, thin piece of cloth or paper. Dorita chose red **ribbon** to wrap the gift. [**ribbons**]

rice (rise)

Rice is a seed that comes from a grass that grows in warm, wet places. The small white or brown seeds are cooked before they are eaten.

bowl of **rice**

rich (rich)

Someone who is **rich** has a lot of money or owns a lot of things. **Rich** people own that huge house on the hill. [**richer, richest**]

riddle (rid-l)

A **riddle** is a kind of question that has a funny answer. A **riddle** is a trick you play using words. **Riddles** are questions like this: What has two legs and no feet? (Answer: pants) [**riddles**]

riding camels

ride (ride)

1. When you **ride** in or on something, you move along with it as it goes from one place to another. People **ride** in cars, vans, buses, trucks, trains, and airplanes to go from one place to another. We **ride** on a bus to school every day. Jerry and Patti spent Saturday morning **riding** their bicycles. [**riding, rode, ridden**]
2. A **ride** is the trip you make when you travel on or in something that is moving. It's a short **ride** from Malcolm's house to Diego's. [**rides**]

fork and napkin on the left, knife and spoon on the **right**

right (rite)

1. The **right** side of something is the opposite of the **left** side. In the United States, we drive on the **right** side of the road. To get to the post office, turn **right** at the corner.
2. Right also means that something is as it should be, without any mistake. Something that is **right** is correct. Do you know the **right** answer to 8 + 2?

ring (ring)

1. A **ring** is also a piece of metal, plastic, or other material in the shape of a circle. Most rings are worn on fingers. Denise likes to wear her silver **ring** with the green stone. The clown hung from two **rings**. [**rings**]
2. To **ring** means to make a sound like the sound of a bell. Did you hear the telephone **ring**? [**ringing, rang, rung**]

rip (rip)

When you **rip** something like paper or cloth, you pull it so that it tears and comes apart. The thin tissue paper **rips** easily. [**ripping, ripped**]

ripe (ripe)

When a fruit is **ripe**, it is ready to be picked, harvested, or eaten. The green tomatoes are not **ripe** yet. **[riper, ripest]**

rise (rize)

To **rise** means to go up, move up, or get up. We watched a balloon **rise** and float through the air. Lea **rose** from her seat and read the poem she had written. **[rising, rose, risen]**

river (riv-uhr)

A **river** is a large amount of flowing water that begins in a higher place, like a mountain, and flows to a lower place, like the sea. The sides of land along a **river** are called banks. **[rivers]**

river

road (rohd)

A **road** is a wide path that people, cars, trucks, and buses travel on. Most **roads** have a hard, smooth surface. **[roads]**

roast (rohst)

When you **roast** something, you cook it in a hot oven or over an open fire. It took four hours to **roast** the turkey. **[roasting, roasted]**

rob (rahb)

To **rob** means to take something that belongs to someone else. The police caught two men trying to **rob** a store. **[robbing, robbed]**

robot sent to Mars

robot (roh-baht)

A **robot** is a machine that is used for dangerous jobs or to do the same job over and over again. A **robot**, called *Sojourner*, was sent to explore the planet Mars. **[robots]**

rock (rahk)

1. Rock is the material that the hard parts of the earth are made of. Large stones or pieces of this material are called **rocks**. Mountains are made of hard **rock**. **[rocks]**
2. To **rock** something means to move it from side to side. Dad is gently **rocking** the baby to sleep. **[rocking, rocked]**

rocket (rahk-uht)

A **rocket** is a long, narrow machine that can fly very fast into space. **Rockets** are used to send satellites and spacecrafts into space. **[rockets]**

rocket

roll (rohl)

1. To **roll** is to move by turning over and over or by having a part like a wheel turn over and over. When Jason let go of his wagon, it began to **roll** down the hill. Martha picked up snow and **rolled** it into a ball. **[rolling, rolled]**

2. A **roll** is a small, round piece of bread. Carrie made a turkey sandwich on a **roll** for lunch.

3. A **roll** is also something that is rolled or wrapped over a tube. Is there a **roll** of paper towels under the sink? **[rolls]**

roof (roof) or (ruf)

A **roof** is the part on top that covers a house or building. Other things, like cars, also have a **roof**. Mr. Mark climbed a ladder to fix the **roof**. **[roofs]**

room (room) or (rum)

1. A **room** is one part of the inside of a house or building. **Rooms** have walls and doors. Many **rooms** also have windows. Sam shares a **room** with his brother. **[rooms]**

2. Room also means space for something to be in, or space to do something in. Is there **room** in the suitcase for this heavy sweater?

rooster (roo-stuhr)

A **rooster** is a male chicken. When the sun comes up, **roosters** make a lot of noise. **[roosters]**

rooster

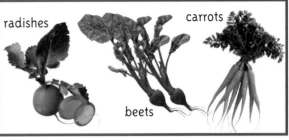

radishes

carrots

beets

root vegetables

root (root)

A **root** is a part of a plant that grows under the ground and holds a plant in the ground. **Roots** get water and food from the ground. **Roots** of a tree are often big and strong. Some **roots** are eaten as vegetables. **[roots]**

rope (rohp)

Rope is strong, thick string made by winding lots of smaller strings together. **Rope** is used to pull or lift heavy things or to hold things in place. The boat was tied to the dock with **rope**. **[ropes]**

rose (roze)

A **rose** is a kind of flower. Most **roses** are red, pink, yellow, or white. Some **roses** have a very sweet smell. The sharp points on the stem of a rose are called thorns. **[roses]**

rough (ruhf)

1. When something is **rough**, there are bumps on its surface. The opposite of **rough** is smooth. The car bounced on the **rough** dirt road.

2. Rough also means not gentle. When the wind started blowing, the sea got so **rough** that boats could not go out. Football is a **rougher** game than baseball. **[rougher, roughest]**

round (round)

Something that is **round** is shaped like a ball or a circle. The earth, rings, and wheels are all **round**. [**rounder, roundest**]

row (roh)

A **row** is a line of people or things side by side or one after another. We all stood in a **row** while Aunt Brooke took our picture. [**rows**]

rub (ruhb)

To **rub** means to press your hand or something else on something and move back and forth across it. Brian began to **rub** his sore elbow with his hand. [**rubbing, rubbed**]

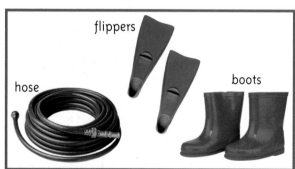
things made from **rubber**

rubber (ruhb-uhr)

Rubber is a strong, hard material that can stretch but doesn't break. **Rubber** can keep water out. Tires, boots, and toys are made of **rubber**.

rude (rood)

Rude means not polite. It is **rude** to push someone out of the way. [**ruder, rudest**]

rug (ruhg)

A **rug** is a mat used to cover part of a floor. [**rugs**]

rule (rool)

1. A **rule** tells you what you have to do or what you cannot do. The **rules** of a country are called laws. There is a **rule** against running in the halls at school. [**rules**]
2. To **rule** means to lead a country and to make laws. [**ruling, ruled**]

ruler (roo-luhr)

1. A **ruler** is a straight, flat tool used to measure length or to draw straight lines. Most **rulers** are made of wood or plastic and are 12 inches long.
2. A **ruler** is also someone who leads a country or makes rules. The **ruler** of a country may be a king, a queen, or a president. [**rulers**]

run (ruhn)

1. To **run** means to move quickly using your legs. People and many animals can **run**.
2. When a machine **runs**, it is working. I hear the washing machine **running**. [**running, ran**]

children **running**

rush (ruhsh)

To **rush** means to go somewhere or do something quickly. If we **rush**, we can get to the movie before it starts. [**rushing, rushed**]

Ss

sad (sad)

Sad means to feel unhappy about something. Krista was **sad** when she had to give away her dog's puppies. [**sadder, saddest**]

safe (sayf)

When you are **safe**, you are away from danger or are being protected and won't get hurt. When something is **safe**, it is in a place where it will not be lost or stolen. The young children felt **safe** crossing the street when the school guard was there to stop traffic. [**safer, safest**]

sail (sayl)

1. A **sail** is a large piece of strong cloth that is attached to poles on a boat. As the wind blows against the **sail**, it makes the boat move. Todd's boat has striped **sails**. [**sails**]
2. When something **sails**, it moves on water using the power of the wind. Michelle went **sailing** on Lake Ontario with her aunt and uncle. Cal **sailed** his toy boat in the pond. [**sailing, sailed**]

sailboat (sayl-boht)

A **sailboat** is a kind of boat that has one or more sails. As the sails catch the wind, they make the **sailboat** move over the water. Some **sailboats** also have a motor, so they can travel even if there is no wind. [**sailboats**]

salad (sal-uhd)

A **salad** is a kind of cold food that is often a mixture of lettuce, tomatoes, carrots, or other raw vegetables. Some **salads** are made with fruit, meat, fish, pasta, or cheese. Ali ordered pasta **salad** with beans. [**salads**]

some **salad** vegetables

sale (sayl)

1. A **sale** is a time when a store sells things for less than they usually cost. The shoe store is having a **sale** on boots.
2. If something is for **sale**, it can be bought. The big house on the corner is for **sale**. [**sales**]

sailboats

salt (sawlt)

Salt is something white that is often added to food to give it a better taste. **Salt** comes out of the ground or from sea water. Natasha put **salt** and pepper on her baked potato. When something has a lot of **salt** in or on it, we say it is **salty**. This popcorn is very **salty**.

same (saym)

1. If two things are the **same**, they are alike in every way. My cousin and I both have the **same** last name. Miki and Cam are wearing the **same** kind of raincoat. **2. Same** can also mean that something has not changed. Is that the **same** book you were reading yesterday, or a different one?

same

sand (sand)

Sand is the tiny pieces of rock that we walk on when we are at the beach or on a desert. **Sand** can be brown, white, pink, or black and looks like powder. Something that is covered with **sand** or full of **sand** is **sandy**. After we came back from the beach, the floor of the car was very **sandy**.

sandwich (sand-wich)

A **sandwich** is a kind of food made with two pieces of bread and meat, cheese, peanut butter, or some other food

sandwich

between them. Justin likes egg salad **sandwiches**. [**sandwiches**]

sank (sangk)

Sank comes from **sink**. The boat filled with water and **sank** to the bottom of the lake.

sat (sat)

Sat comes from **sit**. We **sat** down on the couch to read. While Amy was eating lunch, her dog **sat** on the floor watching her.

satellite (sat-l-ite)

A **satellite** is a kind of spacecraft that travels around Earth, the moon, or another planet. **Satellites** are used to send radio and television signals to Earth and to gather information about the weather. [**satellites**]

playing in the **sand**

save (sayv)

1. To **save** means to help someone escape from danger. The guards at the beach are trained to **save** swimmers from drowning.

2. If you **save** something, you keep it because you want to have it or do something with it later. Mom **saves** all my drawings. **[saving, saved]**

saw¹ (saw)

A **saw** is a tool with a sharp metal edge with tiny points called teeth. Dad used his electric **saw** to cut wood for new shelves. **[saws]**

using a **saw**

saw² (saw)

Saw comes from **see**. We **saw** many tall buildings in the city.

say (say)

If you **say** something, you speak words aloud. "What did you **say**?" "I **said** that we are going to be late if we don't hurry." **[saying, said]**

scale¹ (skayl)

A **scale** is a machine that is used to see how heavy things are. At the store, Bari put the bananas on a **scale** to weigh them.

scale

scale² (skayl)

A **scale** is one of many tiny, hard pieces of skin that often cover fish and reptiles. Alligators and snakes have **scales**. **[scales]**

scare (skair)

Something that **scares** you makes you feel frightened. Tony's frog mask **scares** his little sister. When something **scares** people, we say it is **scary**. We saw a very **scary** movie last night. **[scaring, scared]**

scarecrow

scarecrow (skair-kroh)

A **scarecrow** is something that looks like a person and is put in a field or garden. **Scarecrows** are used to scare away birds so that they will not eat the seeds and plants. The farmer made a **scarecrow** with poles and straw for the body and covered it with old clothes and a hat. **[scarecrows]**

scarf (skahrf)

A **scarf** is a piece of cloth worn around the neck or on the head. In cold weather Brian wears a long wool **scarf** to keep his neck and chest warm. **[scarves]**

school (skool)

School is a place where children and adults go to learn things from teachers. At **school** people learn to read, write, use numbers, and study science, art, computers, and many other things. Tara is learning to subtract numbers and to read maps at **school**. Aunt Kara is at medical **school** studying to become a doctor. **[schools]**

science (sie-uhns)

People study **science** to learn about Earth and other planets, stars, electricity, oceans, the weather, animals, plants, the human body, and other natural things in the universe. **[sciences]**

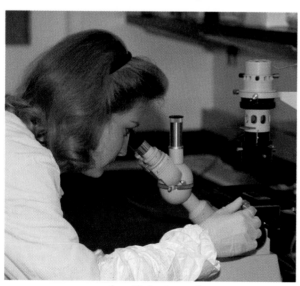

scientist at work

scientist (sie-uhn-tist)

A **scientist** is a person who has learned about some area of science and uses it in his or her work. **Scientists** try to understand how and why things happen. **[scientists]**

scissors (siz-uhrz)

Scissors are a tool with sharp edges used for cutting paper, cloth, and other things. **Scissors** are made of two metal or plastic pieces that fit together, with holes for your thumb and finger.

scissors

scratch (skrach)

1. To **scratch** means to rub with something sharp. Jenny tried not to **scratch** her mosquito bite. A rough edge on the bottom of the bowl **scratched** the top of the table. **[scratching, scratched]**
2. A **scratch** is the mark left on a surface that has been rubbed with something sharp. The cat made **scratches** on the chair with her claws. **[scratches]**

scream (skreem)

To **scream** means to make a very loud sound with your voice without using words. Charlie **screamed** when a big spider fell into his lap. **[screaming, screamed]**

screen (skreen)

1. A **screen** is the front, flat part of a television or a computer that you look at to see pictures or words. Don't touch the computer **screen**.
2. A **screen** is also something that fits over a window and is made of many very thin wires that cross each other. **Screens** let the air come in but keep the insects outside. **[screens]**

scrub (skruhb)

To **scrub** means to rub something hard, often with a brush or rough material, to get it clean. Daryl had to **scrub** the bathtub to clean off the ring of dirt around it. **[scrubbing, scrubbed]**

sculpture (skuhlp-chuhr)

Sculpture is the art of making interesting shapes out of stone, wood, clay, metal, or some other material. A person who creates **sculptures** is called a **sculptor**. Some **sculptures** look like people or animals and some are imaginary shapes thought up by the sculptor. **[sculptures]**

making a
sculpture

sea (see)

The **sea** is the salt water that covers most of the earth. Another word for **sea** is **ocean**. Many kinds of fish, whales, other animals, and plants live in the **sea**. **[seas]**

seal (seel)

A **seal** is an animal that lives in the ocean. Its body is covered with smooth fur and is round in the middle and narrow

seal

at the ends. Its front and back feet are called flippers. A **seal** is a mammal. The mother **seal** called to her baby with loud barking sounds. **[seals]**

search (suhrch)

To **search** means to try hard to find something. We had to **search** the house for our cat and found her in a corner of the basement taking care of her new kittens. **[searching, searched]**

season (see-zuhn)

Season means a time of year with its own kind of weather. The four **seasons** are spring, summer, autumn or fall, and winter. **[seasons]**

seasons

spring

summer

autumn or fall

winter

seat (seet)

A **seat** is something to sit on, like a chair or a bench, or any other place that you can sit. The room was so full that some of us had to take **seats** on the floor. **[seats]**

seat belt (seet belt)

A **seat belt** is a strong belt that you put across your body and attach to a metal piece when you are riding in a car or an airplane. **Seat belts** help to keep people safe if there is an accident. **[seat belts]**

second¹ (sek-uhnd)

A **second** is a very short period of time. There are 60 **seconds** in a minute. **[seconds]**

second² (sek-uhnd)

A person or a thing that is **second** is the next one after the first. We were **second** in line for circus tickets. Marisa asked for a **second** slice of toast.

secret (see-kruht)

A **secret** is something that only one person or a few people know. "If I tell you where I keep my diary, will you keep it a **secret**?" **[secrets]**

see (see)

When you look at something with your eyes, you **see** it. I **see** Jamahl coming down the street. "Did you **see** the program about bees and other insects on television last night?" "No," said Samantha, "I **saw** a puppet show." **[seeing, saw, seen]**

avocado seed
squash seeds
pepper seeds
apple seeds

seeds

seed (seed)

A **seed** is the part of a plant that can grow in soil and make a new plant. We will plant both vegetable and flower **seeds** in the garden this spring. **[seeds]**

seesaw (see-saw)

A **seesaw** is a long board with a piece under the middle part of it. One person sits on each end, and each takes a turn pushing off the ground. **[seesaws]**

selfish (sel-fish)

Being **selfish** means not thinking or caring about what another person wants or feels. It was **selfish** of Joanne not to share her crayons with her friends.

sell (sel)

To **sell** means to receive money for something you give to someone. At the fair, people **sell** different kinds of food and tickets for rides. Does that store **sell** stickers? **[selling, sold]**

send (send)

To **send** means to make someone or something go from one place to another place. Audry and Kris are baking cookies to **send** to their brother at camp. Yesterday, I **sent** a thank-you note to Granny for the birthday present. **[sending, sent]**

sentence (sent-ns)

A **sentence** is a group of words that tells a complete thought. Written **sentences** begin with a capital letter and end with a period, question mark, or exclamation point. There are many **sentences** in this dictionary. **[sentences]**

serious (sir-ee-uhs)

Something that is **serious** is important and needs careful thought. Sometimes **serious** things can be bad or dangerous. Dad's face was very **serious** when he told us that our cat had died.

set (set)

1. A **set** is a group of things that are alike in some way and go together. Dad bought a **set** of tools for the car. I have a new chess **set**. **[sets]**
2. To **set** means to put something down somewhere. Please **set** that chair in the corner.
3. When the sun **sets**, it goes down and day becomes night. **[setting, set]**

seven (sev-uhn)

Seven is the number that comes after six and before eight. **Seven** is written **7**. There are **seven** days in a week. **[sevens]**

sew (soh)

To **sew** means to use a needle and thread to hold two pieces of cloth together or to attach something to a piece of cloth. Jamie knows how to **sew** a button on his shirt. **[sewing, sewed, sewn]**

shadow (shad-oh)

A **shadow** is the dark shape that you see when your body or something else stops the light from shining on an area. As Tina waved her arms, she watched her **shadow** move too. **[shadows]**

shadow on a wall

shake (shayk)

If something **shakes**, it moves up and down or backward and forward very quickly. We watched the dog come out of the lake and **shake** herself dry. The note on the juice container reads "**Shake** well before opening." Mom **shook** hands with my teacher when she met him. **[shaking, shook]**

shape (shayp)

A square, a triangle, and a circle are all **shapes**. Something's **shape** is the way the outside of it looks. Marcel made cookies in the **shape** of hearts. **[shapes]**

share (shair)

1. To **share** is to let other people have some of what you have. When Tony forgot his lunch, I said I would **share** mine with him.
2. To **share** also means to use something with someone else. Roberta and Janet **share** a bedroom. **[sharing, shared]**

blue **shark**

shark (shahrk)

A **shark** is a large fish with a wide mouth and rows of sharp teeth. Some **sharks** are 50 feet long. **[sharks]**

sharp (shahrp)

Something that is **sharp** has a pointed end, like a needle, or an edge that can cut, like a knife. It was easy to cut the paper with the **sharp** scissors. **[sharper, sharpest]**

sheep in a field

sheep (sheep)

A **sheep** is a farm animal with thick, curly hair used to make wool. **Sheep** are mammals also raised for their meat. Young **sheep** are called **lambs**. **[sheep]**

shelf (shelf)

A **shelf** is a board or other flat piece used to put things on. A **shelf** is attached to a wall or is part of a piece of furniture. Rochelle has toys and books on the **shelves** in her bedroom. **[shelves]**

shell (shel)

A **shell** is a hard cover that protects a living thing. Eggs, turtles, snails, and nuts have **shells**. **[shells]**

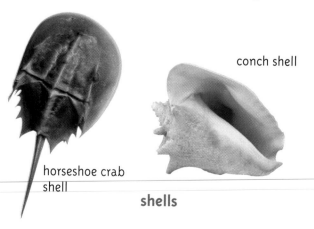

conch shell

horseshoe crab shell

shells

shine (shine)

Things that **shine** give out light or show light on their surface. The sun, the stars, and light bulbs **shine**. Something that **shines** is **shiny**. The jeweler rubbed the silver bracelet until it was **shiny**. [**shining, shone,** or **shined**]

ship (ship)

A **ship** is a large boat that can travel a long way in deep water. My cousin went to Alaska on a big **ship**. That **ship** is carrying oil. [**ships**]

shirt (shuhrt)

A **shirt** is a piece of clothing that is worn on the top half of a person's body. Curtis likes **shirts** with pockets. [**shirts**]

shoe (shoo)

A **shoe** is worn on the foot to protect it. **Shoes** are made of different materials like leather or cloth. Sneakers are a kind of **shoe**. [**shoes**]

shoot (shoot)

1. To **shoot** means to make something go forward or up into the air very fast. It is Marie's turn to **shoot** the basketball.

shooting for a basket

2. To **shoot** also means to hurt or kill using a gun. [**shooting, shot**]

shop (shahp)

1. A **shop** is a store where people go to buy things or to get something done. My aunt works in a flower **shop**. We had to take our television set into a repair **shop** to get it fixed. [**shops**]

2. When people **shop**, they go to stores and buy things. [**shopping, shopped**]

walking along the **shore**

shore (shor)

The **shore** is the land along the edge of a lake or an ocean. The area of sand at the edge of an ocean is called the **seashore**. [**shores**]

short (short)

When something is **short**, it is not far from the top to the bottom or from one end to the other. **Short** is the opposite of tall or long. It's only a **short** walk from here to the top of the hill. "Grandpa, why does your visit have to be so **short**?" asked Casey. Candice is **shorter** than Debra. [**shorter, shortest**]

shorts (shorts)

Shorts are pants that end above the knees. I'll wear **shorts** today.

shoulder (shohl-duhr)

The **shoulder** is the part of the body just below the neck where each arm is attached. Rosa often wears her backpack over her left **shoulder**. [shoulders]

shout (shout)

When you **shout**, you speak very loudly. When her Dad was fixing the car engine, Enid had to **shout** for him to hear her. [shouting, shouted]

shovel (shuhv-uhl)

1. A **shovel** is a tool with a long handle that is used to dig or lift things. [shovels]
2. To **shovel** means to pick something up with a shovel and move it somewhere else. Cindy likes to **shovel** snow. Keanu **shoveled** sand into his pail at the seashore. [shoveling, shoveled]

shoveling snow

puppet **show**

show (shoh)

1. **Show** means to let someone else see something that you have. **Show** also means to explain how to do something. Lorena is going to **show** me her new puppy. Malcolm **showed** Suzy and Jorge how to play a new computer game. [showing, showed, shown]
2. A **show** is a program on television or is something you can see in a theater, circus, or at the movies. Dana likes to be in puppet **shows**. [shows]

shower (shou-uhr)

1. When you take a **shower**, you wash your body while standing under water that falls from above. Georgia took a **shower** and Amy took a bath before getting dressed for the party.
2. A **shower** is also rain that falls for a short period of time. The **shower** was good for the garden. [showers]

shrink (shringk)

To **shrink** means to get smaller. I didn't know my sweater would **shrink** when it was washed, but now it fits my little brother. **[shrinking, shrank, shrunk]**

shut (shuht)

Shut means to move something that is open until it is closed. Please **shut** the car door. The suitcase was so full that Lily couldn't **shut** it. **[shutting, shut]**

shy (shie)

Someone who is **shy** is a little afraid of people and may not want to talk to them at first. On the first day of school, Kwami was **shy** and stood next to his mother and held her hand. **[shyer or shier, shyest or shiest]**

sick (sik)

To be **sick** means not to feel well. Maria won't be in school today because she's **sick** with a bad cold. When our dog got **sick**, the vet gave us medicine to put into the dog's food. **[sicker, sickest]**

side (side)

1. A **side** is an edge or surface of something. A square has four **sides**, and a cube has six **sides**. Rene wrote a letter on one **side** of the paper and drew a picture on the other **side**. Let's walk on the other **side** of the street, where it's sunny.
2. A **side** is also one of two groups of people who are playing a game against each other. Which **side** won the hockey game? **[sides]**

sidewalk (side-wawk)

A **sidewalk** is a raised path with a hard surface along the edge of a street where people can walk. We walked along the **sidewalk** and looked at the store windows. **[sidewalks]**

walking on a **sidewalk**

sign (sine)

1. A **sign** is writing or a picture that gives you information or tells you what to do. A **sign** in front of the Smith's house said they were having a garage sale. **[signs]**
2. To **sign** something, means to write your name on it. We are all going to **sign** the birthday card for Mom. **[signing, signed]**

sign

signal (sig-nuhl)

A **signal** is a way of giving information without using words. When a traffic light is red, it is a **signal** for traffic to stop. **[signals]**

silent (sie-luhnt)

A person or thing that is **silent** does not make any sound. Everyone was **silent** while Aaron read his story, until he got to the part about the haunted house. It is very hard to be **silent** while you are being tickled.

silly (sil-ee)

If something is **silly**, it is funny and not serious. Carmen drew a very **silly** picture of a giraffe dancing with a hippopotamus. That was the **silliest** movie I've ever seen. **[sillier, silliest]**

silver (sil-vuhr)

Silver is a metal that is shiny and has a light color. **Silver** is used for jewelry, coins, and other things.

simple (sim-puhl)

Something that is **simple** is easy to do. Mom showed me a **simple** way to make an apple pie. **[simpler, simplest]**

sing (sing)

To **sing** is to use the voice to make music, often with words. We are learning to **sing** some new songs in our music class. A **singer** is a person who uses the voice to make music, sometimes as a job. **[singing, sang]**

single (sing-guhl)

1. Single means only one. There are three buds on the plant, but only a **single** flower. Eve came home with only a **single** earring because she had lost the other one.
2. Single also means not married. One of my brothers is married and one is **single**.

a **single** house

sink (singk)

1. A **sink** is a container attached to water pipes that is used for washing things. Put the dirty dishes in the kitchen **sink**. We all took turns washing our hands at the bathroom **sink**. **[sinks]**
2. To **sink** means to go below the surface of water. Terry frowned as he watched the boat he built **sink** to the bottom of the bathtub. **[sinking, sank, sunk]**

sinks

sister (sis-tuhr)

If you have a **sister**, she is a girl who has the same parents you have. Doug has one **sister** and two brothers. **[sisters]**

sit (sis)

To **sit** is to rest the lower back part of the body on something, usually with the legs bent. Cheryl likes to **sit** in her father's lap and read to him. Mike **sat** on the edge of the swimming pool with his feet in the water. A cat was **sitting** on the fence watching the birds. **[sitting, sat]**

six (siks)

Six is the number that comes after five and before seven. **Six** is written **6**. An insect has **six** legs. **[sixes]**

size (size)

A **size** is how large or small something is. These toy pandas come in two **sizes**, small and large. What **size** ring will fit on your finger? **[sizes]**

roller skates

in-line skates

ice skates

skates

cross-country **skiing**

ski (skee)

1. A **ski** is one of a pair of long, narrow boards that is attached to a special boot to move quickly over snow. **[skis]**
2. When people **ski**, they use skis to move quickly over the snow. When **skiing**, people also use thin hand poles for balance and to push against the ground. **[skiing, skied]**

skate (skayt)

1. A **skate** is a boot or something you attach to your shoe that has a long, sharp piece of metal, called a blade, or wheels on the bottom. **Skates** come in pairs. You use **skates** to move quickly over ice, a sidewalk, or another flat surface. **[skates]**
2. To **skate** means wearing a pair of skates to move quickly over ice or a flat surface. Tara can ice **skate** backward. A person who **skates** is called a **skater**. **[skating, skated]**

skin (skin)

Skin is the part of a person or animal that covers the outside and protects what's inside. A fruit or vegetable also has **skin** that protects it. The **skin** of fruits like oranges, bananas, or pineapples is taken off before the fruit is eaten. **[skins]**

skateboard (skayt-bord)

A **skateboard** is a small board on wheels. A person stands on a **skateboard** and rides by pushing one foot against the ground. **[skateboards]**

skateboard

skip (skip)

1. To **skip** means to move along by jumping and hopping, first on one foot and then on the other.
2. **Skip** also means to pass over something or not do it. Leilah had to **skip** her swimming lesson today because she has a cold. **[skipping, skipped]**

skirt (skuhrt)

A **skirt** is a piece of clothing worn mostly by girls and women. Skirts hang from the waist. **[skirts]**

skunk (skuhngk)

A **skunk** is a small black animal with a long tail and a white stripe down its back. It can make a very bad smell when it feels in danger. **[skunks]**

skunk

sky (skie)

The **sky** is what you see far above you when you are outside and you look up. The sun, moon, stars, and clouds are in the **sky**. The **sky** is blue when the weather is clear and gray when cloudy or rainy. **[skies]**

skyscraper (skie-skray-puhr)

A **skyscraper** is a tall building with many floors. We took an elevator to the top of a **skyscraper** and looked out over the whole city. **[skyscrapers]**

skyscrapers

sled (sled)

A **sled** is something you sit on to ride over the snow. It has long, thin metal pieces on the bottom. **[sleds]**

sleep (sleep)

To **sleep** means to rest with your eyes closed and your mind not thinking. People dream when they **sleep**. Lauren **sleeps** in a room with her sister. When we camp, we **sleep** in sleeping bags. If you are tired because you didn't **sleep** enough, we say you are **sleepy**. **[sleeping, slept]**

slice (slise)

1. A **slice** is one thin, flat part of something that is cut from the rest of it. Would you like a **slice** of apple? **[slices]**
2. When you **slice** something, you cut it into thin, flat pieces. Let's **slice** this fresh loaf of bread and make sandwiches. **[slicing, sliced]**

slide (slide)

1. To **slide** is to move quickly and easily over the surface of something. It's fun to **slide** down a hill on a sled. **[sliding, slid]**
2. A **slide** is a long, smooth surface to slide down, with a

on a **slide**

ladder to the top. Dad and Eric are going down the **slide** together. **[slides]**

slip (slip)

To **slip** means to slide from a place by mistake and fall down. Jenny **slipped** on the broken stair and fell. The wet plate **slipped** out of my hand. Something you can easily **slip** on or slide on is **slippery**. The sidewalk is **slippery**. **[slipping, slipped]**

slow (sloh)

Slow is the opposite of fast. Someone or something that is **slow** takes a long time to do something or get somewhere. Dan is **slow** at eating. The train we're riding on is **slower** than the one that's passing us. If something is done in a **slow** way, it is done **slowly**. Cars going into the tunnel were moving **slowly**. **[slower, slowest]**

small (smawl)

Small means little or not very big. An ant is a very **small** insect. The pants I got last year are too **small** for me now. **[smaller, smallest]**

small dogs in a basket

smell (smel)

1. To **smell** means to use the nose to find out about something. Many animals can **smell** things that people cannot **smell**. I **smell** cookies baking in the oven. **[smelling, smelled]**

2. A **smell** is what your nose tells you about something. Those roses have a sweet smell. **[smells]**

smiles

smile (smile)

1. When you **smile**, your mouth gets wide and turns up at the corners. People **smile** when they are happy or when they think something is funny. Megan **smiled** to see her kitten taking a nap in the dog's bed. We all **smiled** when Mom took our picture. **[smiling, smiled]**

2. A **smile** is the look your mouth has when you are happy or think something is funny. Charlie had a big **smile** on his face when he saw his birthday cake. **[smiles]**

smoke (smohk)

Smoke is the gray or black cloud of gas that rises in the air when something burns. When we burned the food on the stove, **smoke** filled the kitchen. **Smoke** from a forest fire could be seen in the distance.

smooth (smooTH)

If something is **smooth**, it has a surface that is not rough or bumpy. A baby's skin is **smooth**. The surface of the lake is **smooth** when there is no wind. **[smoother, smoothest]**

snail (snayl)

A **snail** is a small animal that lives in a shell and has a soft, slippery body. Niki found **snails** at the beach and in the garden. [**snails**]

snake (snayk)

A **snake** is a long, thin reptile that has no legs and slides along the ground by moving first one part of its body and then another. **Snakes** have scales, and some have beautiful colors and patterns. [**snakes**]

king snake

boa constrictor

cobra

snakes

sneaker (snee-kuhr)

A **sneaker** is a kind of shoe made with rubber on the bottom and cloth or leather on top. People wear **sneakers** when they play basketball or other sports, when they jog, and for many other activities. My aunt wears **sneakers** to her job as a waitress because she stands a lot. [**sneakers**]

sneeze (sneez)

When you **sneeze**, a lot of air comes out of your nose and mouth very suddenly. "Please cover your mouth when you **sneeze**," the school nurse told us. [**sneezing, sneezed**]

playing in the **snow**

snow (snoh)

1. Snow is tiny pieces of frozen water that are white and soft. **Snow** falls from clouds in cold weather. A **snowball** is made by pressing snow together with your hands. A **snowman** is a shape of a person made from **snow**.
2. To **snow** means to fall from the sky as snow. If it **snows** tonight, let's play in the snow tomorrow. [**snowing, snowed**]

soap (sohp)

Soap is something that you mix with water and use for washing and cleaning things. Some **soap** is liquid and some is solid. When I fell down and scratched my leg, Mom washed it with **soap** and water.

soccer (sahk-uhr)

Soccer is a game played on a field by two teams made up of 11 players each. Players try to get the **soccer** ball into the goal by kicking it or hitting it with any part of the body except their hands or arms.　**soccer** player

sock (sahk)

A **sock** is something made of soft material like cotton and is worn on the foot inside a shoe. The baby was wearing tiny yellow **socks** on her feet that matched her yellow dress. **[socks]**

soft (sawft)

1. Something that is **soft** bends or changes shape very easily when it is touched. **Soft** is the opposite of hard. Baby chicks have very **soft** feathers.
2. Soft also means quiet and gentle, and not loud. As I went to sleep, I could hear **soft** music coming from the radio. **[softer, softest]**

soft feathers

soil (soil)

Soil is the top layer of earth that we plant things in. Mr. Sommers put some new **soil** in the garden this year to help his vegetables grow better.

solar (soh-luhr)

When we say that something is **solar**, we mean that it has something to do with the sun or uses energy from the sun. **Solar** energy can be used to heat water or make electricity. Jackie has a small **solar** calculator that needs light to work.

sold (sohld)

Sold comes from **sell**. We **sold** our house because we were moving to another city. Neil **sold** us his tickets to the baseball game.

soldier (sohl-juhr)

A **soldier** is a man or woman who is in the army. **Soldiers** fight for their country when there is a war. **[soldiers]**

solid (sol-id)

Something that is **solid** is hard and has a shape. If something is **solid**, it is not a liquid or a gas. When the orange juice froze, it was **solid** and we ate it with a spoon. The ice on the lake was **solid**.

some (suhm)

Some means an amount of something or part of a group of people or things. Did you get **some** salad? Most of the snow has melted, but there is still **some** snow under the tree. **Some** of us are going sailing tomorrow.

somersault (suhm-uhr-sawlt)

A **somersault** is a way of moving your body by putting your head down close to your chest, bending your knees, and rolling so that your feet go over your head. Briana can do a backward **somersault**. **[somersaults]**

something (suhm-thing)

Something is a thing that you do not call by name or that you do not know the name of. Do you hear **something** moving in the bushes? Here is **something** for you to drink.

sometimes (suhm-timez)

If you do something **sometimes**, you do it part of the time but not all the time. **Sometimes** I think I'd like to be an astronaut when I grow up, and **sometimes** I think I'd like to be a teacher.

somewhere (suhm-wair)

Somewhere means at a place, but you don't know where. Kim's cousins live **somewhere** in Texas. Jesse lost a glove **somewhere** between his house and school.

parents with their **son**

son (suhn)

A **son** is the male child of a man and a woman. Daddy is Grandpa's **son**. The Bells like to walk in the park with their **son**. [**sons**]

song (sawng)

A **song** is music with words that can be sung. A **song** is also the sounds that birds make. We sang **songs** and played games at the party. [**songs**]

sore (sor)

When a part of your body hurts, we say that it is **sore**. I fell down while I was skating and now my leg is **sore**. Karin has a **sore** throat and a cold.

sorry (sahr-ee)

Feeling **sorry** means to feel sad because of something that is happening or something you have done. John said he was **sorry** he had taken Sis's game without asking. [**sorrier, sorriest**]

sound (sound)

A **sound** is anything that you hear. What's that **sound** coming from the kitchen? We heard the **sounds** of children laughing and shouting. The donkey made a very loud **sound** that scared me. [**sounds**]

soup (soop)

Soup is a liquid food made of water and vegetables, meat, noodles, or other kinds of food.

having **soup** for lunch

Many kinds of **soup** are eaten hot, but some are eaten cold. The Cottons are having **soup** for lunch today. [**soups**]

sour (sour)

Sour is a taste that is the opposite of sweet. Lemons taste **sour**. [**sourer, sourest**]

south (south)

South is a direction on a compass opposite north. When you face the setting sun, which is always in the west, **south** is the direction to your left. The state of South Carolina is south of North Carolina and lies below it.

space (spays)

1. A **space** is any area that is not filled with something. Mom hid the Christmas presents in a **space** at the back of her closet. We found a parking **space** right in front of the store. **[spaces]**

2. Space is also the area high above and all around Earth, where the sun, planets, and stars are. It is sometimes called **outer space**. Astronauts travel in **space**.

astronaut in **space**

spacecraft (spays-kraft)

A **spacecraft** is something that travels into space away from the earth. Some **spacecraft** carry people and some carry only instruments to measure things and take pictures in space.

A **spacewalk** is the activity of moving in space outside the spacecraft. **[spacecraft]**

spaghetti and meatballs

spaghetti (spuh-get-ee)

Spaghetti is a kind of food made of long, thin noodles that are cooked and often eaten with something on top, like a mixture of meat and tomatoes.

speak (speek)

1. To **speak** is to say words. Rose didn't **speak** until she was three years old. You're **speaking** so softly that I can't hear you.

2. To **speak** also means to talk in a language. I **speak** English and Spanish. My friend Ming **speaks** Chinese and English.
[speaking, spoke, spoken]

special (spesh-uhl)

Something that is **special** is different in a good way from what is usual. For my birthday, we had a **special** meal with all my favorite foods. As a **special** treat, Dad took us to the circus.

spell (spel)

To **spell** means to write or say letters in the correct order to make a word. We **spell** *carrot* c-a-r-r-o-t. Marcus can read, but he doesn't **spell** very well. **[spelling, spelled]**

spend (spend)

When you **spend** something like time, energy, or money, you use it. My big sister **spends** a lot of time studying because she wants to do well in school. I **spent** four dollars on a present for my friend. [**spending, spent**]

spiders

spider (spide-uhr)

A **spider** is a very small animal with eight legs and no wings. Many **spiders** spin webs to catch insects to eat. **Spiders** are often black or brown, but some are green or orange. [**spiders**]

spill (spil)

If you **spill** something, you make it come out of a container by mistake. Amanda was careful not to **spill** the hot chocolate. [**spilling, spilled**]

spin (spin)

1. To **spin** is to make a web or a cocoon, or to make thread. The webs spiders **spin** look like pretty designs. The caterpillar **spun** a cocoon for itself.
2. When a person or a thing **spins**, it turns around very quickly many times. As the music got louder and louder, the ballet dancer began to **spin** faster and faster. The car wheels were **spinning** on the ice. [**spinning, spun**]

splash (splash)

To **splash** means to make water or another liquid fly into the air and make something or someone wet. Sheila likes to **splash** in puddles when it rains. Charlie **splashed** us when he dropped the glass of juice. [**splashing, splashed**]

spoon (spoon)

A **spoon** is a tool used for eating some foods. A **spoon** has a round part to hold food and a handle. We eat foods like soup and cereal with a **spoon**. [**spoons**]

sport (sport)

A **sport** is a game that you play to get exercise and have fun. Skating, tennis, basketball, running, soccer, and swimming are all **sports**. Some **sports** are played by one or two people, and some are played by a team. [**sports**]

baseball▲

basketball▲

▼soccer

▼football

sports

spots on a leopard

spot (spaht)
A **spot** is a small dot or mark on something. There's a **spot** on my shirt where I spilled some soup. Gary's dog is white with black **spots**. **[spots]**

spring (spring)
Spring is the season between winter and summer, when the weather gets warmer. Plants come up out of the earth and many trees get new leaves in the **spring**. **[springs]**

square (skwair)
A **square** is a shape that has four corners and four sides that are the same length. A square looks like this: ■. A checkerboard is divided into many **squares**. **[squares]**

squash (skwahsh)
A **squash** is a vegetable. It is often yellow or green and can be long or round, hard or soft. **[squashes]**

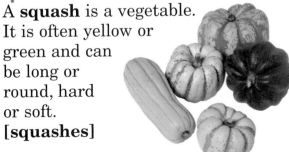

different kinds of **squash**

squirrel (skwurl)
A **squirrel** is a small gray or brown animal with a long, thick tail and small, pointed ears. **Squirrels** live in trees and eat nuts. **[squirrels]**

squirrel

stair (stair)
A **stair** is one of a group of steps used to go from one floor of a building to another. The **stairs** to the attic are steep. **[stairs]**

stamp (stamp)
A **stamp** is a small piece of paper to stick on an envelope or a package to show that you have paid to have it delivered to an address. Some people collect **stamps**. **[stamps]**

stand (stand)
1. To **stand** means to be on your feet, not sitting or lying down. We had to **stand** on the bus because there weren't any more seats. Carlos **stood** up to try out his new skates.
2. To **stand** also means to put something so that it is straight up and down. The broom **stands** over there in the corner. **[standing, stood]**

star (stahr)

1. A **star** is a ball of burning gases out in space. Most **stars** are so far away that they look like tiny points of light in the night sky. The sun, which heats Earth, is our closest **star**. Groups of **stars** that form patterns in the sky are called **constellations**.
2. A **star** is also a shape with five or six points. On the American flag there is a **star** for each state in the United States. **[stars]**

stare (stair)

To **stare** means to look very hard and long at something or someone. Maya **stared** at the colorful fish swimming around in the aquarium. **[staring, stared]**

start (stahrt)

To **start** means to begin to do something or to begin to happen. I can't wait to **start** reading this mystery story. Tennis lessons **start** next week. **[starting, started]**

state (stayt)

A **state** is one of the 50 parts that the United States is divided into. Which **state** do you live in? **[states]**

station (stay-shuhn)

A **station** is a building or place where people work. A gas **station** is a place where gas is sold. Police work out of a police **station**. Radio and television **stations** send out programs that we listen to and watch. **[stations]**

statue of President Lincoln

statue (stach-oo)

A **statue** is a sculpture of a person or animal. **Statues** are often made of stone, metal, wood, or clay. There is a large **statue** of President Abraham Lincoln in Washington, D.C. **[statues]**

states of the United States

Alabama	Hawaii	Massachusetts	New Mexico	South Dakota
Alaska	Idaho	Michigan	New York	Tennessee
Arizona	Illinois	Minnesota	North Carolina	Texas
Arkansas	Indiana	Mississippi	North Dakota	Utah
California	Iowa	Missouri	Ohio	Vermont
Colorado	Kansas	Montana	Oklahoma	Virginia
Connecticut	Kentucky	Nebraska	Oregon	Washington
Delaware	Louisiana	Nevada	Pennsylvania	West Virginia
Florida	Maine	New Hampshire	Rhode Island	Wisconsin
Georgia	Maryland	New Jersey	South Carolina	Wyoming

steal (steel)

To **steal** is to take something that belongs to someone else. John puts his bicycle in the garage at night so that no one will try to **steal** it. [**stealing, stole, stolen**]

steam (steem)

Steam is a gas that is made by boiling water. A long time ago train engines ran on **steam**.

steep (steep)

When something is **steep**, it goes up high and is hard to climb. A mountain, road, or path can be **steep**. Some roofs are **steep**. [**steeper, steepest**]

stem (stem)

The **stem** is the part of a plant that the leaves, flowers, and fruit are attached to. **Stems** are usually long and thin and hold up the plant. When you eat cherries, you have to pull off the **stems** first. [**stems**]

step (step)

1. A **step** is one of the flat surfaces to put your foot on when you go up or down stairs or some ladders. Mae sat on the **steps** to wait for her friend.
2. A **step** is also the distance your foot moves when you walk forward or backward. When Theus walks, he takes small **steps**, but his father takes big **steps**. [**steps**]
3. To **step** is to lift a foot and put it down in another place. Be careful not to **step** on that banana peel! [**stepping, stepped**]

stick¹ (stik)

A **stick** is a long, thin piece of wood or something else. Here is a **stick** to mix the paint. The pet store owner likes to carry his parrot around on a **stick**. Mom put some carrot **sticks** in my lunch today. [**sticks**]

stick² (stik)

1. To **stick** means to attach with something like glue or tape. The package will be ready to mail as soon as we **stick** an address label on it.
2. **Stick** also means to push something sharp into something or through it. Peggy tried to **stick** her fork into the bean, but it slid across the plate. [**sticking, stuck**]

sticker (stik-uhr)

A **sticker** is a small picture on paper or plastic that has glue on the back. [**stickers**]

sting (sting)

When something **stings**, you feel a quick, sharp pain. Sometimes the soap **stings** when it gets into Grace's eye. [**stinging, stung**]

sitting on **steps**

stir (stuhr)

When you **stir** something, you mix it by moving it around in a container with a spoon or a stick. Dad always **stirs** the soup a few times while it is cooking. [**stirring, stirred**]

stomach (stuhm-uhk)

Your **stomach** is a place inside the middle part of your body where food goes after you eat it. If you eat too much, your **stomach** might hurt. [**stomachs**]

stone (stohn)

A **stone** is a small piece of rock. The water made the **stones** on the beach very smooth. **Stone** is also rock that is found in the earth and is used to make statues and other things. [**stones**]

large **stones**

stop (stahp)

To **stop** means not to do something anymore. Justin was told to **stop** teasing his sister. The car **stopped** at the red light. When our computer **stopped** working, we had to have it fixed. [**stopping, stopped**]

store (stor)

1. A **store** is a place to go to buy things. The video **store** we go to has a shoe **store** next to it. [**stores**]
2. To **store** something means to save it or keep something to be used at a later time. The Tays **store** their sleds and skates in the cellar for the summer. [**storing, stored**]

trees blowing in a **storm**

storm (storm)

A **storm** is weather with snow or rain and a lot of wind. There was a loud **storm** last night with a lot of rain, lightning, and thunder. [**storms**]

story (stor-ee)

A **story** is something real or imaginary that a person tells or writes about. Uncle Hugo tells good ghost **stories**. We each wrote a **story** about something we like to do. [**stories**]

stove (stohv)

A **stove** is a large metal container used for cooking food or for heating a room. The wood **stove** kept the cabin warm in the winter. On Saturday we cooked strawberry jam on top of the **stove** while we baked a pie in the oven. [**stoves**]

straight (strayt)

Something that is **straight** does not curve or bend. Brandon has curly hair and I have **straight** hair. It's hard to draw a **straight** line without a ruler. [**straighter, straightest**]

strange (straynj)

Strange means different or unusual. My new school seemed very **strange** until I got to know the other kids. Samantha is very neat and thinks her brother is **strange** because his room is such a mess. Charlie drew the head of a **strange** beast for his Halloween mask. [**stranger, strangest**]

stranger (strayn-juhr)

A **stranger** is someone you do not know. When our car broke down, a **stranger** helped by calling the police. A **stranger** asked Dad where the post office was. We were taught never to go anywhere with a **stranger**. [**strangers**]

straw (straw)

1. A **straw** is a paper or plastic tube through which a person can drink a liquid. Nelly likes to drink milk, juice, and lemonade through a **straw**. [**straws**]
2. Straw is also the dried stems of some plants that is used to make brooms, hats, scarecrows, and other things. Farm animals often sleep on beds made of **straw**.

wearing a **straw** hat

straw basket

strawberries

strawberry (straw-ber-ee)

A **strawberry** is a small red fruit that grows close to the ground. We picked four pints of **strawberries** and made ice cream. [**strawberries**]

stream

stream (streem)

A **stream** is a small river. Sometimes **streams** dry up when it is very hot or when it doesn't rain much. This **stream** flows into a big river a few miles from here. [**stream**]

street (street)

A **street** is a road in a town or a city, often with sidewalks and houses or other buildings along it. I live on Dexter **Street**. Everyone in the parade marched down the middle of the **street**. [**streets**]

stretch (strech)

If you **stretch** something, you change its shape by pulling it and making it longer or wider. Kimberly tried to **stretch** the rubber band around the package, but it was too small and broke. Fred and Tanya **stretch** their arms and legs before they do their exercises. **[stretching, stretched]**

stretching

string (string)

A **string** is a long, thin piece of rope, wire, or plastic. The woman in the bakery tied up the box of cookies with a long piece of **string**. My guitar has six **strings** on it. **[strings]**

stripe (stripe)

A **stripe** is a line of color that is next to a different color. The skunk had a white **stripe** down its back. Lucy's favorite blanket has blue and green **stripes**. **[stripes]**

a shirt with **stripes**

strong (strawng)

Something that is **strong** has a lot of power or is hard to break. Amanda lifted up the chair to show us how **strong** she was. A **strong** wind blew down that tree last week. We mailed the books in a very **strong** box. **[stronger, strongest]**

stuck (stuhk)

Stuck comes from **stick**. When I put my hand in my pocket, I **stuck** my finger on something sharp. In the book, the dinosaur got **stuck** in the mud and her friends had to help her get out.

student (stood-nt)

A **student** is a person who learns from a teacher in a class at school. **Students** in the third grade went to the museum today. **[students]**

studying

study (stuhd-ee)

Study means to work at learning things by reading books and thinking. Justin sat at the kitchen table to **study** for his science test. When you **study** something like art or music, you learn how to do it by practicing. **[studying, studied]**

submarine (suhb-muh-reen)

A **submarine** is a kind of ship that can travel under water for long periods of time. **Submarines** are used to explore things deep in the ocean. **[submarines]**

subtract (suhb-trakt)

When you **subtract**, you take one number away from another number. If you **subtract** two from three, you get one. **[subtracting, subtracted]**

subway

subway (suhb-way)

A **subway** is a train or a group of trains that travel under the ground through tunnels. Many large cities all over the world have **subways**. Many people ride in **subways** to work. **[subways]**

sudden (suhd-n)

Something that is **sudden** happens very quickly and when you did not think it would happen. Cheryl made a **sudden** turn on her bicycle and almost ran into me. All of a **sudden** the lights went out. If something happens in a **sudden** way, it happens **suddenly**. **Suddenly** the rain stopped and the sun came out.

sugar (shug-uhr)

Sugar is a white or brown food that comes from a plant and is used to make other foods sweet. **Sugar** looks like tiny grains or powder. Foods like candy, cookies, and many desserts taste sweet because they have **sugar** in them. **[sugars]**

suit (soot)

A **suit** is a jacket and a pair of pants or a skirt that are made from the same kind of cloth. Maria's mom wore a black wool **suit** with a red blouse to the office today. **[suits]**

suitcase (soot-kays)

A **suitcase** is a flat bag to put your clothes and other things into when you travel. From the window of the airplane, we watched the workers putting the **suitcases** onto the plane. **[suitcases]**

pulling a **suitcase** on wheels

sum (suhm)

A **sum** is an amount of money or the number that you get when you add two or more numbers together. A hundred dollars is a large **sum** of money. The **sum** of six, two, and one is nine. **[sums]**

summer (suhm-uhr)
Summer is the season that comes between spring and fall, when the weather is warmest. Last **summer** I learned how to sail. [**summers**]

sun (suhn)
The **sun** is the bright yellow star that is closest to Earth and gives us our heat and light. The **sun** came up at about six o'clock this morning. People, animals, and plants all need the **sun** to help them grow and be healthy. When the **sun** shines, we say that it is **sunny**.

sunflower (suhn-flou-uhr)
A **sunflower** is a large flower with big yellow petals and a brown center with a lot of seeds in it. Some **sunflowers** grow very tall. [**sunflowers**]

sunglasses (suhn-glas-iz)
Sunglasses are dark glasses that protect your eyes from the bright sun. Many people at the beach were wearing **sunglasses**.

wearing **sunglasses**

sunk (suhnk)
Sunk comes from **sink**. That big log has **sunk** to the bottom of the pond.

sunrise

sunrise (suhn-rize)
Sunrise is the time in the morning when the sun can first be seen in the sky. The birds started singing at **sunrise** and woke me up.

sunset (suhn-set)
Sunset is the time in the evening when the sun goes down and disappears from the sky. We had a beautiful orange and pink **sunset** yesterday.

supermarket (soo-puhr-mahr-kit)
A **supermarket** is a large store that sells all kinds of food and many other things. In a **supermarket** you push a cart around and fill it with things you want to buy, and then pay as you leave. [**supermarkets**]

supper (suhp-uhr)
Supper is a meal that people eat in the evening. Yesterday we had a big meal in the middle of the day and hot dogs for **supper**. [**suppers**]

surface (suhr-fuhs)
The **surface** of something is the top or outside part of it. The **surface** of that table feels smooth on top and rough on the edge. [**surfaces**]

surprise (suhr-prize)
1. A **surprise** is something that happens when you did not know it was going to happen. Getting a puppy for her birthday was a big **surprise** for Anna. [**surprises**]
2. To **surprise** someone means to do something the person did not know you were going to do. Trish and I are going to **surprise** Mom and Dad by making breakfast for them. [**surprising, surprised**]

swallow (swahl-oh)
Swallow means to let foods or liquids go from your mouth down to your stomach. I take a drink of juice to help me **swallow** my vitamin pill in the morning. [**swallowing, swallowed**]

swam (swam)
Swam comes from **swim**. The dolphin jumped into the air and then **swam** around on water.

moose in a **swamp**

swamp (swahmp)
A **swamp** is a place where the land is soft and wet, and trees and other plants grow out of the water. We saw alligators, turtles, and birds in a **swamp** in Florida. [**swamps**]

swan

swan (swahn)
A **swan** is a large bird with a long neck that lives on water. Most **swans** have white feathers. Young **swans** are called **cygnets**. [**swans**]

sweater (swet-uhr)
A **sweater** is a piece of clothing worn on the top part of your body to keep you warm. Paul and Josh buttoned up their wool **sweaters** before they went outside to play. Greta has a matching **sweater** and skirt. [**sweaters**]

sweatshirt (swet-shuhrt)
A **sweatshirt** is clothing worn over the top part of the body, like a sweater. It is often made of heavy cotton. My **sweatshirt** has a zipper, but Jamie's **sweatshirt** pulls over her head. [**sweatshirts**]

sweatshirt and shorts

sweep (sweep)

To **sweep** means to clean dirt off a floor or other surface using a broom or a brush. Mom asked me to **sweep** the dust out from under my bed. Martina **swept** the inside of her dollhouse with a tiny brush. **[sweeping, swept]**

sweet (sweet)

Something **sweet** tastes like something with sugar or honey in it. I had a piece of watermelon that was very **sweet**. The chocolate milk is too **sweet** for Bo, but it's just right for me. **[sweeter, sweetest]**

swept (swept)

Swept comes from **sweep**. I **swept** the leaves off the front steps.

swim (swim)

When you **swim**, you move forward or backward in the water by using your arms and legs. My parents think it is important for us to learn how to **swim**. Karl likes to **swim** in a pool. Whales, dolphins, and many different kinds of fish **swim** in the ocean. We **swam** in a lake last summer. **[swimming, swam]**

swimming

on **swings**

swing (swing)

1. A **swing** is a seat that hangs on ropes or chains from a metal bar or tree. Sitting on a **swing**, a person can go up in the air. Carol pushed me on the **swing** first, and then I pushed her. **[swings]**
2. To **swing** means to move backward and forward or in a circle in the air. I like to **swing** when I'm at the playground. Uncle Ben held Peggy by the hands and **swung** her around off the ground.
3. To **swing** also means to move something quickly through the air. When Jackie **swings** the bat, she tries to hit the ball a long way. **[swinging, swung]**

sword (sord)

A **sword** is a long metal knife used for fighting. Knights used **swords** a long time ago to fight their enemies. **[swords]**

syrup (suhr-uhp) or (sir-uhp)

Syrup is a sweet, thick liquid that is poured over pancakes and other food. Maple **syrup** comes from a maple tree. **[syrups]**

Tt

table (tay-buhl)

A **table** is a piece of furniture that has a flat top and legs to hold it up. It took four people to move the heavy picnic **table** out of the sun and under the oak tree. [**tables**]

picnic **table**

tag (tag)

1. A **tag** is a kind of label. A name **tag** has a person's name written on it. A price **tag** tells how much something costs. All the children wore name **tags** when they went on the field trip. [**tags**]

2. Tag is also a game that children play. The person who is "it" has to touch, or **tag**, another player. The first graders like to play **tag** at recess.

tail (tayl)

A **tail** is the part of the body of some animals that grows from the back end. **Tails** come in many shapes and sizes. Goats, monkeys, dogs, fish, squirrels, and many other animals have **tails**. [**tails**]

tail of a lemur

take (tayk)

1. To **take** means to get something using your hands. Please **take** your brother's hand when we cross the street.

2. Take also means to carry or bring. Remember to **take** an umbrella with you.

3. Take also means to have. Bebe **takes** a bath every night before going to bed.

4. Take also means to use or ride. Christopher **takes** a bus when he goes to day camp.

5. Take also means to need. How long will the photographs **take** to be ready? This cake **takes** an hour to bake. [**taking, took**]

tale (tayl)

A **tale** is a story. Have you heard the **tale** about a frog prince and his magic sword? [**tales**]

talk (tawk)

To **talk** is to say words or to speak. How old were you when you learned to **talk**? We can't **talk** during the spelling test. [**talking, talked**]

tall (tawl)

When something is **tall**, it goes up high above the ground. The opposite of **tall** is short. We could see the clock at the top of the **tall** building from far away. Jean has grown an inch **taller**. [**taller, tallest**]

tame (taym)

When an animal is **tame**, it has been trained to do what a person tells it to do. **Tame** animals do not act wild. They are gentle and friendly. [**tamer, tamest**]

tape (tayp)

1. Tape is a kind of paper, plastic, or cloth with a surface that makes things stick together. Shari put **tape** on the torn piece of paper.
2. Another kind of **tape** has a special surface that can record sounds or pictures. A **tape** that can record sounds is called an **audiotape**. A **tape** that can record both sounds and pictures is called a **videotape**. [**tapes**]

videotape

audiotape

tapes

taste (tayst)

To **taste** means to put some food on your tongue to tell what it is like. Some foods **taste** sweet or sour or salty. Abbey **tasted** the meat to see if it needed more salt. [**tasting, tasted**]

taxi (tak-see)

A **taxi** is a car that has a driver who is paid to take people places. We took a **taxi** to the airport. [**taxis**]

tea (tee)

Tea is a kind of liquid people drink. **Teas** are made from water and the dried leaves from some kinds of plants. [**teas**]

teaching a class

teach (teech)

To **teach** means to help one person or many people learn something. Delany is trying to **teach** her little brother how to tie his shoes. Today Mr. Miller is **teaching** his class about numbers. [**teaching, taught**]

teacher (teech-uhr)

A **teacher** is a person whose job is to teach. The art **teacher** taught the children how to use red, yellow, and blue to make orange, green, and purple. [**teachers**]

team (teem)

A **team** is a group of people who play together or work together. Morgan is glad that she and her friend Lindsey are together on the same **team**. [**teams**]

tear¹ (tir)

A **tear** is a drop of salt water that comes from your eye when you cry or sometimes when you laugh. **Tears** ran down Ken's cheeks when he dropped his ice cream cone. **[tears]**

tear² (tair)

To **tear** means to pull apart. When Madeleine's shirt got caught on the gate, we could hear the material **tear**. **[tearing, torn]**

tease (teez)

Tease means to make fun of someone. Terry felt angry when Tracy started to **tease** him for losing the race. **[teasing, teased]**

teeth (teeth)

Teeth are the hard white parts that grow in rows inside the mouth. **Teeth** comes from **tooth**. We use out **teeth** to bite and chew food.

telephone (tel-uh-fohn)

A **telephone** is an instrument we use to call and speak to a person who is not with us. **Phone** is a short word for **telephone**. A telephone that some people carry with them is called a **cellular phone**. **[telephones]**

cellular phone

desk telephone

telephones

looking at the the stars through a **telescope**

telescope (tel-uh-skohp)

A **telescope** is an instrument that makes things that are very far away look larger and closer. Scientists use large **telescopes** to study the moon, planets, and stars. A **telescope** called the Hubble Space **Telescope** orbits the earth and takes pictures of stars and other things in outer space. **[telescopes]**

television (tel-uh-vizh-uhn)

A **television** shows pictures on a screen while it plays sounds. **Televisions** use electricity to work. We can watch **television** after we finish our homework. **[televisions]**

tell (tel)

1. To **tell** means to say or speak about something. The crossing guard **tells** the children when they can cross the street. If I **tell** you a secret, will you promise not to **tell**? **2.** To **tell** also means to know. When we smelled the food cooking, we could **tell** it was almost time for dinner. **[telling, told]**

temperature (tem-puh-ruh-chuhr)

Temperature is a way of measuring how hot or cold something is. Cold things like ice have low **temperatures** and hot things like steam have high **temperatures**. Do you know what the **temperature** is today? **[temperatures]**

ten (ten)

Ten is the number that comes after nine and before eleven. **Ten** is written **10**. People have **ten** fingers and **ten** toes. If you multiply **10** times **10**, you get 100. **[tens]**

tepees

tepee (tee-pee)

A **tepee** is a kind of tent made of animal skins and shaped like a cone. **Tepees** were first made by Native Americans in North America. **[tepees]**

terrarium (tuh-rer-ee-uhm)

A **terrarium** is a clear container for keeping small plants and sometimes small animals. Kerry has a glass **terrarium** with plants and a pet turtle. **[terrariums]**

playing **tennis**

tennis (ten-is)

Tennis is a game played by hitting a ball back and forth over a long, low net. Something called a racket is used to hit a **tennis** ball.

tent (tent)

A **tent** is a small cloth house used for sleeping or living outdoors. **Tents** are made of strong cloth held up by poles and ropes. Our camping **tent** is big enough for four people. We watched workers setting up a huge **tent** for the fair. **[tents]**

setting up a **tent**

terrible (ter-uh-buhl)

Terrible means very bad. That garbage has a **terrible** smell. Everybody helped clean up after the **terrible** storm.

test (test)

A **test** is a group of questions that are asked to learn how much a person knows about something. A **test** can also show how well a person can do something. David took a swimming **test** to see which class he should be in. **[tests]**

thank (thangk)

When you **thank** people, you are telling them that you know they have done something kind for you. Uncle Keith **thanks** Max whenever Max helps him weed the garden. **[thanking, thanked]**

theater (thee-uh-tuhr)

A **theater** is a place where movies or plays are seen. The puppet show was held in a tiny **theater**. **[theaters]**

thermometer (thuhr-**mahm**-uht-uhr)

A **thermometer** is an instrument that measures temperature. Stephanie looked at the **thermometer** outside the window to see how cold it was. Mom is using a thermometer to take Tim's temperature. **[thermometers]**

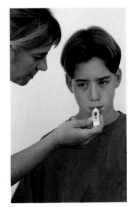
using a **thermometer**

thick (thik)

1. When something is **thick**, it fills a lot of space from side to side or top to bottom. **Thick** is the opposite of thin. Tiesha likes a **thick** layer of peanut butter on her sandwiches for lunch.
2. A liquid that is **thick** pours slowly. Honey is **thick**. **[thicker, thickest]**

thick brush

thin brush

thin (thin)

1. When something is **thin**, there is not much space between its sides. **Thin** is the opposite of thick. The kitten has a **thin** collar around its neck. It's too cold outside for that **thin** coat.
2. **Thin** also means not weighing much. The baby lamb had been sick for three weeks and was very **thin**.
3. A liquid that is **thin** pours quickly. The warm pancake syrup was **thin** and easy to pour. **[thinner, thinnest]**

thing (thing)

If something is not a person and not a place, it is called a **thing**. Animals, plants, cars, furniture, food, and toys are all **things**. All those **things** won't fit in one box. **[things]**

think (thingk)

To **think** means to use your mind, so that you have ideas or believe something. Which song do you **think** we should sing? Lauren **thinks** she would like to be a police officer when she grows up. I promise to **think** about what you said. [**thinking, thought**]

third (thuhrd)

When something is **third**, it comes after second and before fourth. Renee ran as fast as she could in the race and won **third** prize. [**thirds**]

thirsty (thuhr-stee)

Thirsty means to need to drink something. Charlotte likes to drink orange juice when she gets **thirsty**. [**thirstier, thirstiest**]

thought (thawt)

1. When you have a **thought**, you have an idea. Karim wrote his **thoughts** about spring in a poem and then drew a picture to go with it. [**thoughts**]
2. Thought comes from **think**. Isabel **thought** she had a pencil and eraser with her, but she had forgotten to take them.

thread (thred)

Thread is string that is very thin. **Thread** is used for sewing. Let's get a needle and **thread** to shorten your pants. [**threads**]

needle and spools of **thread**

three (three)

Three is the number that comes after two and before four. **Three** is written **3**. A tricycle has **three** wheels. A triangle has **three** sides. [**threes**]

through (throo)

1. Through means from one end or side and out the other. The cars moved slowly **through** the tunnel.
2. Through also means done or finished. The children put the beads back in the box when they were **through** with them.

looking **through** the fence

throw (throh)

Throw means to send something flying through the air. Ken and Sue are not allowed to **throw** balls in the house. The baby **threw** the toy and then ran to get it. [**throwing, threw, thrown**]

thumb (thuhm)

The **thumb** is the short, wide finger on one side of a person's hand. Shelly shut off the radio by pushing the button down with her **thumb**. [**thumbs**]

thunder (thuhn-duhr)

Thunder is a loud noise in the sky that can be heard during some rainstorms right after lightning is seen. Ana's dog ran under the chair and barked when she heard the loud **thunder**.

ticket (tik-it)

A **ticket** is a small piece of paper that shows that something has been paid for. You will need a **ticket** to get into the basketball game. Kara kept her bus **ticket** in her pocket so she wouldn't lose it. **[tickets]**

tickle (tik-uhl)

To **tickle** means to touch someone in a soft, quick way that makes the person laugh. **[tickling, tickled]**

tie (tie)

1. To **tie** means to hold together by joining two ends of something like string, rope, or cloth. Becky decided to **tie** the newspapers before putting them out for recycling. **[tying, tied]**

tying newspapers

2. A **tie** is a long piece of cloth that is worn around the neck and hangs down the front of a shirt. Danny likes the way his red **tie** looks with his blue jacket. **[ties]**

tiger

tiger (tie-guhr)

A **tiger** is a large wild cat. It has orange and white fur with dark stripes. **Tigers** are mammals. **Tigers** live in Asia, but in many places you can see **tigers** in a zoo. **[tigers]**

tight (tite)

1. Something that is **tight** fits too close to something else and does not have enough space around it. **Tight** is the opposite of loose. I need a larger size because the right boot is too **tight**.

2. **Tight** also means to have a strong hold on something. Jana held on **tight** as she climbed the ladder to the high slide. **[tighter, tightest]**

time (time)

1. **Time** is how long it takes to do something or for something to happen. Peter spent a lot of **time** working on his project for the science fair.

2. **Time** is also the hour and minutes when something is happening. What **time** do you want to meet for lunch? **[times]**

tiny (tie-nee)

When something is **tiny**, it is very, very small. From the airplane the people and houses on the ground look **tiny**. Some insects are **tiny**. **[tinier, tiniest]**

tiptoe (tip-toh)

Tiptoe means to walk softly and quietly on the toes of your feet. Clara took off her shoes and **tiptoed** past her brother so that she wouldn't wake him from his nap. **[tiptoeing, tiptoed]**

tire (tire)

A **tire** is a round piece of rubber that is wrapped around a wheel. **Tires** are usually filled with air. Bicycles, cars, trucks, and buses have **tires**. **[tires]**

tire swing

tired (tired)

When you are **tired**, you feel as if you need to sleep or rest. Lara felt **tired** all day and went to bed early.

tissue (tish-oo)

Tissue is a kind of soft, thin paper. Adam wiped his nose with a **tissue** after he sneezed. **[tissues]**

toad (tohd)

A **toad** is an animal that looks like a frog but has rougher and drier skin. **Toads** are amphibians, but they live on land most of the time. **[toads]**

toaster (toh-stuhr)

A **toaster** is a small machine that heats bread and turns it brown. Bread heated this way is called **toast**. **[toasters]**

today (tuh-day)

Today means the day that is happening now. Kelly decided to clean her room **today**.

toe (toh)

A **toe** is a part of your foot. There are five **toes** on each foot. **[toes]**

together (tuh-geTH-uhr)

Together means with someone or something. Karen put apples and pears **together** in a bowl.

tomato (tuh-mayt-oh)

A **tomato** is a kind of fruit. **Tomatoes** are round, red, and filled with juice and seeds. **[tomatoes]**

tomatoes

tomorrow (tuh-mahr-oh)

Tomorrow is the day after today. If today is Friday, what is **tomorrow**? **[tomorrows]**

tongue (tuhng)

The **tongue** is the long part that moves inside the mouth. People use the **tongue** for talking and for tasting and swallowing food. **[tongues]**

took (tuk)

Took comes from **take**. Jake **took** a tennis lesson yesterday.

some **tools**

tool (tool)

A **tool** is something that helps you do special jobs. Dentists use **tools** to clean your teeth. Rakes and shovels are **tools**. **[tools]**

tooth (tooth)

A **tooth** is one of the hard white parts inside your mouth. Mandy's **tooth** is very loose and may come out soon. **[teeth]**

toothbrush (tooth-bruhsh)

A **toothbrush** is a small brush that we use to clean our teeth. A **toothbrush** has a long handle. **[toothbrushes]**

toothpaste (tooth-payst)

Toothpaste is something soft we put on toothbrushes to clean our teeth. **[toothpastes]**

top¹ (tahp)

1. The **top** means the highest part. I'll race you to the **top** of the hill. **2.** A **top** can also be the cover of something. If you leave the **top** off the jar, the glue will dry up.

top² (tahp)

A **top** is also a toy that spins on a point on the bottom. **[tops]**

torn (torn)

Torn comes from **tear²**. Jim's favorite jeans are **torn** at the knee.

tornado (tor-nayd-oh)

A **tornado** is a powerful storm with very strong winds that spin in the shape of a cone. A **tornado** can throw houses and trees high into the air. **[tornadoes]**

touch (tuhch)

To **touch** means to use the hand or sometimes another part of the body to feel something. Ned **touches** the turtle and feels its hard shell. **[touching, touched]**

touching a clay turtle

tow (toh)

Tow means to pull something behind you. A truck that pulls cars that cannot move by themselves is called a **tow truck**. **[towing, towed]**

toward (tord)

When we say **toward**, we mean in the direction of something. When you move **toward** something, you move closer to it. Hope saw her friend Rosa down the street and walked **toward** her to talk with her. The metal nails moved **toward** the magnet.

towel (tou-uhl)

A **towel** is used for drying or wiping something. **Towels** are made of soft cloth or paper. Pete used paper **towels** to clean up the milk he spilled on the table. [**towels**]

Eiffel Tower, a **tower** in Paris, France

tower (tou-uhr)

A **tower** is a very tall, thin building, or the tall, thin part of a building. [**towers**]

toy (toi)

A **toy** is something to play with. Before sitting down for story hour, the kindergarten children put the **toys** away on the shelves. [**toys**]

trace (trays)

To **trace** means to make a copy of something, like a picture, on a thin piece of paper. When you **trace**, you put the thin piece of paper on top and then draw the lines you can see through the paper. Jeannie likes to **trace** pictures from a book and color them. [**tracing, traced**]

track (trak)

1. A **track** is the mark that people or animals make with their shoes or feet. Tires can also make **tracks**. **2.** A **track** is also a long, thin metal piece that trains ride on. [**tracks**]

tractor (trak-tuhr)

A **tractor** is an open truck used by farmers to pull plows and other things. **Tractors** have very large back wheels. [**tractors**]

tractor towing a wagon

traffic (traf-ik)

When we say **traffic**, we mean all of the cars, trucks, and buses moving along a road or street. Emily and Marianne were late for their gymnastics class because there was so much **traffic**.

traffic light (traf-ik lite)
A **traffic light** is a set of lights on a road or street that tells drivers when to "stop" and "go." The green light means "go" and red means "stop." The yellow light means "slow down and get ready to stop." It is against the law to go through a red **traffic light**. [**traffic lights**]

traffic light

trail (trayl)
A **trail** is a kind of path that people can follow. Marci and her cousins followed the **trail** from the lake to their cabin in the woods. [**trails**]

trailer (tray-luhr)
1. A **trailer** is a home that can be moved from one place to another. Colin and his family live in a **trailer**.
2. Another kind of **trailer** can be attached to the back of a car or truck and is used to carry things from one place to another. [**trailers**]

train (trayn)
1. A **train** is a row of railroad cars that are attached to each other. **Trains** travel along railroad tracks to carry people and things from place to place. [**trains**]
2. To **train** means to teach people or animals how to do something. Let's **train** our pet bird to say "hello." Airplane pilots go to special schools to be **trained** to fly airplanes. [**training, trained**]

trap (trap)
1. A **trap** is a thing set up to catch an animal or person. Lobsters and mice are caught in **traps**. [**traps**]
2. To **trap** means to catch someone or something. Spiders use their webs to **trap** insects. [**trapping, trapped**]

lobster **traps**

trash (trash)
Trash is anything that people throw away. Some **trash**, like cans and bottles, can be recycled.

travel (trav-uhl)
To **travel** means to go from one place to another place. Cherie's goal is to **travel** to Africa to see all the animals there. [**traveling, traveled**]

train on tracks

tray (tray)

A **tray** is a flat container used to carry or hold things. Some **trays** have legs and are used as small tables. [**trays**]

treasure (trezh-uhr)

Treasure is things like gold coins and expensive jewelry. In the story, the dragon guarded the **treasure** in the cave. [**treasures**]

treat (treet)

A **treat** is something special that someone gives you or does for you. Mom let Pete and Sandy stay up late as a **treat**. After each show, the seal at the aquarium gets food as a **treat**. [**treats**]

palm **trees**

tree (tree)

A **tree** is a very large plant with strong roots underground. **Trees** have trunks, branches, and leaves. Flowers, fruits, and nuts grow from some **trees**. [**trees**]

triangle (trie-ang-guhl)

A **triangle** is a shape with three straight sides and three points. ▲ and ◣ are triangles. [**triangles**]

trick (trik)

1. When you **trick** people, you do or say something that you want them to believe even though it is not true. We tried to **trick** Dad into thinking we had forgotten his birthday. [**tricking, tricked**]
2. A **trick** is something people do that seems like magic. The clown did a **trick** that made the scarf seem to disappear. [**tricks**]

tricycle (trie-sik-uhl)

A **tricycle** has one wheel in front and two in back and is used for riding. Mario can ride fast on his **tricycle**. [**tricycles**]

tricycle

trip (trip)

1. To **trip** means to bump or hit your foot against something and fall or almost fall. Becky stepped up so she wouldn't **trip** on the crack in the sidewalk. [**tripping, tripped**]
2. When you take a **trip**, you travel to another place. Last winter Jim and his mom went on a skiing **trip**. On a **trip** to New York City, the Hunts visited two museums and the Statue of Liberty. [**trips**]

trombone (trahm-bohn)

A **trombone** is a musical instrument. It is a horn made of a metal called brass. You play a **trombone** by sliding its long, curved tubes to make different sounds. [**trombones**]

trouble (truh-buhl)

1. When people have **trouble** with something, they find it difficult or have a problem with it. I had **trouble** opening the jar. [**troubles**]
2. To be in **trouble** means to have done something you should not have done and that someone is upset about it and may punish you. Megan got in **trouble** for not listening to the baby-sitter.

truck (truhk)

A **truck** is a large machine that has a strong engine and wheels. People drive **trucks** to carry and move heavy things from one place to another. **Trucks** deliver fruits and vegetables to the supermarket. [**trucks**]

trucks

true (troo)

1. True means that something really happened and is not made up. Ellie likes to read **true** stories about children.
2. When something is **true**, it is correct. It is not false. It is **true** that trees called evergreen trees keep their leaves all winter.

trumpet (truhm-puht)

A **trumpet** is a musical instrument. It is a horn made of a metal called brass. You play a **trumpet** by blowing in one end and pressing the finger buttons on top. Steve plays the **trumpet** in the school marching band. [**trumpets**]

playing the **trumpet**

trunk (truhngk)

1. A **trunk** is the thick, hard center part of a tree that grows above the ground. It has branches growing out of it and roots underground. The squirrels chased each other around the **trunk** of the tree.
2. A **trunk** is a large container or space for holding things. Grandma keeps extra blankets in a wooden **trunk** in the guest room. We put the groceries in the **trunk** of the car.
3. Trunk is also the name for an elephant's long nose. Elephants can spray water from their **trunks**. [**trunks**]

trust (truhst)

When you **trust** people, you believe that they will tell the truth and do what they say they will do. Kelly **trusts** her friend to take good care of her fish whenever she goes away. [**trusting, trusted**]

truth (trooth)

The **truth** is what really is. When you tell the **truth**, you say what really happened. Sal told the **truth** when he said he pushed Pete and Pete pushed him back. **[truths]**

try (trie)

To **try** means to do something for the first time or a little at a time until you get better at it or see if you like it. Janine was ready to **try** riding her bicycle without training wheels. **[trying, tried]**

wearing **T-shirts**

T-shirt (tee-shuhrt)

A **T-shirt** is a light cotton shirt that is round at the neck and covers only part of the arm. **[T-shirts]**

tub (tuhb)

1. A **tub** is a large, open container used for washing things. Misha's mother filled the **tub** with soap and water to wash the work clothes.
2. A smaller kind of **tub** is used to hold foods like ice cream. **[tubs]**

tube (toob)

A **tube** is something that is long and round on the outside and hollow inside. **Tubes** can be made of rubber, plastic, metal, or glass. Pipes are **tubes**. Toothpaste, paint, and glue come in **tubes**. **[tubes]**

tug (tuhg)

tugging at a rope

Tug means to pull. In a game of tug of war, two teams tug at a rope until one team is pulled over a center line. **[tugging, tugged]**

tugboat (tuhg-boht)

A **tugboat** is a small boat that pushes and pulls larger boats. **Tugboats** have very strong motors. The little **tugboat** pulled the big ship out of the crowded harbor. **[tugboats]**

tugboat pulling a barge

tulip (too-luhp)

A **tulip** is a plant with a long stem and a flower in the shape of a cup. **Tulips** bloom early in spring. **[tulips]**

tunnel (tuhn-l)

A **tunnel** is a long path that has been dug under the ground. **Tunnels** can also be built underwater or through mountains so that people can travel faster from one side to the other. Some animals dig **tunnels** and live underground. **[tunnels]**

turkey (tuhr-kee)

A **turkey** is a large bird with a long neck. Some **turkeys** have feathers that look like a fan. **[turkeys]**

turkey

turn (tuhrn)

1. To **turn** means to move in a different direction or in a circle. **Turn** right at the traffic light. The baby **turned** over and opened his eyes.
2. **Turn** also means to change the way something is. A caterpillar **turns** into a butterfly. Please **turn** on the lamp and **turn** down the radio. **[turning, turned]**
3. A **turn** is a chance to do something. It's your **turn** to throw the ball. **[turns]**

turtle (tuhrt-l)

A **turtle** is a reptile with a large, very hard shell. A **turtle** can pull its head, legs, and tail inside its shell to protect itself. Some **turtles** live in the water and others live on land. **[turtles]**

head · shell · claw · legs

turtle

twig (twig)

A **twig** is a small, thin branch of a tree. The birds built a nest of twigs high up in the tree in the yard. **[twigs]**

twin (twin)

A **twin** is one of two people who are born at the same time to the same mother and father. Some **twins** look alike, and others do not. Do the **twins** in the picture look alike? **[twins]**

twins

two (too)

Two is the number that comes after one and before three. **Two** is written 2. **Two** things that go together are called a pair. People have **two** eyes, ears, arms, hands, legs, and feet. **[twos]**

ugly (uhg-lee)

Ugly means not nice to look at. **Ugly** is the opposite of pretty or beautiful. Things that are **ugly** to one person may not be **ugly** to another person. Ethan thought his ripped jeans looked great, but his grandmother thought they were **ugly**. [**uglier, ugliest**]

umbrella (uhm-brel-uh)

An **umbrella** is made of a round piece of cloth or plastic and is held over the head to protect a person from the rain or sun. An **umbrella** has a long handle and metal pieces that open out or fold down. [**umbrellas**]

uncle (uhng-kuhl)

Your **uncle** is the brother of your mother or father. The husband of your aunt is also your **uncle**. [**uncles**]

under (uhn-duhr)

Something that is **under** is lower than something else. **Under** is the opposite of over. Peg put the napkin **under** the fork when she set the table.

underground (uhn-duhr-ground)

Underground means under the ground. Carrots and potatoes grow **underground**. Trains that run **underground** are often called subways.

understand (uhn-duhr-stand)

To **understand** means to know what something means. Mrs. Jones hopes Ned **understands** that he is not to cross the street alone. [**understanding, understood**]

octopus ▲

moray eel ▲

▼starfish

▼stingray

animals that live **underwater**

underwater (uhn-duhr-wawt-tuhr)

Underwater means under the water. When something is **underwater**, no part of it shows above the surface of the water. Ebony wears goggles when she swims in the lake so she can watch the fish **underwater**.

underwear (uhn-duhr-wair)

Underwear is clothing made to be worn under other clothes. Joel puts on clean **underwear** every day.

unhappy (uhn-**hap**-ee)

Unhappy is another word for sad. **Unhappy** is the opposite of happy. Shavonne was **unhappy** when her best friend moved away. **[unhappier, unhappiest]**

unicorn (**yoo**-nuh-korn)

A **unicorn** is an animal in stories. It is not real. A **unicorn** looks like a white horse with a long horn coming out of the front of its head. In school Maya drew a picture of a **unicorn** and told a story about it to her class. **[unicorns]**

uniform (**yoo**-nuh-form)

A **uniform** is clothing that people wear to show that they are part of the same group or do the same kind of work. Police officers, firefighters, and some teams wear **uniforms**. The high school basketball team wears **uniforms** with dark red shorts and blue T-shirts. **[uniforms]**

wearing **uniforms**

unusual (uhn-**yoo**-zhuh-wuhl)

When something is **unusual**, it does not happen very often. It often snows in the mountains in May, but it is **unusual** to see snow in the valley in May.

up (uhp)

When something goes **up**, it goes from a lower place to a higher place. The squirrel ran **up** the tree to escape the cat chasing it.

upset (uhp-**set**)

To be **upset** is to feel unhappy, angry, or sad about something that has happened. We were all **upset** when Grandpapa fell off a ladder and had to go to the hospital.

upside down (**uhp**-side **doun**)

Upside down means that the top of something is at the bottom and the bottom is at the top. Josh was very proud that he could stand **upside down** on his head.

upside down

use (yooz)

To **use** means to do something with. After washing her hair, Malka **uses** a hair dryer to dry it. The carpenter **used** a saw to cut wood to make new steps. **[using, used]**

usual (**yoo**-zhuh-wuhl)

When something is **usual**, it happens very often. In the state of Maine, it is **usual** for the winter to be cold.

usually (**yoo**-zhuh-wuh-lee)

Usually means most of the time. We can **usually** see the moon at night.

Vv

vacation (vay-kay-shuhn)

Vacation is time away from school or work. Miguel visited his grandmother in Puerto Rico during his **vacation** from school. Katiana likes to camp out on **vacation**. Hugo likes to stay home and build things with his father when they are on **vacation**. **[vacations]**

on **vacation**

valley (val-ee)

A **valley** is an area of low land between hills or mountains. A **valley** often has a river in it. **[valleys]**

van (van)

1. A **van** is a small truck shaped like a box, used for moving things. The plumber took tools from the back of his **van**.
2. A **van** is also a kind of small truck used for carrying people and things from one place to another. Some **vans** have windows on the side or in back and sliding doors on the side. We rode in a **van** to the airport. **[vans]**

vanilla (vuh-nil-uh)

Vanilla is a flavor that comes from the seed of a plant. It is used in ice cream, cakes, and other foods.

VCR (vee see ahr)

VCR is short for **videocassette recorder.** A **VCR** is a machine that plays and records videotapes. A **VCR** is attached to a television so that the videos can be seen on a TV screen. **[VCRs]**

vegetable (vej-tuh-buhl)

A **vegetable** is a whole plant or part of a plant that is grown for use as food. Carrots, corn, and potatoes are **vegetables**. **[vegetables]**

veterinarian
(vet-uh-ruh-**ner**-ee-uhn)

A **veterinarian** is a doctor trained to take care of animals that are sick or hurt. A short word for **veterinarian** is **vet**. The **vet** helped Ari's sick dog get well. **[veterinarians]**

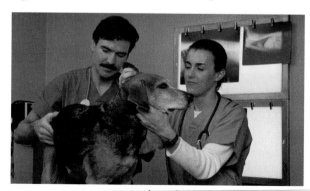

veterinarians

video (vid-ee-oh)

A **video** is a tape with sounds and pictures. **Video** is short for **videotape** or **videocassette**. Some **videos** have movies or television programs recorded on them. Some **videos** are made with camcorders. It's raining today — let's turn on the VCR and watch a **video**. Would you like to see the **video** Mom made of my ballet class or of our soccer game? **[videos]**

violin (vie-uh-lin)

A **violin** is a musical instrument that is made of wood and has four strings. Jasmine holds the **violin** with one hand and plays it by moving a long, thin piece, called a bow, across the strings. **[violins]**

violin and bow

visit (viz-it)

To **visit** means to go somewhere or see someone and stay there for a time. The Turners are going to **visit** the city of Victoria in Canada on their vacation. Moishe **visited** his friend Neil, who is in the hospital. **[visiting, visited]**

vitamin (viet-uh-min)

A **vitamin** is something that the body needs to be healthy. There are **vitamins** in fruits and vegetables and other kinds of food. Some people take **vitamin** pills to be sure they are getting enough **vitamins**. **[vitamins]**

voice (vois)

Voice is the sound you make when you speak or sing. Heather has a beautiful **voice** and likes to sing songs while she plays the guitar. **[voices]**

volcano erupting

volcano (vahl-kay-noh)

A **volcano** is a hole in the earth through which hot melted rock, called lava, is pushed up to the surface from deep inside the earth. As the lava flows and cools, it often forms a mountain shaped like a cone. **[volcanoes]**

vote (voht)

To **vote** means to choose one person or thing over another. Every four years, people in the United States **vote** for the president. The people in Jameel's town **voted** to put a traffic light on the corner near the school. **[voting, voted]**

voyage (voi-ij)

A **voyage** is a long trip that is taken on water or into space. The **voyage** from Africa to North America took many days by ship. **[voyages]**

Ww

pulling a **wagon**

wagon (wag-uhn)

A **wagon** is a box on four wheels that is used to carry people or things. A children's **wagon** has a handle for pulling it. In the past people carried things in large **wagons** pulled by horses. [**wagons**]

wait (wayt)

When you **wait**, you stay in a place until a person arrives or until something happens. We have to **wait** for the sun to set before the fireworks begin. [**waiting, waited**]

waiter (wayt-uhr) and waitress (way-truhs)

A **waiter** is a person who gets your food for you in a restaurant. A female **waiter** is called a **waitress**. The **waitress** asked us what kind of ice cream we wanted for dessert. The **waiter** got another fork for me when I dropped mine on the floor. [**waiters; waitresses**]

wake (wayk)

To **wake** means to stop sleeping. I **wake** up by myself in the morning, but my brother needs an alarm clock. [**waking, woke** or **waked, waked** or **woken**]

walk (wawk)

When you **walk**, you move by putting one foot in front of the other. I can **walk** to my friend's house in three minutes. Marco is blind and uses a cane when he walks. [**walking, walked**]

walking with a cane

wall (wawl)

1. A **wall** is one of the sides of a room or building. Most rooms have four **walls**. Uncle Brett painted the **walls** of his office light green.
2. A **wall** is also something that divides an area. On the other side of that **wall** is a beautiful garden. [**walls**]

want (wawnt)

If you **want** something, you feel that you would like to have it or do it. Charlene **wants** a soccer ball for her birthday. Dan **wants** to be a musician. [**wanting, wanted**]

war (wor)

War is fighting between the armies of different countries or between groups of people in the same country. Soldiers and other people get killed in **wars**. Morgan's father received a medal from the president for being so brave in the **war**. [**wars**]

warm (worm)

Something that is **warm** is cooler than something that is hot. Something **warm** has heat but is not hot. We ate the bread while it was still **warm** from the oven. These mittens will keep your hands **warm**, even on the coldest days. [**warmer, warmest**]

wash (wawsh) or (wahsh)

To **wash** means to clean something with soap and water. Ray helped Carlos **wash** his car yesterday. Remember to **wash** your hands with soap and water before eating lunch. [**washing, washed**]

washing the dog

waste (wayst)

When you **waste** something, you use more of it than you need to, or you throw away part of it that can be used. We don't turn on the dishwasher until it's full so we won't **waste** water. Marcy **wastes** paper when she writes on one side only and then throws the paper away. [**wasting, wasted**]

watch (wahch)

1. A **watch** is a small clock often worn on the wrist. My **watch** shows the time and the date. [**watches**]
2. When you **watch** something, you look at it for a period of time. Please **watch** your little sister so she doesn't fall down the stairs. We **watched** some cartoons on television and then went to bed. [**watching, watched**]

water (wawt-uhr)

1. **Water** is the liquid that comes from rain or melting snow. **Water** is found in oceans, rivers, and lakes. Plants, animals, and people need **water** to live.
2. To **water** is to put water on something, like a plant or a garden.

watering plants

We **water** the plants once a week. [**watering, watered**]

watermelon (wawt-uhr-mel-uhn)

Watermelon is a large, sweet fruit that is green on the outside and red, pink, or sometimes yellow on the inside. **Watermelon** often has small, flat seeds. **[watermelons]**

eating **watermelon**

wave (wayv)

1. To **wave** means to move your hand and arm from one side to the other a few times. Monica **waves** to her friend as she goes by in the car. **[waving, waved]**

2. A **wave** is a moving line of water that comes rolling into the shore of the ocean or other water like lakes or pools. After the storm, we watched the high **waves** hitting against the rocks. **[waves]**

riding a **wave**

wax (waks)

Wax is what candles and crayons are made of. People put other kinds of **wax** on cars and floors to make them shine. **[waxes]**

weak (week)

Weak means easy to break or not very strong. The old chair was so **weak** that it broke when Gus sat on it. **[weaker, weakest]**

wear (wair)

When you **wear** clothes, you have them on your body. Lori likes to **wear** her sneakers to school. **[wearing, wore, worn]**

weather (weth-uhr)

The **weather** is how hot or cold it is outside and what it is like outside in other ways. Sometimes the **weather** is sunny, or it is snowing or raining. We've been having a lot of cool, windy **weather** this week. Cindy likes hot **weather** because she likes to go fishing.

web (web)

A **web** is a net of very thin threads that a spider makes to catch flies and other insects it eats. Insects get stuck in a

web

web and can't get out. **[webs]**

wedding (wed-ing)

When a man and woman have a **wedding**, they get married. Mollie wore a pink dress and carried flowers at her aunt's **wedding**. **[weddings]**

weed (weed)

A **weed** is a plant that is growing where it is not wanted and might hurt other plants. We pull **weeds** from our flower garden to help the flowers grow. [**weeds**]

week (week)

A **week** is a period of time made up of seven days. The names of the days of the **week** are Sunday, Monday, Tuesday, Wednesday, Thursday, Friday, and Saturday. There are 52 **weeks** in a year. [**weeks**]

weigh (way)

To **weigh** means to measure how heavy or light something or someone is. Ann and Trina are using a scale to **weigh** a bag of blocks. [**weighing, weighed**]

weighing blocks

weight (wayt)

The **weight** of something is how heavy or light it is. When I go to the doctor, she always measures my height and **weight**. [**weights**]

well¹ (wel)

1. To do something **well** is to do it in a good way. Charlotte can skate **well**. I think I did **well** on the spelling test. **2. Well** also means healthy and not sick. Jon was sick for two days, but now he is **well** enough to go to school.

well² (wel)

A **well** is a hole that has been dug far into the ground to get water, oil, or gas. In Oklahoma, we saw many oil **wells**. [**wells**]

west (west)

West is the direction on a compass opposite east. When the sun sets in the evening, it goes down in the **west**. The Pacific Ocean is on the **west** coast of the United States.

wet (wet)

1. Something that is **wet** has water in it or on it. Dad and Emily got their pants **wet** in the water. **2. Wet** also means not dry. Watch out for that **wet** paint on the door! [**wetter, wettest**]

wet

whale (hwayl)

A **whale** is a very large animal that lives and swims in the ocean, but breathes air. **Whales** are mammals, not fish. The largest animal on the earth is the blue **whale**. [**whales**]

killer **whale**

209

wheat (hweet)

Wheat is a tall grass plant that is used to make flour, pasta, and some kinds of breakfast cereal. Jay's uncle grows **wheat** on his farm.

wheat

wheel (hweel)

A **wheel** is something round that turns around and around and helps things work or move. Bicycles, cars, and some machines have **wheels**. I counted 18 **wheels** on that big truck. [**wheels**]

using a **wheelchair**

wheelchair (hweel-chair)

A **wheelchair** is a chair that moves on wheels. People who are not able to walk well use **wheelchairs** to move around. Sometimes a **wheelchair** has a motor. At the special games last Saturday, two teams in **wheelchairs** played basketball against each other. [**wheelchairs**]

whisper (hwis-puhr)

When you **whisper**, you talk in a way that is very soft and quiet. When I told a secret to my friend, I tried to **whisper** so that other people wouldn't hear me. [**whispering, whispered**]

whistle (hwis-uhl)

1. A **whistle** is a small instrument that makes a loud sound when you put it in your mouth and blow on it. At camp, when someone blows the **whistle**, we all have to stop swimming. [**whistles**]

whistle

2. When you **whistle**, you make a sound by moving your lips in a special way and blowing air through your mouth or teeth. Caleb likes to **whistle** the same song over and over again. [**whistling, whistled**]

white (hwite)

White is the lightest of all the colors. Snow, milk, and some clouds are **white**. A swan has **white** feathers. [**whiter, whitest**]

whole (hohl)

Whole means all of something, with nothing missing. The **whole** class went to a concert. Did you read the **whole** book, or only some of the stories? Margaret and her friends ate a **whole** box of cookies by themselves.

wide (wide)
If something is **wide**, one side of it is far from the other side. That stream is too **wide** for us to jump across. [**wider, widest**]

wife (wife)
When a man and a woman marry, the woman becomes the man's **wife** and he becomes her husband. [**wives**]

wild (wilde)
Plants and animals that are **wild** live in nature and grow without people taking care of them. **Wild** animals, like lions, tigers, and giraffes, can be seen out in nature or at a zoo. There are a lot of **wild** berry bushes growing along that dirt road. [**wilder, wildest**]

win (win)
When you **win** a contest, game, or race, you are the best player or did the best. Wendell is hoping to **win** the race today. Our team **won** the baseball game yesterday. [**winning, won**]

winning a race

wind (wind)
Wind is air that moves fast. The **wind** blew the small sailboats across the lake. When the **wind** is blowing, we say that it is **windy**. It was so **windy** today that my umbrella blew away. [**winds**]

wiping the **window**

window (win-doh)
A **window** is an open place in the wall of a building that lets in air and light. Most **windows** have glass in them. I closed the **window** because the rain was coming in. Buses, trains, planes, and cars also have **windows** in them. I looked out the **window** of the airplane and saw the Rocky Mountains below. [**windows**]

wing (wing)
1. A **wing** is the part of the body that an animal uses for flying. Birds, bats, and many insects have wings. The bird moved its **wings** up and down and then flew into the air. **2.** An airplane also has **wings**. The **wings** of an airplane stick out from its sides and help it to fly. [**wings**]

parrot's wings

moth's wings

wings

winter (wint-uhr)

Winter is the season between autumn and spring. **Winter** is the coldest season, when it snows in many places. In **winter** Pat's family goes skiing. [**winters**]

wipe (wipe)

Wipe means to rub something to make it clean or dry. Laura, please **wipe** up that milk you spilled. Mom asked the twins to **wipe** their feet on the rug before coming into the house. [**wiping, wiped**]

wire (wire)

A **wire** is a thin piece of metal that bends. **Wires** are used to tie things together, to carry electricity from one place to another, and to make things like screens and fences. Our hamster runs on a **wire** wheel. Christine wears tiny **wires** on her teeth to make them straight. [**wires**]

hamster on a **wire** wheel

wish (wish)

1. A **wish** is something that you want very much to happen or to have. If you could have three **wishes**, what would you ask for? [**wishes**]
2. If you **wish** for something, you want to have it or for it to happen. I **wish** that I could have a little kitten. I **wished** that Grandma would come to see us, and she did. [**wishing, wished**]

witch (wich)

A **witch** is an old woman in a story or a movie who has magical powers. In many stories **witches** are mean and scary, but in some stories there are also good **witches**. The **witch** in the cartoon rode on a broom and had a black cat. [**witches**]

wizard (wiz-uhrd)

A **wizard** is a man in stories or movies who usually has a long white beard and is a magician. The **wizard** in Jason's book wears a tall hat that comes to a point on top and has stars on it. [**wizards**]

woke (wohk)

Woke comes from **wake**. The birds **woke** me up very early this morning. Josh **woke** up at nine o'clock and was late for school.

wolf (wulf)

A **wolf** is a wild animal that looks like a large dog. **Wolves** are mammals that live in groups and hunt other animals to eat. Young **wolves** are called **cubs**. [**wolves**]

wolves

woman (wum-uhn)

A **woman** is a female person who has grown up. Girls grow up to become **women**. [**women**]

won (wuhn)

Won comes from **win**. Hank ran the fastest and **won** the race.

wonderful (wuhn-duhr-fuhl)

Wonderful means very, very good or exciting or unusual. We had a **wonderful** time at the fair last Saturday. The acrobat at the circus did **wonderful** tricks on the high wire.

wood (wud)

1. The trunk of a tree and its branches are made of **wood**. People use **wood** to build houses and furniture and to make paper and other things. Bert made an owl from a piece of **wood**.
2. A place where many trees and bushes are growing close together is called the **woods**. We took a walk in the **woods** and saw some deer. [**woods**]

woods

weaving cloth from **wool**

wool (wul)

Wool is the thick, soft hair that grows on sheep and some other animals. **Wool** is used to make yarn for sweaters and scarves, and cloth for blankets, coats, and many other warm things. Nicky's warmest jacket is made of **wool**.

woolen (wul-uhn)

Woolen means made from wool. Latoya wears a **woolen** sweater under her **woolen** coat on very cold days.

word (wuhrd)

A **word** is a group of letters or sounds put together to mean something. When you speak or write, you are using **words**. Tim is trying to think of **words** that rhyme for the poem he is writing. Rosita has taught her friend Diana many **words** in Spanish. [**words**]

wore (wor)

Wore comes from **wear**. Evan **wore** goggles in the water. Josie **wore** a long skirt to the party.

work (wuhrk)

1. Work is the job that a person does to earn money. Mom doesn't have to go to **work** tomorrow because it's a holiday.
2. Work is the energy that you use to get something done. Painting the chair was hard **work**.
3. To work is to do a job and get paid for it. Carol's dad **works** as a firefighter.
4. To work also means to use your energy to get something done. If we all **work** together, we can finish cleaning out the garage today. Someone who **works** is called a **worker**.
5. We say that a machine **works** if it does what it was built to do. The refrigerator **works** when it keeps food cold. [**working, worked**]

world (wuhrld)

The **world** is another name for the planet Earth. All the water, land, people, plants, and animals on Earth are part of the **world**. Beth has a map of the **world** with the names of all the countries on it. [**worlds**]

earthworm

worm (wuhrm)

A **worm** is a long, thin, soft animal that lives in the ground. **Worms** do not have legs but move by turning from side to side. Birds and fish like to eat **worms**. [**worms**]

farmer▲

astronaut▲

gardener▲

athlete ▲

▼office worker

▼police officer

▼nurse

▼mechanic

people **working** at different jobs

worn (worn)

Worn comes from **wear**. Why have you **worn** such a heavy jacket on such a warm day? Kevin knew he had **worn** his sunglasses to the beach, but he couldn't find them when it was time to go home.

worry (wur-ee)

When you **worry** you think a lot about something bad that might happen and you feel a little afraid. Don't **worry**, I'll come back to pick you up after your piano lesson. Marie was **worried** about her cat until it was found. **[worrying, worried]**

worst (wuhrst)

Worst is the opposite of best. If something is the **worst**, it is as bad as it has ever been. My best friend is the **worst** speller in the whole class. The hurricane on the island was the **worst** hurricane in 50 years.

wrap (rap)

To **wrap** means to cover something on all sides with something else. I think I'll **wrap** Jennifer's birthday present in this yellow paper and put a bow on it. Mike **wrapped** himself in a blanket to keep warm. **[wrapping, wrapped]**

wrapped in a blanket

wrinkle (ring-kuhl)

A **wrinkle** is a line or a bump where skin or cloth folds. When you frown, you can see **wrinkles** on your face. I ironed this shirt, but it still has **wrinkles** in it. **[wrinkles]**

writing

write (rite)

When you **write**, you put words or numbers on paper, a chalkboard, or something else. People often use a pencil, pen, or piece of chalk for **writing**. We are going to **write** the names of animals that live in the ocean. Sarah **wrote** a short story about her horse. People who earn money by **writing** are called **writers**. Benjamin's dad is a **writer** for a television station. **[writing, wrote, written]**

wrong (rawng)

1. Something that is **wrong** is not true or correct. That's the **wrong** answer to the question, but I can tell you the right answer.
2. Wrong also means not nice or not right. It was **wrong** of you to take Brandon's toy away from him.

X ray (eks-ray)

An **X ray** is a kind of picture that shows the inside of the body. The **X ray** showed that

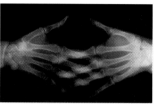

X ray of hands

Camille had broken her finger when she fell off her skateboard. Sometimes the dentist takes **X rays** of my teeth. **[X rays]**

xylophone (zie-luh-fohn)

A **xylophone** is a musical instrument made of narrow pieces of wood of different lengths. The pieces are hit with small hammers to make sounds. **[xylophones]**

xylophone
hammers and bars

yard (yahrd)

A **yard** is the area of ground that goes around the front, back, or sides of a house. Let's play in the **yard** until dinner. I like the way the **yard** smells after the grass has been cut. **[yards]**

yarn (yahrn)

Yarn is a kind of string that is made of pieces of thread that are wrapped around each other. Wool, cotton, and nylon **yarn** are used to make cloth, sweaters, socks, rugs, and other things. **[yarns]**

yawn (yawn)

To **yawn** is to open the mouth wide and slowly breathe air in and let it out. People **yawn** when they are tired. The dog **yawned** and went to sleep. **[yawning, yawned]**

year (yir)

A **year** is the period of time it takes Earth to go around the sun. People measure their lives in **years**. There are 12 months, 52 weeks, or 365 days in one **year**. The first day of the **year** begins on January 1 and is called New Year's Day. **[years]**

yell (yel)

To **yell** is to speak or call out in a very loud voice. Your sister forgot her lunch, so please **yell** and see if you can catch her. Brad **yelled** at his dog because it had taken food off the dining room table. The basketball players **yelled** "Yea!" when their team won the game this week. **[yelling, yelled]**

yellow (yel-oh)

Yellow is a color. The skin of bananas and lemons is **yellow**. Butter and the round center of an egg are **yellow**. Some daisies have a **yellow** center. The petals of buttercups and daffodils are **yellow**.

yellow tulips

yes (yes)

Yes is the opposite of no. People say **yes** when they agree with something or think it is true. Please say **yes** and come with us to the party. **Yes**, I think I will.

yesterday (yes-tuhr-day)

Yesterday is the day before today. I played games inside **yesterday** since it was raining, but today I want to play outside. If today is Saturday, **yesterday** was Friday. **[yesterdays]**

yogurt (yoh-guhrt)

Yogurt is a soft food that is made from milk. Tad likes fruit in his **yogurt** because plain **yogurt** has a sour taste. **Frozen yogurt** is made from **yogurt** and is like ice cream. **[yogurts]**

young rhinoceros with its mother

young (yuhng)

Young means that someone or something has lived for a short time. **Young** is the opposite of old. A person who is **young** has been alive for only a few years. Many **young** animals stay near their mothers. Do you have a **younger** sister or brother? Kim is the **youngest** child in her family. **[younger, youngest]**

yours (yorz)

Something that is **yours** belongs to you. Here, this green coat is **yours**, not mine.

yo-yo (yoh-yoh)

A **yo-yo** is a small toy made of two round pieces of wood or plastic that move up and down on a string. **[yo-yos]**

yo-yo

Zz

zebra (zee-bruh)

A **zebra** is a wild animal that looks like a horse but has black and white stripes. **Zebras** are mammals that live in Africa. The lion moved slowly in the grass toward the **zebras** that were drinking from the water hole. **[zebras]**

zebras

zero (zir-oh)

Zero is a number that means there is nothing. The number **zero** is written **0**. Two plus **zero** equals two. The number ten (10) is written with one **zero**, and the number one hundred (100) has two **zeroes**. The TV weatherperson said the chance of rain today is **zero**. **[zeroes]**

zigzag (zig-zag)

A **zigzag** is a pointed line made of shorter lines that go up and down. Jarrell made a picture of a storm with gray rain clouds and a yellow **zigzag** line to show lightning hitting a tree. **[zigzags]**

zipper (zip-ur)

A **zipper** is made of two pieces of metal or nylon that fit together when the **zipper** is closed and come apart when the **zipper** is opened. **Zippers** are sewn into things like pants, skirts, jackets, backpacks, and tents to allow them to open and close. **[zippers]**

backpack with **zippers**

zoo (zoo)

A **zoo** is a place where wild or tame animals are kept. People go to **zoos** to watch animals and learn about them. Some **zoos** have cages and fences. The children petted animals at the children's **zoo** and then visited the peacocks. **[zoos]**

visiting a children's **zoo**

How New Words Are Created

New words are formed in different ways. Sometimes they are created by putting two words together. The words *birthday, firefighter, skateboard, sunglasses,* and *toothpaste* were made by joining two words. There are many other words in the dictionary that were also created from two words. Can you find them?

Prefixes. Sometimes a word or a word part is added to another word to make a new word. A word or word part added to the beginning of a word is called a **prefix**. The prefix **re** means "again" and **un** means "not." Can you figure out the meaning of the new words below made with these prefixes?

re	un
re + fill = refill	un + afraid = unafraid
re + heat = reheat	un + fair = unfair
re + sell = resell	un + happy = unhappy

Suffixes. A word or word part added to the end of a word to make a new word is called a **suffix**. Below are some words that are created by adding the suffixes **ly** and **y** and the suffixes **er** and **r**. The suffixes **ly** and **y** are added to a word to mean "how" or "in what way." The suffix **er** and is added to some words (verbs) to mean "someone who" or "something that." The suffix **er** is added to other words (adjectives) to mean "more."

y	er
dirt + y = dirty	lead + er = leader
sleep + y = sleepy	play + er = player
wind + y = windy	teach + er = teacher

ly	er
friend + ly = friendly	fast + er = faster
quick + ly = quickly	soft + er = softer
sudden + ly = suddenly	tall + er = taller

Contractions. Sometimes two words are put together to form one shorter word called a **contraction**. *I'm, don't,* and *let's* are contractions. A contraction is made by taking out one or more letters and using an apostrophe instead. Here are some words that are used to make contractions:

am becomes **'m**, as in *I'm*
are becomes **'re**, as in *we're, you're, you've, they're*
have becomes **'ve**, as in *I've, we've, they've*
is becomes **'s**, as in *he's, she's, it's*
will becomes **'ll**, as in *I'll, he'll, she'll, it'll, you'll, they'll*
not becomes **n't**, as in *don't*
us becomes **'s**, as in *let's*

Forming Plurals

Plural means more than one. Most nouns become plural when the letter **s** is added to the end of the word, as in *oceans, trains, farms, schools, pandas, hands, states, trees, skis, shoes,* and *pies.*

Sometimes the letters **es** are added to a noun to form its plural, as in *buses, glasses, brushes, inches,* and *boxes.*

When a noun ends in **y**, sometimes **s** is added, as in *monkeys* and *days.* With some words the **y** is changed to **i** and **es** is added. Story becomes *stories* in the plural, and sky becomes *skies.* Penny, berry, and daisy become *pennies, berries,* and *daisies* in the plural.

Nouns ending in **o** are made plural by adding **s** or **es**, as in *radios, potatoes,* and *heroes.*

When a noun ends in **f** or **fe**, an **s** is often added to form the plural, as in *roofs* and *giraffes.* Sometimes the **f** or **fe** is changed to **v**, and **es** is added, as when scarf becomes *scarves* in the plural, and loaf, knife, and wife become *loaves, knives,* and *wives.*

Some words do not change when they become plural, as in *deer, sheep,* and *spacecraft.*

Some words change their spelling completely when they become plural. Child changes to *children* in the plural, foot changes to *feet,* man to *men,* mouse to *mice,* tooth to *teeth,* and woman to *women.*

Words That Sound Alike

Some words sound alike but have different spellings and meanings. These words are called **homophones**. You can look for these words in the dictionary if you don't know what they mean.

ate, eight	know, no	sail, sale
bear, bare	mail, male	see, sea
break, brake	meet, meat	son, sun
deer, dear	night, knight	stair, stare
flower, flour	pair, pear	tail, tale
heel, heal	plane, plain	toe, tow
hole, whole	right, write	week, weak

How Words Work in Sentences

The words in English are divided into eight basic groups called **parts of speech**. Parts of speech show how words are used in a sentence. The names of the parts of speech are noun, pronoun, adjective, verb, adverb, conjunction, preposition, and interjection.

Noun. A noun is a person, place, or thing. Words like *house, teacher, city, country, boy, girl, star, dog, people, pants, anger,* and *pizza* are nouns. A noun tells who or what. Names of people and places are also nouns.

Pronoun. Instead of repeating a noun, a word called a pronoun can be used. The words *he, she, it, I, we, you, they, him, her, them, me,* and *us* are pronouns.

Adjective. An adjective tells something about a noun or a pronoun. Words like *hot, soft, ugly, sweet,* and *large* are adjectives. So are words like *happy, happier, happiest,* and *good, better, best.*

Verb. A verb is a word that describes action or tells what is or what is felt. Words like *move, play, bark, is, are, go, run, smell, feel, eat,* and *hug* are verbs.

Adverb. An adverb tells something about a verb or an adjective. Words like *slowly, now, quickly, everywhere, forward,* and *gently* are adverbs.

Conjunction. A conjunction is a word that joins other words together or joins parts of a sentence together. The words *and, or, because,* and *but* are conjunctions.

Preposition. Words like *under, from, by, to,* and *with* are prepositions.

Interjection. An interjection is a word we use to show strong feelings about something. Some interjections are *Great! No! Ouch! Oh! Wow!* and *Hi!*

Sample Sentences

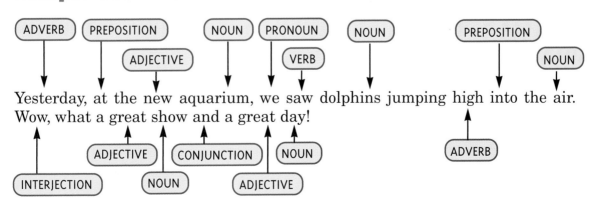

Measurements

People in the United States measure things in inches, feet, miles, cups, quarts, gallons, and pounds. These measurements are part of the U.S. Customary System of measurements. Many other countries measure things in meters, kilometers, kilograms, and liters, which are part of a measurement system called the Metric System.

MEASURING LENGTH

U.S.

1 foot = 12 inches
1 yard = 3 feet or 36 inches
1 mile = 5,280 feet

Comparison

1 foot = 0.305 meter
1 yard = 0.914 meter
1 mile = 1.609 kilometers

Metric

1 meter = 100 centimeters
1 kilometer = 1,000 meters

Comparison

1 meter = 39.37 inches
1 centimeter = 0.394 inches
1 kilometer = 0.621 miles

MEASURING LIQUIDS

U.S.

1 cup = 8 ounces
1 pint = 2 cups
1 quart = 2 pints or 4 cups
1 gallon = 4 quarts

Comparison

1 cup = 0.236 liter
1 pint = 0.473 liter
1 quart = 0.946 liter
1 gallon = 3.78 liters

Metric

1 liter = 1,000 milliliters

Comparison

1 liter = 1.0567 quarts
1 milliliter = 0.0338 ounces

WEIGHING THINGS

U.S.

1 pound = 16 ounces
1 ton = 2,000 pounds

Comparison

1 pound = 453.6 grams

Metric

1 gram = 1,000 milligrams
1 kilogram = 1,000 grams

Comparison

1 kilogram = 2.205 pounds

Index of Picture Labels

Photo Credits